A GROUP ANALYTIC APP
UNDERSTANDING MASS VIOLENCE

A Group Analytic Approach to Understanding Mass Violence makes an analytic examination of the enactment of genocide by Nazi Germany during World War II to explore how mass and state-sponsored violence can arise within societies and how the false beliefs that are used to justify such actions are propagated within society. Bennett Roth makes use of Bion's concept of 'Hallucinosis' to describe the formation of false group beliefs that lead to murderous violence.

Drawing on both group analysis and psychoanalysis, Roth explores in relation to genocide:

- how people form and identify with groups
- the role of family groups
- how conflict can arise and be managed
- how violence can arise and be justified by false beliefs
- how we can best understand these dysfunctional group dynamics to avoid such violence.

A Group Analytic Approach to Understanding Mass Violence will be of great interest to all psychoanalysts and group analysts seeking to understand the role of false beliefs in their patients and society more generally. It will also be of interest to students and scholars of Holocaust studies programs or anyone seeking to understand the perpetation of genocide in the past and present.

Bennett Roth, PhD, is a Faculty member at the Department of Psychiatry, Mount Sinai Hospital and maintains a private practice in New York City, USA. He has lectured internationally on group therapy, psychoanalysis and film, and on the work of Wilfred Bion.

A GROUP ANALYTIC APPROACH TO UNDERSTANDING MASS VIOLENCE

The Holocaust, Group Hallucinosis and False Beliefs

Bennett Roth

LONDON AND NEW YORK

First published 2019
by Routledge
2 Park Square, Milton Park, Abingdon, Oxon OX14 4RN

and by Routledge
711 Third Avenue, New York, NY 10017

Routledge is an imprint of the Taylor & Francis Group, an informa business

© 2019 Bennett Roth

The right of Bennett Roth to be identified as author of this work has been asserted by him in accordance with sections 77 and 78 of the Copyright, Designs and Patents Act 1988.

All rights reserved. No part of this book may be reprinted or reproduced or utilised in any form or by any electronic, mechanical, or other means, now known or hereafter invented, including photocopying and recording, or in any information storage or retrieval system, without permission in writing from the publishers.

Trademark notice: Product or corporate names may be trademarks or registered trademarks, and are used only for identification and explanation without intent to infringe.

British Library Cataloguing in Publication Data
A catalogue record for this book is available from the British Library

Library of Congress Cataloging in Publication Data
Names: Roth, Bennett E., author.
Title: A group analytic approach to understanding mass violence : the Holocaust, group hallucinosis and false beliefs / Bennett Roth.
Description: Abingdon, Oxon ; New York, NY : Routledge, 2019. | Includes bibliographical references and index.
Identifiers: LCCN 2018028637 (print) | LCCN 2018032400 (ebook) | ISBN 9780429460005 (Master) | ISBN 9780429862410 (Web PDF) | ISBN 9780429862403 (ePub) | ISBN 9780429862397 (Mobipocket/Kindle) | ISBN 9781138625280 (hardback : alk. paper) | ISBN 9781138625297 (pbk. : alk. paper)
Subjects: LCSH: Genocide--Psychological aspects. | Mass murder--Psychological aspects. | Holocaust, Jewish (1939-1945)--Psychological aspects.
Classification: LCC HV6322.7 (ebook) | LCC HV6322.7 .R683 2019 (print) | DDC 303.6--dc23
LC record available at https://lccn.loc.gov/2018028637

ISBN: 978-1-138-62528-0 (hbk)
ISBN: 978-1-138-62529-7 (pbk)
ISBN: 978-0-429-46000-5 (ebk)

Typeset in Bembo
by Taylor & Francis Books

CONTENTS

Introduction   vi

1   The problems with Freud's Group Theory   1

2   The Role of Non-Kin Cooperation, Weapons that Kill at a
    Distance and Shared Beliefs in Group Formation   15

3   A New Evolutionary Basis of Group Development   29

4   War Group Development and the Nazi Path to Violence   42

5   The Nazi Platform of Group Hallucinosis   58

6   Hallucinosis and Perversions   69

7   The Historical Range of Mass Murder and the uniqueness of
    the holocaust imaginary threats and violent solutions   84

8   Summary and the Imaginary Nation   98

9   Addenda   117

Appendix A. Himmler's Speech at Poznan   *126*
Appendix B. Friedrich Jecklen   *128*
Appendix C. The Kovno Massacre   *130*
Appendix D. The EinsatzGruppen   *133*
Bibliography   *134*
Index   *150*

INTRODUCTION

> The personification **of** the devil as the symbol **of all** evil assumes the living shape **of** the **Jew**.
>
> *Adolf Hitler*, Mein Kampf
>
> Anti Semitism is the same as delousing. Getting rid of the lice is not a question of ideology, it is a matter of cleanliness.
>
> H. Himmler, April, 1943

There are unique risks in writing about the mass murders in World War II given the vast array of perspectives of these horrific events in Europe. Although the amount of written material is overwhelming, from a psychological perspective it is insufficient in explaining the motivation of the Germans. In many ways this is a special kind of detective story in which we know the murderers and estimate the victims but have problems with the scope of the motive(s). Historians of World War II have been transformed in their understanding by a series of events: the ethic cleansing in the Balkans, Cambodia, Indonesia and Rwanda, the release of Soviet documents and the appearance of the exhibition in Hamburg "Crimes of the Wehrmacht." These recent events were a decisive impetus for a re-examination of the interactive levels of participation in the Nazi killing and torture machinery and the morality of mass murder. In contrast, there have been no comparable transformations in the psychoanalytic interests in the mass murders. To say that psychoanalytic theory has turned its back on violence is an understatement. In its place studies of survivors and intergenerational transmission of trauma defensively continue. In addition, the wealth of specialist studies has also fragmented the picture of the Nazi apparatus and behavior. It is now almost impossible to see how all the elements and historical figures fit together into a coherent series of events. Wachsmann (2015, p. 14) describes the resulting effect as "a giant unassembled puzzle with new pieces added all the time" without any connection to the wider public or deeper understanding. Only in the last few years, with a new generation of German historians entering the field, Roseman (2007) reports, has the term "perpetrator" entered the historical literature. Psychoanalytic theorizing, both from an individual and group perspective, remained distant from the faces and acts of violence (Pick, 2012) focusing attention on the study of trauma and the humanity of the survivors. Survivor accounts by Jews and non-Jews are a separate category of response to the horror; they are inevitably painful and moving yet incomplete in their view, no matter the injustice and horror, as the perspective is often narrow and personal. At the same time the preoccupation with victims' wrenching descriptions obscured, in part, the real consequences of the Nazi violent past and an understanding of the interactive psychology of mass movements with violent willing perpetrators. The fusion of "racist" ideology and state violence resulted in the deaths of millions.

One reason why the Holocaust has refused to recede into the historical past was that "victimhood" was made "a central reference point for identity, assertions and restitution claims" (Bartov, 2003a, p. 321) Much of what we find repulsive about violence cannot be explained by psychoanalytic theory. Ideas about sanity and democracy were closely bound together following 1945 (Pick, 2012). Insanity as evil could be found in communities, small groups and nations. Nurturance, security and secure attachment were the cure for the authoritarian and sadistic super-ego. War was defined as mad, beyond analytic logic and fought by the obedient and sacrificial. Creative technology enhanced the capacity to kill while ignoring the unconscious motivations and inner meanings of murder and mass victims. Psychoanalysis' claim to export humane and democratic values and free humanity from the human capacity for destructive violence remains unmet.

In counter point the term perpetrator is singularly important in literature, film and the designation of madman. At the same time it carried an implicit meaning granting ownership to the murderous crimes across all of the divisions of cooperation within the Nazi systems. Within the Nazification of Germany there were a vast number of players in this system who not only moved between desk jobs and being active in the killing fields (Roseman, 2007, p. 93) but also moved from normal family life to killing apparatuses back to family life to find sanctuary after the war. The still ongoing discovery of the sheer diversity of the participants and their fates after the war questions whether discussions of "the perpetrator" or a single cause for these mass murders are possible. Wachsmann's (2015) recent extensive history of the concentration camps reveals the complexity, locations and numbers of participants in one organizational structure of the Nazi terror. What is not in doubt is the central role the Jews played in the Nazi *Imaginaire* over and above the racism, violence and murder of other groups (Bartov, 2003a). This was most evident in the collective Nazi obsession of the imaginative fantasy that Jews had the power to pollute the Aryan race.

Contemporary historians now recognize and annotate the huge diversity of institutions, organizations and significant numbers of civilian organizations that were parts of the machinery that killed, terrorized and looted Jews (Mazower,

2009). The result is to complicate enormously any profound sense of who the perpetrators were, what motivated them and what their personality traits were. Certainly Flick (industrialist), Eichmann and Frank (Nazi Governor of Poland) had very different personalities. From the *Gangsterland* civilian administration in the Lublin district (Musial, 2000) to Wildt's (2009) *Sicherheitsdienst* (intelligence service), Lifton's doctors (1986), and Dicks' unrepentant sadistic killers (1972), the German military and storm-trooper units, the *Fieldpolizei* to the large range of different criminal and regular police units; and all this to understand in addition to the Nazi Party and its supporting organizations. Roseman (2002), the historian of Wannsee, concludes the intensive search for *a perpetrator* has demonstrated that there was neither a single explanative phenomenon for the Nazi cumulative radicalization nor were all the killers sadistic monsters. While there is no dispute to the vast collective literature concerning the Holocaust the deeper "motivation" question remains unanswered.[1]

Through this entire post-war period of discovery psychoanalysts of every persuasion have remained mostly silent or a few were bound to either wildly speculative psychoanalytic guessing and leader centric explanations (Kernberg, 2003a, 2003b) that were "diagnostic" and obscured more than they revealed (Ornstein, 2012). This current effort seeks to remedy the absence of analytic insights oddly initiated by Freud (Pick, 1993) in his famous letter to Einstein. Remarkably Freud (1993) appears to nearly anticipate mass murder in a remark that focused on the outcomes of war: "if the victors' violence eliminated his opponents permanently – that is to say killed him. This had two advantages: he could not renew his opposition and his fate deterred others from following his example" (p. 204) To annihilate a group of opponents in order to enforce subjugation, remove partisans and inflict terror is secondary to eliminating an unarmed widespread community politically controlled by a state (Semelin, 2009, p. 335).

With all of this history still appearing at a time when unmediated memories of the Holocaust are becoming rare, important probing questions remain unanswered that cast a shadow on the past, the present and history (Bartov, 2000). Among them are 1) what allows or motivates people in groups to kill unarmed people? 2) What galvanized Hitler's vast army of helpers to murder Jews up to the last minute of the war? 3) What is the relationship between Nazi ideology and murder? 4) Can psychoanalytical clinicians and theorists contribute to Holocaust studies? I hope to further this discussion. A partial answer rests in expanding our understanding of how an individual's values, beliefs, character and identity are formed and transformed by a (political) ideology or false belief system. Psychoanalysis as a theory has not had much interest in personal desire expressed through political beliefs and demands. Yet, it is clear that belief in Nazism—inseparable from war and mass violence—destroyed the old Europe and impacted the world as we knew it.

For the best part of the last century, psychological theories and common sense views were in agreement in identifying significant experiences with parents as pivotal in shaping individual identity. The three primary socializing agents of children in western society that made contributions in shaping identity were families, peer groups and schools. Ignored in this putative description are the effect of mass cultural movements and the cultural patterns of risk that affect the unfolding of identity within a culture that often lead to violence. A case will be made that one primary evolutionary function of all cultures is to moderate emerging psychosocial experiences relevant to individual expression of psychological character and endowment (Allen and Fonagy, 2006). Within this broader social context individual acts of violence are usually viewed as a signal of the failure of normal developmental processes (Fonagy, 2003). Studying the Nazis leads to the conclusion that a political culture/ideology can elicit, use and harvest violence for its own purposes (Bessel, 2009), much as any president can make false claims. Ideologically based mass violence may be best understood as the outcome of and inaugurated by a radical shift in cultural beliefs and embedded group dynamics that are a "frightening mystery." Hitler's ride to power and preoccupation with murder remain a continuing mystery.

It seems appropriate that this proposal was submitted around the dates of 9/11. Living in Lower Manhattan I was deeply affected by the unfolding of the WTC attack and its repercussions. Among my responses was becoming a consultant to a well-known high school, of more than 5,000 students and faculty, that was evacuated near the WTC site. The school was the group patient.

Within a short time the Center for Disease Control tested everyone looking for PTSD and a consultant came to brief the teachers likening the events in New York to the events that took place with the high school shooters in Columbine. The convergence of these two events led to my questioning whether psychoanalysis, group and individual, had any deep reckoning of group violence and perpetrators. This culmination of events stimulated a number of questions that first emerged when I treated a man who claimed he had killed someone as a child and I found almost nothing in the psychoanalytic literature on murderers and zero on kid killers. Editors of a well-known analytic journal did not accept that paper.

I began a quest to understand violence and to distinguish intimate violence (one to one) from violence between groups of people. I began naively to read on the Germans in World War II and to review Bion's theoretical work on groups and his personal history. I questioned whether Bion was engaged in the British de-Nazification program and contacted Dr. Pick, author of *The Search for the Nazi Mind* (2012). This led to a paper re-evaluating Bion's group theory and questioning his omission of personal or intimate violence.

Very slowly, over considerable time and with considerable mental struggle with my own post-war Jewish identity, I engaged in reading about the Nazis and my ideas slowly formed. Not until this past year did they take sufficient shape and coherence after many false starts. The current struggles with ISIS and the reaction to the Syrian refugees in Europe quickened my search and efforts, as there is a dynamic repetition of group racial behavior and violence. Certainly the current political situation seems ripe for an examination of "false beliefs."

Now, with world events unfolding, continued mass shooting in schools, there is a belated interest in violence in the psychoanalytic associations, the group therapy associations and other venues. Hopefully this effort will have some impact.

PS. I have no direct relationship to the Holocaust other than being Jewish and that a British cousin of mine more than 25 years ago married a man who was a Nazi hunter and an Israeli spy. I think it would be very difficult to describe the personal process of writing this book. Psychoanalytic investigation is a process of complex encountering leading to integration and not the collection, organization and recitation of related historical narratives, facts and sequences of events. I had no idea where my initial inquiry into perpetrators in 9/11 would lead me and, in particular, how that encounter would affect me: social power and dynamics are unstable and at times like these any individual is at its mercy. It likely would take more time to examine my experience then I am willing to write about and reveal. Finally, this book is a challenge. It is a challenge to think in group dynamic terms and it was a challenge to emotionally face the terrifying topic of this book: to recognize the powerful malignant group dynamics at work that changed a range of emotional hatreds into mass acts of extermination that remain disturbing. One major impediment to this effort was the ongoing failure of psychoanalytic theorists to move beyond the early conceptualizations of "aggression" and their failure to "understand" the significance of negative beliefs. To understand acts of murder, injury, rape, medical experimentation on people by other people, cannot be psychoanalytical comprehended by the concept of aggression, calling them "evil" or by appeals to diagnostic categories. Violence and other acts of harm are not explainable by phobic responses.

The memory of these events will blur and fade to be supplanted by other tragedies of state organized violence. This effort seeks a different emphasis than currently exists in the analysis of the dynamics of the Nazi regime. Like the latent content of a group dream the deep dark emotional meanings of the Holocaust or Shoah remain unexplored. The personal and violent desires expressed in ideological groups, while commonplace, are seldom recognized because they engender emotional discomfort and existential pain. Because mass murder is external to the sanctioned social discourse of psychoanalysis, repeated murderous behavior is called evil or psychopathic to filter its impact and separate us from its extreme meanings. Unlike personal violence, large group violence is driven by constellations of beliefs that are mostly false and constructed to elicit, harvest and condone violence. The current political situation in the United States lends some urgency to the understanding of beliefs and "false beliefs."

As I was preparing this final draft I came upon "My Parents' Bedroom," a short story by Uwem Akpan (2009) concerning genocide in Rwanda that in a simple frame captures the powers that hide behind racial genocide.

Note

1 A new book by Dan Plesch (2017) was published recently.

1

THE PROBLEMS WITH FREUD'S GROUP THEORY

> I am talking about the evacuation of the Jews, the extermination of the Jewish people; it is one of those things that is easily said. "The Jewish people is being exterminated" every Party member will tell you, "perfectly clear, it's part of our plans, we're eliminating the Jews, exterminating them, a small matter."
>
> H. Himmler, Posen Speech 1943

In Freud's attempt to understand human social, political and cultural life, he proposed to examine life in the horde, often mistranslated as "group" ("Massen").[1] Freud employed early-tribal imagery to describe the dynamic of the leader (father imago) of the horde killed by his sons, allegedly because he would not let his sons have sexual access to the women of the horde. His libidinized imagery is reminiscent of *Totem and Taboo*'s despotic and brutal leader who monopolizes all assets, destroys all rivals, and in turn must be destroyed to meet his fate (Freud, 1915). Freud's speculative and primitive description of the horde has generally been ignored by evolutionary theories despite their co-existence in time with analytic theory. Continuing psychoanalytic attempts to understand more complex group behaviors consisting of desire, ideology and moral prohibitions have been caught in the intellectual quicksand of Freud's primitive imagery that mistakenly confined groups to the same developmental progression as children. The contributions of humans' unique "groupishness" was not necessarily liberated by Bion's (1961) theories of regression to unconscious group processes that focused on unconscious impediments to work and cooperation in reality or Kaes' (2007) notion of security (links) in groups (Roth, 2013).

It is now evident that Freud was preoccupied with applying his theory and validating the meaning and imagery of the father-king he cherished in the ancient literary Oedipal trilogy. In this Greek dynastic epic Freud found not only evidence of (his) patricidal guilt and incestuous yearnings, two of the stanchions of his emerging theory, but he also attempted to tie our human social uniqueness directly and simply to repression of sexual desire and the death instinct. Upon deeper reflection while he acknowledges the influence of unconscious forces, it is possible to see in his images the meat-eating head of a pack of carnivores described by Darwin, lurking in the shadows of the Freudian and Kleinian unconscious. Later in his writings (*Why War?* 1932), Freud seems too preoccupied by personal moral considerations and unable to directly face the abhorrent results of the violence between nations in World War I and the carnage they left behind. Where Freudian theory required that sexuality was developmentally stage related, he avoided considering that destructive wishes and acts be considered in the same manner. War and genocide are forms of group violence instigated by differences in beliefs. Often the differences between friend and enemy, kin and non-kin can become violent if the leaders of human groups take these differences seriously enough that they will kill or die for them.

To appreciate the dynamic interactive complexity of human bio-social organisms living in large and small-scale societies, rather than reducing and distancing them as primitive hordes, requires a wider understanding of multilevel cultural evolution and the dynamics of a variety of within-group human civilizing processes. Although Freud suggested there are interactive cultural influences on the individual psychic moral development of the super-ego, psychoanalysis remained fundamentally based on both pre-Oedipal and Oedipal theories of repressed group dynamic behavior and ignored the embedded social/cultural aspect of his speculations. Families are embedded in cultures that are variable and supply the external anchors in reality for both conscious and unconscious desires, individual roles, mutuality and identity (Kegan, 1982). In addition, the less the individual members of the family are in touch with themselves the more they unconsciously view the world in terms of their inner reality.

Anthropological evidence supports the basic idea that larger groups of non-kin humans living in cooperation created new evolutionary problems to resolve—among them ensuring the coordination of supplies required the suppression of self-serving behaviors to ensure individual and group security, mutuality and survival in vastly different environments. Some groups solved these problems better than others, and the more successful adaptations spread, by warfare, economic superiority and imitation. Importantly, the successful adaptations in group-level functional organizations included warfare, a topic avoided by most psychoanalysts and developmental theories (Fornari, 1974; Pick, 2012). When psychoanalysts dare to speculate about war, it is still viewed as destructive or criminal or is reduced to psychotic, barbarian behavior, while they search for the causes of war within an individual psyche or focus on its intergenerational traumatic effects. Unlike psychoanalysts, anthropologists consider killing as natural to humans (Wrangham, 2006, p. 44): anyone can kill, not just psychopaths and sadists. Individual killing is complex and includes weapons, intentions or sudden rage (Cartwright, 2002), while group killing more often requires politicized language with symbolic and violent group behavior. Organized combative killing or battles includes clashes among several groups or polities in various forms of alliances or conflicts. Importantly, the history of war, revolution and insurrection, crime and mass murder is primarily the history of man living in groups and contesting competitively with other human groups for various resources or in response to attack or humiliation. While lethal state-organized warfare is an evolutionary novelty among mammals, at the same time it is a constant and transglobal occurrence in our human history. One possible conclusion is that the neuro-psychology of adult males is historically and genetically adapted to take advantage of helpless rivals by killing them because of the long-term advantages of being physically or militarily superior (Wrangham, 2006, p. 57). Primitive war was likely different from organized warfare and driven by resource scarcity and coercion from leaders. Predatory killing in human males may activate a neural reward system as well as social and homosocial rewards and is held in restraint by enforced codes of punishment or prosocial mores. Predatory animals kill parsimoniously, only out of immediate need and not for sport or war. In sum, Cunnliffe (2009) concludes that only a thin tissue of social constraint, carefully nurtured and evolved within group mores, keeps us civilized and there is ample evidence that this constraint breaks down regularly. It is necessary, I believe, to consider how social constraint emerged in human groups and to understand how it breaks down among males when the benefits of lethal aggression outweigh the costs of that aggression.

Before being able to answer this important question regarding violence in groups, a better understanding of human group evolution is necessary. One implication of viewing human cultural and familial history as a process of multilevel group evolution and selection is that the focus shifts from the narrow perspective of the individual psyche and its development to changes that are inherently diverse, but follow patterns of increasing complexity in interactive human group dynamics. Any common psychoanalytic assumption that human nature may be reduced to a list of individual psychological or unconscious psychoanalytic universals that result in human universals, such as incest avoidance or violence, appears speculative when diversity among individuals and groups is considered. Wilson (2015), from the perspective of his theory of evolutionary biology, claims "while humans share a single genetic heritage, including psychological universals ... they result in cultural diversity, not uniformity" (p. 145). Conceptions of health and development are not unbiased when considering the problems of living in different cultures and when emergencies and conflicts require that our evolutionary truce be renegotiated (Kegan, 1982, p. 110).

The fundamental question and processes of how human groups became functionally socially organized, and the process by which these groups adapted, became complex non-kin aggregates and thrived, are not satisfied by Freud's speculations on hordes nor by Darwin's notion of natural selection as simply the survival of the fittest.[2] In general, emergent group mechanisms must minimally coordinate group safety, social relations and resources, while preventing disruptive forms of self-serving behavior or conflicts of interest through all the emerging levels of social hierarchical organization and cultural roles. Emerging human adaptive social mechanisms of group cooperation may have been determined by the evolution and establishment of what Bion (1961) called specialized work groups, but they in turn were dependent upon the slow emergence of group psychic links establishing non-kin security and safety (Kaes, 2007). In other words the evolution of human kinship-independent cooperation produced tensions in hierarchical organizational strata dealing with power, patronage, resources and trust: leading to or co-evolving with the development of communication, trade and commerce between non-kin groups. Over many generations of adaptive struggle this non-kin group adaptation became relatively successful until it is both common and vulnerable to outbreaks of violent conflict in most human groups. Kinship and ethnic familiarity have provided a psychological structure for predicting social and sexual exchanges while serving as a primary source of social identity. Confounding the sense of the construction of identity was the emergence of poly-ethnic group coalitions and competing ideologies that determined who rightfully belongs.

In the following, I will present theoretical evidence from evolutionary theory dealing with the emergence of the idea of modern states that will describe the dynamics of warfare in general, and the mass murders by the Nazis in particular. Modern states historically emerged from poly-ethnic empires and intensified the dynamics and conflicts of being a citizen. In order to acknowledge and accept a group analytic level of understanding it is necessary to recall Ostow's (1986) caution that individual psychoanalytic theory fails to account for Nazi group violent behavior. In group dynamics when there is an affinity between a group and an individual, it is largely a result of that individual's conscious or unconscious recognition and identification with the inscriptions of the values, desires and goals of that coalition. Elias (1969) suggested that the reality of interdependence was severely and defensively underestimated by psychoanalysts.

The emergence and accelerating nature of Nazi organizational antagonistic policy and behavior toward Jews from 1933 onward makes simple dynamic understanding of Nazi rhetoric and behavior difficult. Confounding our understanding is that organizational behavior was multifaceted, as was the Nazis' cultural means at their disposal to justify and implement racist and imperial goals. Anti-Jewish policy became a progressive violent process made of pieces in a vast puzzle that resulted in deportation, war, genocide and the destruction of Jews and Jewish culture in Europe. Anti-Jewish policy and murder was enacted differently within the various countries in Europe. Earlier attempts to grapple with this widespread dynamic destructive process lack a critical understanding of the dynamics and spread of progressive terror evolving into mass murder. While we cannot access the perpetrators and interview them, I can provide a model for understanding its group dynamics, force and contagion of violence.

Freud (1915, p. 122) observed:

> In 1912 I took up a conjecture of Darwin's to the effect that the primitive form of human society was that of a horde ruled over despotically by a powerful male. I have attempted to show that the fortunes of this horde have left

indestructible traces upon the history of human descent; and especially that the development of totems, which comprises in itself the beginnings of religion, morality and social organization, is connected with the killing of the chief by violence and the transformation of the primal horde into a community of brothers.

Importantly and reductively, Freud goes on to hypothesize that "human groups exhibit once again the familiar picture of an individual of superior strength among a troop of similar companions dominating the group."

While the status of totemism has remained somewhat vague and unrefined in anthropology, the concept of the horde has retreated into the background to be replaced by a concept of political community or polity. Narroll (1964) defined polity as being a group of people whose membership is defined in terms of occupancy of a common territory and who have an official with the specific function of announcing group decisions at least once a year (p. 286), and are not included in a larger political unit. Eller (2006) later stated: "a polity is a sovereign political entity usually but not necessarily a state" (p. 213). Within this distinction is a range of loose or structured human organizations that vary from households, agricultural villages, chiefdoms, monarchies, early states and modern states (Otterbein, 2004, p. 81). Each individual social polity structure is both different and with different degrees of complexity and conflict within its boundaries and can range from primitive tribal structures to complex unions of state-like organizations. As the social structures become more complex there was the greater possibility for armed or competitive conflict with another (neighboring) social-political structure, whether kin or non-kin. With emerging complexity and greater numbers of inhabitants, our ancestors learned to negotiate and cooperate and to suppress disruptive forms of within-group non-kin competition: making forms of benign within-group selection the primary human evolutionary force. Group selection theory describes natural selection operating between or within groups of organisms, rather than only between individuals. Group or multi-level selection produces adaptations that benefit the functioning or survival of the group or other kin, rather than the individual. Darwin's evolution theory rejected the idea of group selection in favor of individual selection. Most humans evolved and live, however, in a variety of complex social group coalitions in proximity to other coalitions. Another major distinction ignored by Freud's group theory is that it is only in human groups that paternity emerged as important. In multi-male and female animal groups females mate promiscuously and paternity is mostly irrelevant rendering the Oedipal conflict a purely human construction although there may be other benefit from between group matings.

When considering the dynamics of human group selection distinctions between coercive, disruptive and benign forms of within-group non-kin, social cooperation is critical to understanding the evolution of larger successful human social entities (Bingham and Souza, 2009). It became, and remains, evolutionarily necessary for all human social groups to develop systems and symbols to preempt transgressions and instill a sense of fear for the consequences of anti-group and anti-family behavior. This was accomplished by inflicting real or social harm to those defying varying codes of protection. From infancy individuals emerge first within their intimate and subsequent larger social structures seemingly aware of, learning and internalizing the coded signals to avoid social punishment. This learned adaptive function prepares individuals to adapt to expanding social scenarios and interdependent roles.

The more successful or productive group(s) selection functions are within larger social groups and culture, the more they will harvest socially adaptive cooperating individuals. Such successful adaptations foster growth in population, create more material culture and are likely to control more territory and resources, yielding more offspring with extended kinship. The less successful groups are vulnerable to exploitation, dispersal and annihilation.

When reconsidering Freud's hundred-year-old theory it is necessary to make important distinctions between group cultures in which the important dominant individuals appropriate the best mates and resources due to strength or power, and those where individuals achieve high status in social groups through kinship, earned behavior or adaptive sophistication (competence). According to Freud's untested scenario, within the primary family parent-offspring antagonisms (conscious and unconscious) were, from *infancy,* reducible to rivalry with the same sex parent over access to the opposite sex parent. When human intergenerational conflict is viewed as competitive, the Oedipal myth and other folk tales acquire an expanded significance. Most often written by men for males, they do not persist simply to convey themes of the unconscious significance of desire, such themes must also appeal to a larger social purpose (group): rulers and parents struggle to subdue competitive others (Daly and Wilson, 1988). Current evidence suggests that open competition for sexual mates as Freud described occurs primarily at the time of sexual maturity and parent-offspring conflict begins to be openly and conflictingly concerned with same sex rivalry over reproductive status (Daly and Wilson, 1988).

It is important to recognize that violent competition, as Freud speculated, was not restricted to seeking sexual access but importantly to attain resources in emerging or ancient social groups. Such competitions became violent with or against other coalitions for access to self-sustaining resources, symbolic icons and conflicts over authority. Self-interested kin and non-kin hierarchical coalitions within a larger polity added complexity to competition by forming independent sub-groups that competed in open and hidden ways. Eventually attempts were made to organize competition by laws, rules or agreements to modify the costs of conflict and losses.

Where psychoanalytic theory constructed an internal source of "inhibition and prohibition" in the morally governing super ego, its theories ignored the important idea that it was necessary for people living in large social groups to struggle to develop prohibitory mechanisms that included symbols, weapons/punishments, that aimed to suppress conflicts of interests of a wider range: violence and greed. These cultural suppressors appeared on larger group stages at low cost to the human social groups. The development of social suppressors allowed groups to bond and expand while requiring the development of new forms of coercive mechanisms for suppression of "selfish" self-interest (Bingham and Souza, 2009). Increases in the population of human groups living among non-kin placed an evolutionary premium on individuals who were better able to predict their social environment scenarios, adaptively sustain themselves among other individuals and avoid conflicts of interests with non-kin. The emergence of protective and restrictive coercive laws and law enforcement became a self- and group-interested moral development as well as social reinforcement necessary for cooperation and insured the maintenance of the group's beliefs and culture. At the same time similarity and shared beliefs increasingly brought people cooperatively together with less fear of conflict, while coercive enforcement sought to eliminate or marginalize those unable to maintain group and cultural values and beliefs. Enforced kinship-independent cooperation was the result and yielded an entire suite of traits and systems we think of as essentially human that include complex language, our unique sexual and child-rearing practices, and our elaborate ethical and political cultural sense. However these evolutionary developments did not liberate humans from competition between large groups or polities for necessary resources coincident with the emergence of coercive or violent military coalitions. Nor did it protect those within a group or class of persons from seeking solidarity and enjoying superior intellectual, social, military or economic status: of an elite with status and power. Often status was awarded to performance in war that was offensive or defensive. Political complexity was motivated by men's pursuit of status that usually refers to dominance and culture bound forms of prestige and status.

Often the competition and conflict between coalitions, elites or belief systems resulted in recognition of significant difference and armed conflict or forces for splitting apart a polity appeared, improvement in the tools of warfare emerged dependent on advances in weaponry and wars became a larger life-and-death group struggle. War between coalitions is likely a product of human natural selection and expresses the respective communities' willingness to risk lives to back a specialized social structure, a belief system or to secure resources. This creates the recognition of public allies and enemies through two opposing armed forces or armies. Contesting communities created symbolic identifactory and social value beliefs to justify and encourage the violent risks taken in pursuit of these elite interests. If the nation is on the verge of collapse or finds enemies without and within that are intolerable, a unitary executive power often seeks a violent solution. Often this decision rejects the notion of a just or unjust war.

On a fantasy (psychic) level, however, members of each community, in order to use and justify violence, learned to adaptively assign their residual anxieties, aspects of selves and "bad impulses" onto the accepted enemy, who in turn absorbs them. Community members rid themselves of violent impulses by projecting them onto their armies (Bion, 1961), which in turn deflect them, directing them against their external enemy (Jacques, 1955). The members of each warring social group express this integrating war dynamic and must support their group interests with few exceptions or exemptions. Each warring group develops a war culture that includes group war myths, heroes and beliefs about the meaning of war and death in combat. Bingham believes that written language may have coincided with the recording of successful battles (Bingham and Souza, 2009).

For the defeated in warfare, this could result in the destruction of the polity or coalition, a change in group boundaries, the killing or enslavement of the survivors, and the loss of material resources and territory. For example, Julius Caesar's armies likely killed one million and captured another million in his wars from 58 B.C. to 51 B.C. (Cunliffe, 2009, p. 79). For the victor, there were also losses to mourn and usually gains in power and its symbols, heroes and resources. War-conflict with another polity psychologically contributes to enforce cooperation within each warring group and fosters ethnocentric bonding that dynamically socializes and limits that polity for war with its personal and social demands for the sacrifices of its members. Such within-group ethnocentric beliefs in turn contribute to a sense of personal alliance and social identity, while fostering and discharging negative beliefs and psychic elements identified with the other polity's combatants. The violent attack on or eradication of another culture or part of a polity in war is often expressed by a polarity: lauded as a noble act sanctioned by God and or glorifying the State by its perpetrators (Bartov, 2003) and viewed as crimes against humanity or morality by its victims and observers. Idealization of each war group's elite leader and its live and dead heroes also occurs while the rival other is negatively cast as a monster (Money-Kyrle, 1951). The mourning of human losses from violent conflict, usually symbolized as "the fallen soldier" or war hero, is a constant with war and tempered by belief in within-group interests and ideals as just and group or kin protective of the non-combatants. Mourning for the vanquished is more complex as it also brought shame and in order to survive the vanquished often had to renounce their identity and beliefs. Mourning for a culture, state or its symbols is expressed through archaeological interests, memorials and war museums.

In order to view group dynamics on this grand scale, certain individual biases must first be addressed. The idea that human society is dynamically equivalent to a single human development, an insect colony or a horde, belongs to earlier nineteenth-century reductionist thinking. From an evolutionary perspective the primary function of all human groups over time included physical activities such as childcare, food acquisition, predator defense, trade, and warfare with other group coalitions. Emerging cultures also provided support and response to increasing human mental and environmental development, and activities made possible by the emergence of a larger frontal cortex that is distinctly human, contributing to our capacity for symbolic thought, language, and concrete and abstract symbolization. This evolutionary development not only extended human childcare and development but also included the enhancement of neural mechanisms to transmit beliefs and information over and within generations. It followed that such cognitive development facilitated the establishment and communication of significant cognitive and emotional bonds within kin and non-kin groups who shared common languages and symbols. Over time such cooperating groups constructed an imagined written or venerated history that became enhanced as a shared and guiding culture and history. The shared language supported not only the creation of a group's history but also led to the creation of a "sacred" history of origin that is usually group enhancing.

Identifier and inhibiting symbols (e.g., flags, statues, etc.) within most groups emerged to serve as objects of identification in warfare and appear as abstractions or iconic symbols requiring recognition and ritual observance by group participants. With these developments emerged the significant and necessary ability of unrelated individuals to bond to and with these symbols and cooperate in groups to form a safe cooperative group identification and coalition. The evolutionary emergence of an increased neuro-cognitive capacity for symbolic thought, including but not restricted to language, led to a quantum leap in human ability to adapt to its environment and to develop useful implements of identification. Since symbolic thought invokes the creation of mental relationships that persist in the absence of concrete environmental stimulation, the use of symbols for prestige and kin and non-kin groups spread. Stated another way, the mental symbolic representation not only stands for the original and valued object within the kin and non-kin group, but also fosters the idea of a recognizable link to personal and shared distinct group identity, prestige and history. In addition, representation in symbols also allows for abstraction and metaphoric expansion concurrent with emotional attachment to the ideals and rituals that display, reinforce and contain the cultural identifier symbols. All of these serve to display and reinforce group attachment bonds and contribute to recognition of a distinct positive or negative social identity.

Compared with these original unique human "groupishness" developments and achievements, most other primate species are very smart as individuals, but their intelligence is based upon distrust, and they may only function as a cooperative cultural group when predatory, attacked, sated or instructing their young. Importantly, other primates are limited in that they have coded limited communication, but do not develop extensive symbolic or abstract social identifiers. While some primate groups can not tolerate "outsiders," importantly there is only one primate that developed complex weaponry and weapons that kill at a distance: humans (Bingham and Souza, 2009).

The historical development of weaponry is significant to most group developments. Weapons are instruments that increase the efficiency of particular activities associated with hunting, crime, law enforcement, self-defense, sports and war. It is likely that, among human groups, distrust, fear and competition with other non-kin groups for resources led to the employment of hunting implements being turned into instruments of warfare and violence against other individuals or groups. The evolution of the rifle from flintlock to missile launcher within a relatively short period of time is one instance of this evolution. Over time and transglobally across cultures, weapons evolved that could be effectively used or discharged at greater distances, thus providing safety from threats in intimate battle and greater destructive power (Bingham and Souza, 2009; Boot, 2006). Although it is often unrecognized, humans are the unique mammals to employ this evolutionary adaptation from food hunting to group violence and uninhibited excess killing.

Not only do humans kill with weapons effectively at an increasing distance and safety, they kill repeatedly beyond the immediate need.

As the capacity for larger scale violent killing emerged in early non-kin groups and resources became more available, the groups also increased in size and productivity. This in turn led to the establishment of a warrior and hero class with the creation of centralized tiered social structures that included efforts to prevent and suppress within-group disruptions and control access to weapons. As more complex and larger political aggregates evolved deterrence took on both a hierarchical structure and supported an increasing individual specialization, permitting expertise and experts a division of labor that included warriors, or specialists at warfare. In this new militant structure a devoted warrior elite[3] formed, based on material, expertise, kinship and the capacity to suppress within group conflicts and make war. Spoils, plunder and forms of taxation of a lower social class usually supported the warrior class. As political states emerged and their requirements for alliance and deterrence became more complex, cost-effective law enforcement became separated from the capacity to make war between non-kin related entities. Groups of all sizes exploited accidental new technologies for war making in their self-interest, leading to a long human history of violent conflicts with increasingly sophisticated and distancing weaponry (Bingham and Souza, 2009; Boot, 2006). This in turn led to larger evolving social organizations, including the creation of military warfare systems among political units of different sizes. The creation of and devotion to warfare systems is a variable among polities that is likely the result of underlying dynamics associated with the experience of threat and readiness to respond to conflicts with violent solutions. Violence or force that was once exclusively used to secure a mate became part of group selection.

War, and the capacity to make war as either conquest or deterrent, although highly disruptive and costly, is as important in our human history as kinship and the family, religious structures and personalities, and the economy and modes of exchange. Military organizations and war technologies, along with codes of laws and courts, are recognized major components of any social structure or polity (Otterbein, 2004). These social structures exercise coercive force, threat and power as a deterrent to within group disruptive behaviors and protect against between group violence. Between group violence was called war.[4]

Warfare erupted as a result of group cultural differences (non-kin coalitions), when larger diverse entities broke up (e.g., the Ottoman Empire) into smaller entities or polities joined to assure trade or protective alliances, or a polity was humiliated usually by force or insult. Almost all polities have a history of making war and that requires the political will to revert to extreme counter-democratic violent means to realize or actualize the group elite's interests and goals: usually warfare dominates a social political formation and unleashes and magnifies deeply embedded human violent potentials. In all of these war situations large numbers of combatants are sacrificed and non-combatants also die who are unable to flee and are usually unarmed. World War I was recognized as expanding the era of non-combatant casualties by the use of weapons from a distance. From a historical perspective all of the political states now in existence since 1500 owe their existence to warfare (Boot, 2006).

It is important to note that war does not simply start with the onset of actual hostilities. First a symbolic polarity that signifies an Enemy-Other needs to be created or reinforced, which in principle requires painful detachment or construction of that enemy from the non-kin interacting group alliances. Ideology and belief provide an anesthesia that blocks the pain of this detachment and denigration. From a humane perspective this is "a blow to the basic tissues of social life that damages the bonds attaching people together and impairs the prevailing sense of communality" (K. Erikson, 1996, p. 153). State organized perpetrated violence against a within subgroup of that state cannot occur unless it is preceded by symbolic and real acts of hostility and disengagement. In distinguishing war and genocide, it is important to understand that the evidence clearly exists that while a social and political structure emerged for wars, genocidal mass murder is more likely related to predatory killing that proceeded from an overwhelming advantage over victims (Jones and Fabian, 2009). Humans are more likely to kill other humans than many other mammals are to kill members of their own species.

Under normal social conditions most group coalitions attempt to inhibit violence, war-making and killing. Kaes (2007) broadly enabled a more definitive view of the normal complex intrapsychic relationships (links) in group coalitions. Relationships between an individual and a group in regard to basic dependency (protective) wishes, and importantly, individual and group defenses against bad or malignant psychic objects inside and outside the group allow normalized social interactions. While these below conscious psychic links usually protect individuals against solitude, threat and fear, Kaes suggested that these psychological attachment or links also function as a dynamic container in which structuring, defensive, aggressive and violent psychic individual alliances are normally psychically bound with varying potential to act. Socially performed rituals and articulated threats initiated by a group elite can be psychologically understood to serve to loosen that protective function and direct hidden (shadow) or suppressed violent actions against a targeted polity or individuals made different. The evidence for this becomes starkly clear in the real and psychological irrationality of actual targeting in "witch hunts." This form of targeting signals and prepares members of the polity for a violent categorical change in group moral beliefs and initiates radical otherization in which a newly defined enemy is often redefined as if it were an infectious disease to be eliminated or isolated. Most names assigned to such dangers or enemies aim to convey negative, dangerous and malicious threats: usually subhuman.

Preparing a polity psychologically for either war or genocide requires the creation of a specific group mindset with sufficient cause to enforce the psychological exclusion necessary for increased threat and violence to emerge. Such social dynamics are now generated through a series of familiar verbal and symbolic rituals, a language of disgust or revenge aimed at redefinitions of values and beliefs as preparation for within-group sacrifices and violent acts. At this point it is important to understand the massive restructuring of the values and beliefs in German society by the Nazis' repetitive propaganda, not openly evident in other societies (Bytwerk, 2004). The pressures to publically conform within a totalitarian system led to public falsifying preferences out of fear (Kuran, 1995) and to group pressure. People tailor their public choices and behaviors to avoid real social threat and political consequences making it harder for others to voice discontent. One important consequence is that the targeted group is redefined as different, antagonistic or dangerous to the other group's values, goals and existence and these acts are conformed to. For males another public response is a coercive call for military training including compliance with a new ideological requirement for permission for killing and for the targeting of those to be eliminated at little personal risk. This group behavior is constructed to be in the service of the larger polity, a belief system or a dominating elite group and should not be confused with individual sadism, in which cruelty is its own reward. One frightening example of this behavior is the speech of H. Himmler in 1943 to SS members in praise of callousness toward Jews (reprinted in K. Taylor, 2009, pp. 57–58). Unarmed civilians preparing for war also engage in the performance of "security" bonding rituals to reduce fear and annihilation anxiety in preparation for sacrifices to the elite military interests and for the unknown trauma to come. This also accomplishes a binding of within-group identity, while simultaneously denying (splitting off) the threat of destroying their collective identity. Often in war bystanders and civilians are exposed to cruel murderous events such as one described by Taylor (2009, p. 19) in which fifty Jewish men were beaten to death in Lithuania in front of an applauding crowd while their national anthem played. This event reveals not people who are coerced into watching, but a public preference for brutality embedded in a display of violence through the brutal killing of designated victims. The justification for the brutal killing was a political fabrication or preference falsification of revenge for political misdeeds. Such preferences are based on the perceived risks associated with oppositional responses. A common effect of preference falsification is the preservation of widely disliked structures and beliefs. Another is the conferment of an aura of authority and stability on structures vulnerable to sudden collapse. When the support of a policy, tradition or regime is largely contrived out of threat, its defeat can lead to immediate collapse of values and further preference falsifications for personal protection. Falsifications can be extreme and yet believed by Nazi soldiers. For examples see the recorded conversations of British captured Nazi solders who tell of a wide spectrum of beliefs including Jewish blood collecting rituals and mass rapes as if they were witnessed and real (Neitzel and Welzer, 2012).

The Nazi performance of violent security rituals coupled with the protective rise in group ethnocentrism has a deeper dynamic purpose. War leaders and their elite representatives seemingly contain the duality of the morally justified wish to eliminate the other and its opposite, a latent perceived threat to one's own self and/or one's group annihilation: to kill in war or to be killed. These large group behaviors and rituals protectively serve to "hide" fears of retaliation and revenge against the violent perpetrator. For example, Waite (1977) mistakenly argued that only Hitler possessed a psychological duality of destroy or be destroyed. But the symbolic idea of dying for a just cause, an ideology or religious belief or an elite warrior being carried back on his shield is quite ancient; all war makers ask their followers to join such risky and fearful violent tasks.

Coincident with the increased ritualization of war through the rise of avenues for media and symbols in the last hundred years there has concurrently been the development of transformational technologies and the rise of different structures of polities: nationalism, dictatorships and democracy that generated slow or sudden intergroup paradigm shifts in group tensions and conflicts from one set of moral and intergroup interests and ideological assumptions to another. These ideological shifts all led to warfare, civil war and revolution becoming an omnipresent social trauma, part of the experience of redefining polylingual polities or controlling resources regardless of political structure and ideological content.

Conflicting ideological beliefs change moral paradigms within the polities, causing them to become grounded in the key moral binary opposition of good versus evil that overwhelmed earlier designations of dynastic or religious based identity. The interests of each group became opposed to those of all other groups. Simultaneously with these ideological developments, the capacity to kill remotely geometrically increased over the last hundred years. Boot (2006) argues that polities that have successfully mastered the evolution in precise coercive technology and threat from a distance have redrawn the map of the world's destructive power. However, Boot also points out that technology is often not a prime mover, but a second-order consequence of food surpluses, urbanization, secularism, political stability and other conditions that create a fertile climate for innovation in weaponry. Boot is unknowingly describing the surprising fruits of successful non-kin collective cooperation in which actual military "threat" plays an increasing role in shaping technology.

With the technical development of increases in the potential to kill at a distance was the formation of sub-elite coalitions devoted to "special" violent warfare. Under certain conditions, highly specialized work groups emerged that formed a psychopathic alliance with political leaders: a sub-elite within the warrior elite to carry out extreme violent activity in defense of within-group interests. This unique work group carried its own uniforms and recruitment process, and seemingly operated outside the "rules" of war. They represented the special function of the psychopathic pact to kill and to threaten to kill. Such groups, like the SS and contemporary elite war units, are highly attuned to social signals of power and status, while their extreme violence is seen as pragmatic and devaluing of the victims' worth and humanity. However, it is essential to remember that this is a group of people who may receive different rewards for their cruel and murderous acts: they may be sadists, opportunists, executive planners, newly recruited novices, criminal types and ideological zealots wishing to please superiors. In fact, almost any reward can be linked with cruelty and violence in humans (K. Taylor, 2009). Following World War II such covert killing groups appeared in Chechnya, Thailand, Peru, Egypt and Kenya with the support of their sovereign government; their victims numbered in the thousands.

This evolutionary model of group coercion and control of weaponry when applied to Germany and the Holocaust reveals certain important and distinctive psychological patterns integral to mass murder. With the emergence of Hitler as chancellor came an increasingly number of legal acts against the Jews in over an extended time period, from 1933 to 1944, that sought to radicalize the image of Jews first as not German and as dangerous and then to be annihilated. The Nazi leaders constructed a redemptive struggle against imaginary world domination by "the Jew." This "legal" effort ended in the attempt to eradicate all the Jews in Europe that was integrated within the wider Nazi empirical war effort. During these years Hitler initiated a slow starting but rapidly escalating pattern of social/economic eliminative behavior that was not met with any opposition of equal force. The absence of organized opposition is a characteristic of successful governmental genocide: that there is no equal antagonistic force to stop the eliminative process once it starts. All governments have access and control of various military and coercive powers that have the potential to become violently abusive, but the question of how this coercive power apparatus turns violent and against a particular and designated segment of the within group is essential to understanding mass murder. Further, it is necessary to understand what specific cultures are prone to within-group violence and which individuals willingly carry out the mass killing of unarmed portions of the population. In militarized states individual and collective liberties are traded for military values (Mann, 2000) and cruelty in an early step toward genocide.

Notes

1 "Massen" in German is crowd or horde, society ("Gesellshaft") and community ("Gemeinschaft") are organized with boundaries and horde is an undifferentiated mass.
2 Over generations it is successful traits that survive, not individuals, and their survival depends on the abundance of their progeny. Freud failed to grasp that implication of Darwin's theory and turned the metaphor of "king" on its head. Freud's paternalism models itself on a relationship of genuine dependence on the father and the incapacity of the helpless child ignoring patronage in which each party has leverage (Van den Bergh, 1985).
3 "Elite": a select group that is superior in terms of ability or qualities to the rest of a group or society. A group or class of people seen as having the most power and influence in a society, especially on account of their wealth or privilege.
4 Ares the God of the insatiable violent unarmed aspect of war was distinguished from Athena who represented strategy and generalship.

2

THE ROLE OF NON-KIN COOPERATION, WEAPONS THAT KILL AT A DISTANCE AND SHARED BELIEFS IN GROUP FORMATION

> Just like the spirochete bacteria that carries syphilis so are the Jew the carriers of criminality in its political and apolitical form … The Jew is the true opposite of a human being, the depraved member of subracial mixing … He is the embodiment of evil that rises against god and nature … The devil.
>
> *(Keller and Anderson, 1937, quoted in Confino, 2014, p. 7)*

> The central fact which dominates the relations of Jew and non-Jew is that the Jew is "different." He looks different. He thinks differently. He has a different tradition and background. He refuses to be absorbed. Every Jewish money-lender recalls Shylock and the idea of the Jews as usurers. And you cannot reasonably expect a struggling clerk or shopkeeper, paying 40 or 50 per cent interest on borrowed money to a "Hebrew Bloodsucker," to reflect that almost every other way of life was closed to the Jewish people.
>
> *(Winston Churchill, 1937)*

Freud attempted to build his speculative theory of the evolution of human groups on the influence of unconsciously inherited predispositions to real and internal family psychic conflicts. His theoretical challenge of a wider cultural history was cast as if the dynamics of a "family," influenced by the unconscious power of fixed psycho-Lamarckian inherited developmental and cultural repetitions, replayed on a larger, royal cultural stage. It was a common misconception among early psychoanalytic theorists to simply interpret the modern state and its sovereign as being analogous to the conflicts within a family and its paternal leader. Father figure and dynastic head of the state were equated as if all states had male monarchies and were capable of and competing to produce offspring. However, a national state or republic is a more complex, centralized, dynamic entity conducting both domestic and international economic and political relations in its own interest. Freud's outdated and often-uncorrected theoretical Oedipal group theories were clinically and intellectually generative though they had an inhibiting effect on the study of organizational behavior, violence and war (Pick, 2012). Within the limited scope of the Freudian view murders were incorrectly cast as patricide and as driven by Oedipal and sexual dynamics. In addition, the reluctance of Freud, as the founder of the psychoanalytic movement, to leave Vienna in response to the threat of the Nazis had a chilling effect on the analytic establishment, which in turn mostly ignored the psychological significance of the Nazi terrors and mass murders. Analytic group theorists, who flourished during the war and after the Nazi period, suffered from a similar scotoma in terms of examining violence (Roth, 2013), failing to distinguish between the vast differences in the different expressions of aggression and mass violence. Psychoanalysts have remained handicapped in the study of violence because few of them have really been exposed to the naked form in which it commonly appears (Federn, 1940; Hyatt-Williams, 1998) As few violent offenders opted for therapeutic treatment, except under unusual circumstances, both psychoanalysts and group therapists defensively clung to their theories of aggression ignoring important psychic distinctions among human levels of aggression and between acts and fantasies of bodily harm, rape and murder. Aggression as a concept is usually associated with arousal and movement (forward) while violence refers to destructive attacks on bodies or minds as objects in reality frequently to eliminate their life or physical structure. Harmful violence is both expressed and threatened in a variety of direct and indirect forms among intimates, ideologically different coalitions, and kin and non-kin groups. While unlawful violence frequently is adjudicated, the existence of a threat of violence can also be understood as a forceful deterrent. However violence has prosocial and protective influences. From an evolutionary perspective the rise of safe human coalitions required means to establish varieties of internal and social deterrents to ensure security and generativity. The suppression and social management of varieties of human violence and self interest within human social groups and against other human groups was and is required to ensure social safety. However, all violence was not suppressed and organized violence between large social, religious and political groups frequently emerged as forms of terror and warfare.

From an evolutionary perspective survival of human group coalitions that were without the presence of immediate threat required access to the inexpensive means to suppress non-kin conflicts of interest on a large scale (Bingham and Souza, 2009, p. 105). This emergent force of suppression of asocial and antisocial conflicts served to limit and stabilize non-kin communities as protected and safe while yielding the variety of our vast cooperative societies with their varied supporting moral/judicial structures. Bingham and Souza (2009) and Otterbein (2004) believe that there is strong anthropological evidence that continued evolution of remote killing capabilities among early and modern societies were directly responsible for the emergence of social codes of threat/suppression on a wide scale (law enforcement). As non-kin societies emerged an armed military played a conspicuous role in maintaining social order. Enforced codes of conduct helped to establish a necessary suppressive prosocial structure with sufficient prohibitions that allowed non-kin larger groups to promote cooperation and reduce self-interested behavior. Group fitness or multilevel group selection theory (Wilson, 2015) proposes that each member of the social group likely received some social and real benefit from their suppression of violence which yielded cooperation and in return secured relative safety and generativity for their kin and cooperative groups. Bingham (Bingham and Souza, 2009) assumed that group fitness required the long-term self-interested use of the appropriate means of (social) inhibition and coercion that yielded or contributed to the framework upon which social cooperation and safety among non-kin groups relied and thrived. Social cooperation in human groups is self-interested only if substantial numbers of other individuals in the larger groups make the same choice to avoid censure (Wilson, 2015) and self-interested rule breakers are knowingly restrained, punished or expelled. Organized key individuals often promoted and benefited from codes of censure, venture and inter-societal warfare. In the nineteenth century in the U.S. laws were passed to regulate social behavior in which there was a growing sense of justice that included a right to a fair trial. The idea of a disinterested, fair and intelligent hearing when claims of right are presented is fundamental to a rule by law.

Coercive suppression of recurring dangerous, violent or undesirable behavior in non-kin groups enabled the emergence of many necessary prosocial governing structures. These included the growth of internal and external psychological inhibiting suppressors of behavior or moral constructs such as the prohibition against killing. As an important socializing by-product, organized ethical structures emerged through the interplay of biology and culture, giving rise to moral sentiments and codes of behavior that biased cultural evolution. Importantly with the rule of law, humans are the first animals in history to have access to individually inexpensive non-intimate violence, threat and restraint against individuals of the same species (conspecifics) that also enables large-scale excess killing. While social mores are recognized as essential, varied forms of interactive social coercions also exist in families and self-interested cooperating groups and organizations. These codes of behavior derive from social prohibitions, moral codes and enforcement as an important social by-product of most non-kin groupings. Social and family groups carry many adaptations to this inhibiting dynamism, among them our sense of cleanliness, purpose, cooperation and justice always to the advantage of the restraining elite class. From an evolutionary perspective conflicts of interests between healthy adults and between parents and children must be sufficiently suppressed in large groups so that the selfish strategies among related and unrelated individuals and other kin groups are no longer openly perceived as the best options. This in turn contributes to a psychologically significant feeling of being a part of something larger than an individual or family and a nascent sense of the proper distribution of the fruits of social cooperation among members. In contrast to other mammals, humans developed interactive psychological mechanisms when individuals tried to parasitize the cooperation ("free riders") or those with a high benefit-to-contribution ratio and internalized psychological mechanisms to help avoid potentially lethal or painful consequences for non-cooperation. Kegan (1982) recognized that this social adaption contributed to an important sense of belonging to and bonds within a culture as a significant developmental stage of group and individual identity. Kegan is suggesting that as individuals mature within kin and non-kin groups they develop progressively more awareness and appreciation of expected social (rule bound) behavior. Sharp and Fonagy (2008) provocatively suggested that there is a genetic predisposition for social cognitive capacity that likely sets the stage for and separates socially successful individuals and families from those who produce social delinquents or outsiders.

Often overlooked in group and social formation is the emergence of an elite. As elite strata developed within early human groups, the democratic expectancy of social and economic equality often wasn't fulfilled leading to the evolution of within group status, social stratification and conflicts. Elite status among humans remains an economic and social problem. Elite status varies across cultures while investing individuals or coalitions with real privilege and social powers over assets, coercive practices and opportunities. Hereditary rulers, landowners and priestly castes had great advantages (Wilson, 2015) in determining social rights and wrongs. Natural selection theory struggles to explain elitism and Freud only distinguished the "masses" who give vent to their appetites and those who restrain themselves to maintain their integrity. More rational cultural systems occurred through the influence of "great men" or the ongoing power of the "dead father": the covenant with the father after his death can be experienced as liberation or loss. Throughout Freud's theory is the remarkable bias of the dynamics of the father in a kin related family.

An accumulation of anthropological evidence suggests that elite authorities and leaders emerged in human coalitions with varied beliefs and devised selective punitive codes of conduct or "rules" in their interest for people to respect and follow. At a conceptual level these rules helped connect mental codes of interaction with social codes of behavior that helped keep people safe and alive (Berreby, 2005) and contributed to the formation of status or privilege subgroups in regimes. Social rules and various self-interested coalitions emerged sharing common values and beliefs. An important by-product of cooperative social status and moral rule making was establishing the means by which newcomers were taught accommodation and "group cooperation" along with information to help them survive, experience and learn their interpersonal environment cues to avoid the real pains of rule breaking. Cooperative schooling and social and religious codes contributed to a wide sense of group safety and identity along with means of suppression of disruptive forms of behavior. Kin and non-kin culture-bound rules co-mingled with parental education and interventions with children, constantly form(ed) behavioral guidelines for the psychological internalization of "ought," "good" (safe) and "bad" (punishable) constructs supporting safe child socializing behavior interacting with kin and non-kin social interactions. Cooperating social groups also established codes and characteristics for and boundaries of membership defining status and often excluding non-members violently. The sense of self can then be described in terms of moral, legal and ethical group values. This dynamic reappears in all group formation.

On a larger scale Bingham (Bingham and Souza, 2009) also claimed that the continued accidental and planned evolution of remote killing techniques produced and helped establish a wholesale complex reorganization of human societies and their social/competitive interactions. Privilege and status expanded from resources and birthright to include weaponry and successful competition. Warfare has never received the attention that is its due because killing and destruction are an embarrassment to disciplines that assume that humans are basically good. Advances in weaponry not only supported new and widespread evolutionary social patterns of large dominant non-kin aggregates and group violence, with the storage and use of vast resources necessary for mothers and children to survive. Innovations in weaponry contributed to potential military threat, warring and "the balance of power" among different polities. When considered with the co-emergence of complex language and cognitive capacities, the suppression of self-interest (to the point of individual and group safety) helped foster larger often-complex competing human social (non-kin) aggregates. Along with social complexity, a necessary functional and symbolic policing with external moral/judicial structures emerged for managing rule breakers. These achievements required liminal social learning and the teaching and sharing of correct cooperating behavior. As human cognitive capabilities enlarged, productive societies with resources created access to and social support for small and large technical innovations that increased individual life span, group security and the ability to subdue and exploit other polities. Coincident with these social group changes were the enhanced capacities for coercive violence and state warfare at an increasing (non-intimate) distance with increased sacrifice. In other words, Bingham and Souza (2009) argued, many of the features of expanded genetic evolutionary changes that emerged with psychological safety in communities are thought of as occurring on a platform of "a single group origin, an expanded scale of (interdependent) social cooperation" (p. 333). This evolutionary social growth of cooperative societies coincided with and was dependent upon the creation and adaptation of forms of suppressive weaponry useful at a distance with its varied social and coercive by-products (Bingham and Souza, 2009, p. 339). This perspective vastly differs from the "Law of the father" perspective of Freud.

The evolutionary emergence of actual and liminal self-policing functions and use of state authorized coercive force within human social aggregates of different ideological structures is a major human prosocial achievement. However, abuses of state organized coercive or punitive forces by any colonial, competitive or authoritarian state or the forces being turned against a specific segment of a polity (genocide) are all too common. In order to more deeply understand exclusionary coercive processes and absolutist demands for obedience it is necessary to move beyond Freud's theoretical Oedipal conceptions of groups and address the important idea of world shaping beliefs (Taylor, 2009). Psychoanalytic theorists seemed to ignore the function and varied purposes of an intrinsic human need for beliefs and belief systems for individuals. Britton in a series of papers (1998) uniquely addresses the role of beliefs in individual psychoanalytic treatment and its connection to unconscious fantasies. On a broad level shared prosocial beliefs and the formation of belief systems facilitated safe social attachments and bonding for individuals in groups while establishing various forms of transient or long-term communities. However, not all beliefs are prosocial as they only bias information. Beliefs can range from devout to superficial and are oriented to either process or end goal. In contrast to psychoanalysis, social psychologists have typically studied the societal function of beliefs and antisocial attitudes but have ignored their important unconscious functions and origins. It is evident that "beliefs" also serve a constant interpersonal orienting function not only to the unique environment and other elements as a particular social aggregate but to its co-inhabitants. Individuals and groups can "hold" contradictory beliefs, which often are not subject to external proof or integration. Confirmation bias and disconfirmation bias, a prejudged search for confirming evidence, are powerful weapons of collective and individual judgment.

The need for constant human social orientation developed because human beings evolved as inveterate "mind readers" in an interpersonal environ (Baron-Cohen, 2011), attributing meaning and intent to events and people in their environment. In addition, repetitive events elicited feeling, anxiety and beliefs about others or events in that environment, which in turn influenced perceptions of reality and other people in the social environment. Further perceptions easily became shaped by constellations of internal beliefs and triggered emotional responses throughout all psychic levels and expectancies. Aesthetic judgments and interpretative beliefs are thought to coincide with the emergence of human groups' tendency to repeat experiences or acts in concert, fostering expectancy and emotional preparation among participants about future outcomes of those acts and beliefs. Importantly, beliefs help people organize their perceptions of the social world, give meaning and context to inner stimulation, and recognition, appreciation and/or fear of the real and symbolic objects and events in that world. Beliefs then serve as practical guides or frames for perception, comprehension, value, decisions, emotion, affinity and response. Beliefs seemingly help solve a person's anxiety and adaptive problems while performing necessary acts of living in reality by declaring, categorizing and organizing distinctions needed to understand some perceived elements in oneself (reflection and reaction) and/or reality. However, despite being vital, beliefs are not factual and their strength is dependent on psychic conflict, prior experience, authorities and a variety of expectancies that have conscious and unconscious elements. Often categories or systems of beliefs are unexamined for proof. Additionally there are disorders of the belief function that give rise to psychic impairments or risk taking by influencing perception and judgment (Gorman and Gorman, 2017). Such impairments may either be transient or protracted (Britton, 1998) or arise from accommodations to anxiety in response to threat or earlier trauma and the search for an explanation for irrational or unexplainable behavior. Belief systems are often concerned with the existence of non-existence of conceptual entities, biological occurrences or future behaviors—birth, God, democracy, nations, witches, the unconscious—and rely on other believers and group dynamics for support and confirmation. Although beliefs exist in the absence of proof, they often influence discovery, expectations and outcomes and may reduce or exaggerate anxiety, violence or cooperation.

Almost all individuals have a hierarchy of beliefs, about themselves and other individuals or groups and values. Beliefs dynamically range from strongly held to weak and include basic expectancies of safety and survival at "home" and in other environments. In addition, beliefs are necessary for a wide variety of individual anticipations and determination of pleasure, disgust, illness, danger, arousal or threats. Beliefs prepare behavioral and psychological responses to a range of stimulating occurrences either in fantasy or reality and they influence perceptions and accommodation to new information.

Shared beliefs prepare and organize groups of like-minded individuals to form joint collectives to exchange and support these beliefs which are not always observable in reality and may or may not be learned. Any ideology, political, religious or scientific, can then be understood as a constructed and knowingly shared set of related beliefs and ideals thought to be coherent and distinctive by the believers, that organize and make sense of the social or actual world and usually require some form of acknowledgement, action and emotional response. Some beliefs are rooted in anticipations or interpretations of "facts" or actions, while others are invented, predictive or learned; beliefs vary in intensity from central to peripheral. Culture and political movements are understood as conceptual containers for certain constant and variable sets of interacting beliefs, and serve as an invisible barrier to significantly different competing or systems of beliefs. While conceptual and abstract beliefs cannot be proven, neither can they be disproven by evidence; thus, they may serve as guides for or barriers to acquiring information. Beliefs function as instrumental, process oriented or end goal. Almost all beliefs have a causal component; that is that something (A) is caused by something (B) and supplies some form of incentive or meaning. Or if one (A), (B) will occur. The dynamic of transference might be considered a particular form of belief concerning an individual based on the experiences or dynamics of one's conscious and unconscious history.

In contrast to beliefs, human psychological responses such as disgust and reactions to contamination are likely hardwired into humans and when triggered in the context of beliefs are powerful stimulants for fear, threat-safety behavior and otherization. These responses were historically used as quick and powerful emotional explanations for dangers and threats posed to an individual, family group or nations; they were also used as signals and beliefs to explain maladies or direct activities towards social goals, the need for punishment or distinguish the boundaries of "kin-ness." One of the best-known and most lethal cooption of such belief/threats occurred during the years leading up to and including the mass murders in World War II in which state organized false beliefs led to organized mass murders (Taylor, 2009). The Nazis cast the Jew as spreading racial and political pollution that undermined and restructured the values of the German state and people. The Jew's aim, in this Nazi fantasy, was an external projection of the real Nazi aim: to achieve world domination and actively subdue all of humanity. For the Nazi, the Jews were to be punitively punished for their imagined threat.

The Nazi ideological group leaders and media used a variety of evocative primitive threat terms to establish and enhance the belief in an impending Jewish threat and to change or enhance beliefs that designated significant others were dangerously "different." Jews were cast outside the social group's social-legal safe contract by the chancellor, rendering them vulnerable to a set of new increasing coercive and retributive acts and laws. This simultaneous state redefinition of the usual social contract of citizen led to the withdrawal of varieties of group cooperative empathy for this constructed malignant "other" so that former safe/tolerated group members were not accorded the protective continuity of his or her "I." The sharply differentiated segment of the large group was simultaneously constructed by elite politicals as a stranger or an antagonistic, dangerous enemy and hence unknowable, hateful, expendable or exploitable through collective malignant projective processes and false science. They were designated unclean, lethal, vermin, devils, excommunicated, exiled, inferior, not-me and therefore objectified as an anal (Chasseguet-Smergel, 1984; 1990) demonic soul-less thing to be cleansed or lived off in a lethal parasitic relationship (Patterson, 1990). The elite racial group used all of these vivid disparagements of Jews in the service of transforming the recognized mental/social code into a fantasy belief of blame, disgust and danger, drawing upon and resonating with other historical emotional sources of primitive fears. This Nazi-led change in beliefs fostered large-scale group-splitting behaviors, changing perception of and affinity for Jews and creating a dangerous yet vulnerable external "them." State radical otherization fostered the expression and condoning of a variety of violent actions against Jews by both individuals and designated national "protective" groups. These mnemonic devices can be understood as gathering unconscious traces in the history of the development of human societies into a politicized racial ideology of dangerous difference and betrayal in order to instill fear and promote the acceptance of violent militarized solutions as a preventive remedy. That racial ideology appropriated the rituals and ceremonies of a faith and a discipline's religious fervor offering rhetoric without proof or legal hearing. Proof was politically supplied by the creation of national racial exclusionary laws. The Nazi catechetical message was forcefully re-enacted by Nazi leaders following Hitler's repeated depiction of Jews as the disease or threat that infected Germany and was responsible for prior humiliations and defeats (Bytwerk, 2004). As the Nazi state created, employed and monopolized weapons and other means of human destruction, the increasing utilization of these killing devices against unarmed, unorganized Jews was promoted and justified within this false belief system. Cooperation among the members of the German state was required to enforce protective and lawful discrimination and violence. Once punitive otherization as part of a belief system is accepted, moral codes are changed and the victims were mythically constructed as inhuman depraved monsters (Taylor, 2009, p. 185) that must be removed or purged (Frankfurter, 2006).

This eliminative, racist behavior coincided with a Nazification of eugenics, which spread to other countries after the Nazification of conquered territories and the extended use of violent coercive practices that defined unarmed and unorganized Jews as continued threats. In this violent dynamic, which accelerated over more than eight years, Nazi leaders promoted this destructive fantasy (false belief) by repeating excited, emotional language that found deep resonance among a wide range of European group members. Germans profoundly "identified" with the ideological leader, his rhetoric and his providential goals, aimed at creating a violent society (Gerlach, 2010) that accepted a violent mythic cure. Europeans from all levels of education made themselves psychologically available to the Nazi illusion and lies and were attracted to become secondary components of action or organizational leaders. The Nazi rhetoric included accepting Hitler's fantasy millennialist solution and beliefs (Bytwerk, 2004; Kaes, 2007; Roseman, 2007; Mazower, 2009) as a fantasy end product of racial purity. This destructive coalition of an ideology of threat, violence and millennialist fantasy resulted in a widespread combination of spontaneous criminal acts and organized exploitation through the Nazi multipoint network. A media system controlled and organized by the Nazis carried conjoined violent fantasies and lies about unarmed Jews, with the openly expressed goal to eventually eliminate their existence. Without observable remorse or guilt, knowing enough to know that they did not want to know more or require proof, Germans constructed a façade of justified belief, enhanced by the Nazi regime's Machiavellian manipulation of all sources of communication within the country. This resulted in a widespread German belief and allegiance to a wider imaginary racial cause, acquisition of power over who shall live, and the reversal of the defined negative (monstrous) evil: to kill so as to cure (Lifton, 1986). In other words, for Germans to accept the hallucinotic belief that the murder of the Jewish evil was a path to a pure German empire.

It is important to understand how this imaginary belief system emerged. In Germany beginning with Hitler's ascent in 1932 the normal state coercive practices ensuring safety and lawful behavior were in disarray and were brought under Hitler's personal control, exaggerated and turned against the Jews in Germany. As Hitler gained power he exercised an accelerating coercive separation of Jews from the social and economic lives of Germans through racial laws and crafted illusions to their active threat in speeches and media before the mass killings began. For a regime dependent on constant mobilization, the Jew served as the necessary constant mobilizing (paranoid) threat (Friedlander, 2007, p. xix) usual to a paranoid political process. The actual number of laws passed against Jews in Nazi Germany has been estimated to number between 400 and 2,000, creating a social and legal atmosphere in which Jews specifically were made socially, educationally and economically vulnerable. All of these actions were engineered through the Nazification of the judicial systems and often involved courts, local police, the Gestapo, work camps and willing informers, building an unspoken but open legal and visible division in the country between Germans and Jews. Normal legal (inhibiting and coercive) practices in German society were tactically and willingly manipulated to separate, stigmatize and plunder Jews without any threat of punishment to the attackers. This was all exercised in conjunction with the open expression of a salvatory ideology of racial difference and imagined German superiority from a

Fuhrer who promised relief and salvation through retributive military action. Bingham (Bingham and Souza, 2009) and Bessel (2009) believed that exploiting the Jews also yielded economic gain that was necessary for the Nazi war effort and economy. Friedlander (2007) believed that Hitler became a providential leader fighting against his constructed metaphysical enemy, drawing upon beliefs of the purity of the state, the battle against dreaded Bolshevism and the ultimate millennialist redemption in the future German empire.

This creation of a composite dangerous "them" was partially made possible by Hitler's ideological orthodoxy which had made overarching claims, from the 1920s onward, based on a monopolistic set of ideological imperatives with the unique feature of personal loyalty: belief in Hitler was to be loyal to his racial beliefs and goals (Hitler's *Volkstaadt*).[1] Unquestioned loyalty to the leader was central to elite totalitarian systems (Adorno, 1973; Bytwerk, 2004) and coincided with the open removal of any political opposition in a manner much like early religions purged pagans. Hitler's status as an outsider also lent support for the promise of a new Germany and an attack on a failed earlier Weimar regime. Often when seeking to implement his "beliefs" or ideology. Hitler successfully made personal appeals for loyalty based on his political status accompanied by his potential and history of carrying out his violent threats. Within the increasingly coercive totalitarian atmosphere in Nazi Germany that restricted choice, that "threat" and stigmatization converted into terror and mass murder with little open opposition or disobedience (Gellately, 2001; Friedlander, 2007). Central to his Nazi ideology propaganda and rhetoric was the melding of an imaginary "World Jewry" and "World Bolshevism" as imaginary joined twin enemies conspiring against the rightful redemptive return of a future Nazi German empire: the Third Reich. These false beliefs, combined with a willing and controlled media and judiciary, fostered informal and formal social cooperation within the German population from 1932 onward creating and drawing upon a latent Anti-Semitic culture. A paranoid explanation, with Jews/Bolsheviks at its center, was found for prior German ills and the loss of the earlier war. From 1939 onward, as Germany became a militarized country "at war" these causes accelerated into escalating murderous violence. Central to this violent Nazi war state mentality was eliminating or murdering their internal and external enemies (armed or unarmed) beyond the rule of law, blurring any distinction between dispassionate warfare between states and dispassionate execution of unarmed people and children (Pergher and Roseman, 2013). Such blurring of prohibitions against what are usually criminal acts in war provided new possibilities and opportunities for local authorities and common criminal groups to implement a range of their deepest violent racist aspirations against Jews: shattering most fundamental social prohibitions without penalty and often openly cooperating with Nazi goals. Homes, businesses, assets and objects given for safekeeping disappeared into German ownership. Books and religious articles were destroyed or confiscated as if to erase history.

Hitler's self-proclaimed role and status as oracle and redeemer was encouraged and vividly constructed on the repeated (false) idea of the promise to destroy the

Jewish threat (and all other threats) both inside and outside of Germany. This imaginary Jewish threat was structurally indispensable to the idea and image of national savior and empire builder (Redles, 2008) and the murder of non-military Jewish citizens uniting the people to recognize and act against a common enemy. Individual violent wishes are "harvested" by this paranoiac political process and ideologically organized by the leader creating opportunities for the expression of violence, retribution and redemption.

Significantly the Nazi "new order," both within Germany and their stunningly conquered countries, displaced prior state organs with Nazi governors and laws, creating autocratic fiefdoms of violence and corruption. Nazi group dynamic actions, which were sanctioned by a belief in "delegated by the Fuhrer" and "by the will of Hitler," kept the Nazi predation forceful. The ideological hubris of the Nazi predators swept away critical social and moral thinking. The constant and threatening hierarchical demand for compliance to Nazi belief systems and symbols also helped cover the dangerousness of Hitler's international goals for a competing empire for the German people. The appeal of and the deification of Hitler's Utopian vision (vowed future goals and beliefs) fostered an almost ceaseless "impunity of thought and violent action" (Aly and Helm, 2002) until violently defeated. Once defeated, recognizing the immorality of the actions came at a heavy price for Germans confronting the régime's criminal actions. Powerful illusions are difficult to mourn.

The Nazi system of group national and future beliefs, within a millennial and criminal moral system, fermented irrational ethnic hostility combined with what appears as group arrogance of impunity. This created a special form of an extremely violent society (Gerlach, 2010) based on a conspiracy theory of an illusionary enemy as well as real enemies. These false beliefs persisted to the end of the war.

A closer look at conspiracy theories is revealing. The interplay between pre-existing widespread psychological vulnerability and uncertain or prior attack on social cultural beliefs often leads to the vulnerability necessary for the emergence of conspiracy theories as a political tool. Such theories are alternative explanations for the real or imagined threatening future or a particular threat. Often the imagined conspiring agents are described as attempting to destroy or circumvent deeply held or imaginary cultural beliefs or symbols. The function of a prophetic leader is naming the threat that "makes" it recognizable and distinct from a virtuous opposite authority. Hitler's anchoring and objectification of the Jewish threat helped define Hitler as an expert and made the threat he articulated dynamic and real. In this semi-paranoid process misinformation becomes real, forming a frame of separation and inclusion that moves groups into action, recruits bystanders while demotivating the targets or enemies (Tarrow, 1994).

Any assumption that many individual Nazis had deviant personalities within such a violent society is missing an essential issue. Diagnosis of individual pathology serves as a screen or icon to hide the wide range of participants attracted to various elements and opportunities possible within such a widespread illusory group belief system. Racism and psychopathology have some common features. However, people whose self-esteem has been attacked with low levels of trust are most vulnerable to conspiracy theories and social violence. Such individuals in groups are particularly vulnerable to vivid emotional appeals for sponsored revenge for imaginary injustices, violations of sacred beliefs or sites, and past enemies (Gorman and Gorman, 2017). Hitler's reparative racist empirical goals used many of these devices to bond anxious Germans. In addition, some of the most dangerous and violent forms of political paranoia, the idea that sinister forces are secretly engaged in elaborate plots, are a magnet for an ecosystem of beliefs that promises to return order and control. The promise is a false or totalitarian one and historically led to violence.

Embodied in the imaginary Nazi racial solution were the uniforms, images and symbols of the Nazi threat as a bond and stimulant to predatory violence: essentially the Nazi state assumed power over who should live and that power filtered down as an individual's right. Any predatory violent action that emerged among the diverse elements of the Nazi party, army, SS, industrialists, physicians and professional classes was constructed as legally justifiable and in the Fuhrer's and Germany's service. Jews in such a violent society were expendable targets as the primary purveyors of evil and this allowed spontaneous expressions of violence against any. In the medical society, Jews were treated as inferior animals that ethics did not apply to.

Extreme violence became a Nazi radicalization of political and military-state political and coercive power. Within an illusory and conspiratorial belief system that limits choices for all individuals, whether perpetrators or victims, caught in its initiatives and reach, violence easily spreads and ignites among and within prepared group coalitions. Few righteous individuals or groups dared to stand up for decency or truth. At the same time the norm for followers of Hitler's authority and beliefs in the Nazi ideology was anticipation of the Fuhrer's destructive violent wishes creating extended fiefdoms of violence in occupied areas and privatized industrial companies. Through a fantasized interactive merging of wished-for empirical goals and obsessions with their leader's beliefs, numerous and imaginative forms of collaborations and horrors took place. Kaes (2007) and Lifton (1999) explain that from a group perspective, a group of any size can become the means of realizing various hallucinatory goals of its members and/or symbolic all-knowing leader. The individuals in harvested groups must be in a heightened emotional state to be receptive to such a prophetic goal. The hallucinotic goal of a Third Reich and a Nazified Europe offered its believers diverse forms of emotional identifications with real or imaginary violent gratifications regarding race and betrayal. The Nazis created a violent empire by assuming total military power over masses of people in Europe, their assets and authority over whether they lived. Believing in, joining or acting within any aspect of such an extended violent group, even temporarily, required an unconscious pact with the symbolic leader and his imaginary beliefs and violent end goals. Lifton (1986) examined such a racial pact and belief in negative eugenics made among the Nazi doctors. Individual differences in the integrity of psychological identity among Germans doctors as well as their relative need for an external leader, mission or conspiracy may have determined their willingness to join with the Nazi malevolent false belief system. However, important distinctions regarding the transformations by violentization (Athens, 2003) is necessary to distinguish levels of beliefs, and active participation among the doctors as criminal needs to be made. The willing and continuous mass killing of and experimentation on unarmed people requires a deeper psychoanalytic explanation than Lifton's use of doubling as a defense to avoid guilt (1986, p. 421). Once the German doctors accepted the false belief of the Jew as a disease, as having the same ethical status as a laboratory animal, then they were reactive to this hallucinotic belief that they were removing a disease. A delusion of a disease made a healer into a killer.[2] Proctor (1988) concluded that the Nazis' health activism ultimately came from the same "twisted root" as their medical crimes: the ideal of a sanitary pure racial utopia reserved exclusively for pure and healthy Germans.

Hitler's central aim of racially purifying the German community through purifying execution (Semelin, 2009) was violent from its early inception. This aim encouraged direct license for "sleeper needs" (needs expressed only when normal social rules are suspended)[3] to be expressed openly masquerading as science. For example, German medical journals openly expressed the need to find a "final solution" to Germany's Jewish and Gypsy problems. An ideology of purification accelerated into sweeping tentacles of a racial struggle turned murderous and exploitative. Without any moral or military opposition, one product of this dynamic destructive authoritarian system was that the longer the regime lasted, the more megalomaniacal grew its aims, and the more unlimited its mass destructiveness. The relationship between the Nazi regime's megalomaniac utopian goals, preoccupation with and capacity for war, and use of murder as a solution remained embedded to differing degrees in Nazi individuals wherever they assumed control over lives. However, the image of all Nazis as jack-booted fanatics fails to account for the extent to which it appealed to intellectuals, academics and physicians; the degree to which they used the imagery of science in their propaganda appeals and the disturbing degree that Nazism infiltrated science (Proctor, 1988, p. 283).

Stated simply in Bion's (1961) group terms, conscious and unconscious cooperation among individuals was considered a prerequisite for any group to be effective in its task(s): even when the task was violentization or mass wholesale murder. When the task was a megalomaniacal violent eliminative fantasy, all the group members, no matter their role, shared individually in that omnipotent power of their leader. This megalomaniacal fantasy helped the Nazi recruiting efforts in their extended war against Jews[4] by attracting and enhancing latent anti-Jewish sentiment in their allies and conquered areas. This murderous appeal can only be traced by trying to grasp the effects of a collective group nationalistic military processes that combined millennialist utopianism, false science and illusory conspiratorial beliefs with an empirical revolutionary spirit to persecute and tyrannize distinct civilian racial populations. The problem of psychologically analyzing the wide range of personalities among perpetrators and persecutors in order to comprehend when obedience to a (false) belief system turns from a virtue into a murderous crime remains highly problematic. While the term "genocide" is arguable better replaced by Gerlach's "extremely violent societies" (Gerlach, 2010) in which large-scale physical violence targets various population groups, a variety of motives remain explicit. It is clear that as the Nazis initiated acts of war initially against Poland, other countries and then Russia, the Nazis and their cooperating followers, knowingly or unknowingly, crossed a violent murderous threshold. This included developing methods for mass killings, forced removal and expulsion of people, forced starvation and labor, collective rape and strategic bombing and imprisonment. The Nazis were not the first political state to justify individual or mass murder with an illusory or false belief. The continued use of false belief systems to historically organize state sponsored murder is a human phenomenon throughout the history of nation building, colonization and ethnic cleansing. The common ideology features appear to be a belief in a closed system of "purity" with the real or imagined threat of "difference" parsed through false beliefs and a Machiavellian leader with exclusive access to the apparatuses of murder.

Notes

1 A German compound term meaning Hitler's people's state.
2 "Don't be misled into thinking you can fight a disease without killing the carrier, without destroying the bacillus. Don't think you can fight racial tuberculosis without taking care to rid the nation of the carrier of that racial tuberculosis. This Jewish contamination will not subside." Speech by Hitler to Nazi doctors, 1920.
3 Most riots occur when there is the belief that normal social rules have been abridged and there is a "threat."
4 There were more victim groups than Jews. Persecution and murder varied throughout German controlled Europe. It was structured by a variety of actors and interwoven logics and carried out in a variety of ways (Gerlach, 2010); the link between warfare and genocide is significant and will be explored.

3

A NEW EVOLUTIONARY BASIS OF GROUP DEVELOPMENT

Ernst Janning: There was a fever over the land. A fever of disgrace, of indignity, of hunger. We had a democracy, yes, but it was torn by elements within. Above all, there was fear. Fear of today, fear of tomorrow, fear of our neighbors, and fear of ourselves. Only when you understand that – can you understand what Hitler meant to us. Because he said to us: "Lift your heads! Be proud to be German! There are devils among us. Communists, Liberals, Jews, Gypsies! Once these devils will be destroyed, your misery will be destroyed."

The Nuremberg Trials. *Movie (1961), S. Kramer, Director*

If Gandhi's enormously powerful and successful strategy of non-violent resistance had met with a different enemy—Stalin's Russia, Hitler's Germany, even pre-war Japan, instead of England—the outcome would not have been decolonization but massacre and submission.

H. Arendt (2014, pp. 160–161)

Understanding the evolutionary basis of human group cooperation and its violent disruptions is far more than an academic or historical issue; such an understanding is critical to understanding the ever-present dynamic effects of state-sponsored armed conflict or war and mass murder. To expand our dynamic knowledge of these calamities it is essential that a comprehensive description of individual human development be clarified that includes specific attention to the development and dynamics of social/group membership that emerge from benign and enforced- socialization. The dynamics of safe and violent large cultural group behavior is not only crucial to the dynamics of individual identity as formulated by Erikson (Schwartz, 2001), Kegan (1982) and Quinn (2005), it plays a hidden and significant role in the formation and power of such diverse group behaviors as the establishment of group beliefs, ideologies and mass murders.

From a developmental perspective the evolutionary emergence of helpless human infants is coincident with a protective environment supplying intense parental and alloparental care within the various configurations of human kin groups. The human baby does not need to be physically precocial. Rather than investing in the development of locomotion, defense and food acquisition systems that function early in the development of other organisms, the human infant works instead toward building a more effective phenotype: the set of observable characteristics or traits derived from a unique genetic code interacting with its human and social environment. The human neonate brain develops and continues interactive rapid growth with its corresponding orchestrated cognitive competencies largely directing attention toward the immediate interpersonal and social environment. Plastic neural systems readily adapt to the nuances of the local community such as its unique language components, facial expressions, emotions, food, symbols and the gradual introduction of prohibitions. In contrast to the slow development of the ecological survival skills of movement, fighting and feeding, the human child quickly develops early and ongoing interactive skills acquiring the complex communication system of human verbal and non-verbal language. The extraordinary information transfer abilities enabled by emerging linguistic competency in infants and children provide an expanding conduit to the information available from other human minds and intentions (Baron-Cohen et al., 2008; Baron-Cohen, 2011). The emergent capability for intensive and extensive communication potentiates and sharpens the social characteristics of intimate infant human interactions between individuals and eventually within kin groups. Social interactions provide verbal and non-verbal mechanisms for essential expanding patterns of social learning and basic genetic and neural driven environment interactions. The child's growing cursive pattern recognition and abstract symbolic representation central to *animate* linguistic competencies enable the open-ended, creative and flexible information-processing characteristic of humans, especially of children (Summers, Szanto and Crespi, 2013). For the emerging child, cultural information and social behavioral patterns are especially interactively dynamic because they are a fundamental aspect of embedded human social coalitions and collaborations. These early interactions are supported by the nature of the reverie and active containing functions between mother and child along with the crucial protection of pair bonding. Pair bonding allowed children to recognize their fathers fostering the recognition of kinship networks and cooperative behavior.

Human culture is not just a pool or source of information: it is an arena and theater of social interaction, manipulation and competition enabled by levels of cooperation and learning. Success at social cooperation is a continuing learning task and individuals bear a cost for social cooperation and interaction. However, unlike other species, humans are capable of bonding and competing with their own species for supplies other than food. Wars, genocide, murder, bullying, injustices are the result of hyper-competitive or hyper-patriotic behavior such that other humans living in groups are historically the most hostile force in nature (Scaruffi, 2006; Pinker 2011; Summers, Szanto and Crespi, 2013). It is essential to accept this notion in order to establish a path to understand the dynamics of mass killing of unarmed humans and the emergence of extreme violent societies. Culture is contested because it is a contest and requires adaptive skills to negotiate. Human infants need sufficient time to prepare for entry into cultural arenas (Quinn, 2005) and the rapid stimulating impingements on individuals that are created by the variety of shared social encounters. It is the explicit aim of child rearing to enable that immature human to become functional and a self-sufficient adult in their community (Kegan, 1982). From the start of their existence all children are immersed in a cultural world that has a moral force within which its safe practices are imbued: approval and disapproval. What occurs in all childrearing are predispositional priming and evaluative messages necessary for a culturally distinctive self and survival of that self (Spitz, 1957; Quinn, 2005). Early regulation of the child is based on parental reaction that is embedded within an affective culture that contains risk. Learning the restrictions and prohibitions of a primary kin group is the way of demonstrating that the individual belongs to that group and is not easily explained by individualistic motives. The child's motivation to conform to intimate social behavioral norms stems from learning to avoid the "pains" of disapproval and punishment. This group oriented behavior suggests the possibility that group oriented behavior is not driven by individualistic or "selfish" interests which suggests the existence of prosocial motives for preserving the group. This is likely the aspect of personality that Bion (1961, p. 169) referred to as "groupishness"—a kind of innate inner group-minded awareness and concern.

The emergence of and compliance with the dictates of the internal emerging superego from a psychoanalytic perspective is something quite different from bonding to a group, group mentality or a social IQ. Social IQ develops from interactions with other people and learning from success or failure in socially bound environments with individuals and groups.

Alongside these normal supportive and learning enhancements for children are the ongoing presences of coercive practices (social prohibitions and rules—laws) emphasized by Bingham (Bingham and Souza, 2009). These restrictive practices that include cleanliness and language acquisition vary among different families and cultures. The presences of symbols of restrictive inhibition/laws in both family and local culture become more significant as development and mobility continues and eventually are internalized as part of human moral development as a range of external, verbal and social prohibitions with varied consequences. This formulation of the social contributions to morality is significantly different from the classical psychoanalytic formulation of the emergence of a morality attained through bodily control and identification by emphasizing the role of interactive social cues in a communicative field that contains perceived limit setting and concern for the fears of inclusion and exclusion from the group.

Group, family, economic class and culture membership support representations of an emerging complex self-identity as well as average morality and group values in a reciprocal relationship. This psychical identity earns expression in a socially complex manner as dynamic internal constructs: "You, Me, Us, We" (Zahavi,

2015). Cultural and family values and morals determine the components of each interpersonal category. The relationship between the similarities of beliefs usually indicates a common origin or group identity (We). Over time more than one "We" identity emerges as social membership becomes more varied and flexible. Individuals who through group selection "run afoul" of culturally proscribed group mores or rules are described as atypical, criminal, delinquent or socially dysfunctional. Severe early personality pathology arises not only when the psychological mechanism of attachment is disorganized or dysfunctional and cannot fulfill the biological function of preserving the intactness of emerging self, severe pathology may arise when there is an incapacity to develop a safe "We." When an individual physically violates kin and non-kin values, morals or codes of behavior they are likely subject to forms of restraints and censor. If an individual is a member of a social minority the "We" identity reflects the perceived status of that minority.

Mental health interventions in Western societies are usually directed at violent or inadequate rule breakers but rarely at failures to find either a group identity or a reciprocal self-interest group that results in extreme forms of social withdrawal, isolation and failures in intimacy (Us) and securing employment or resources. Overly violent and immature individuals during development are subject to shaming, punishment and often protective separation from their kin and non-kin group. In contrast, isolated individuals struggle to find a peer group identity. The Nazis sought to purify their "We" identity by eliminating children and adults who were physically incapacitated as biological rule breakers as if a predatory society that could not tolerate free riders or risk the spread of inferiors. Free riders are persons whose reward ratio is larger than work ratio by choice or by deficit.

The amount of time and resources necessary to build adaptive forms of social and psychological based individual and group identity that includes social consequences vary within specific cultural complexity. Social identity is best understood as an ongoing individual psychic process and struggle within the overt and covert demands of being a participant member of social groups and adapting to their beliefs, values and intentions.[1] On an intergroup level, from an evolutionary perspective (Summers, Szanto and Crespi, 2013), whatever drove humans to bond together in non-kin groups of all sizes must have been ominous given our prolonged period of social learning and the constant violence between non-kin coalitions and groups. Between group violence is usually based on mutual declarations of "We" and "Them" formed by the real and imaginary projections of differences between the groups.

Mature self-reflective capacities have frequently been described as a developmental outcome of adolescence as a sense of inner solidarity with one's groups' ideals, the consolidation of elements that have been integrated into one's sense of self from one's own psyche and family, including social groups to which one belongs. Social identity is often described as group identity in the social psychological literature. External aspects such as native language, country of origin and racial background would be considered under the concept of a complex group identity (Schwartz, 2001). Important outcomes of individual development or "ego identity"

(Erikson, 1956) are the product of differing childrearing practices interacting with genetic endowment within varying family structures and values. Parents usually raise their children to encourage the development of those qualities they believe are needed for survival and success in their particular cultural/political niches. Totalistic or democratic cultures produce very different outcomes of child rearing behaviors (Quinn, 2003). When children's survival and/or subsistence are at risk, parenting practices will be tailored towards maximizing their physical well being and safety rather than promoting their autonomy (McElhaney and Allen, 2001). Although the achievement of a personal identity may be considered a universal developmental goal, the link between sociocultural context and identity formation (group and individual) is dynamically complex and culturally variable. For current purposes the relationships between large groups, coalitions or polities with conflicting belief systems have not avoided the imagined malignant threats that leads to violent clashes. warfare and prejudice.

From an evolutionary perspective, the chances are extremely remote that non-kin groups evolved without "managing" competitive aggression, beliefs and non-kin violence as well as attempts at integrating gregarious cooperation and coercive threat (Otterbein, 2004). Awareness and ritualization of predatory threat and coercive practices are considered as crucial to ongoing group cooperation as gregariousness and cooperation (Otterbein, 2004). Perhaps only in humans have such complex violent abilities or behaviors combined and contributed to a selective premium for individuals able to promote social cooperation while improving their weaponry: to form kin and non-kin war group alliances (Alexander, 1948; Bingham and Souza, 2009; Otterbein, 2004). Only Fornari (1974) among psychoanalysts ventured to say that warfare is the externalization and articulation of shared unconscious processes in fantasy. This psychic organizer is primary among the fantasies associated with real and imagined threat or the securing of resources: I must kill in order to save the self or by identification, I protect the nation I identify with.

It is possible to summarize the major conflictual points of non-kin social group development through the life cycle as being the management of and integration of gregariousness and different forms of self-interested competition through the emergence of individual (kin) interests. Emerging individual internal representations of identity, interests and choices must be supported and constrained by the development of a psychic-social independent identity. This (I) identity must include the awareness of consequences for selfish/violent interests at some personal cost. A few psychoanalytic theorists have addressed the internal balances and integrity between the emergence of individual identity and a separate but coexisting group or "We" identity, yet both are significant for adaptive success in any social reality. Often the most socially adaptive, those with the capacity to correctly read and negotiate their social environment are viewed as "normal" when required to find a self-interest group that allows for a continuity of life and character fitness. Such individuals read and negotiate their social non-kin environment with great skill and avoid negative consequences.

As articulated by Erikson and his followers (Schwartz, 2001), I have been careful to separate group identity development from that of individual identity in accord with Zahavi's (2015) conceptual distinctions of "You, Me, Us and We" distinguishing different interpersonal aspects of a functional identity with attachments to others. From a psycho-diagnostic perspective the imbalance between the stronger group (We) than individual (I or me) identity may be both an adaptation to various trauma, and responsible for much of the pathology attributed to perpetrators, cult members and other selectively antisocial individuals. In other words, those who seek membership in violent and non-violent authoritarian/millennial groups with dualistic worldviews are likely attempting "repair" or stabilizing a faulty or weak inner sense of individual identity through highly structured and prescriptive violent external group membership. In addition, such persons are described as susceptible to believing theories that resolve anxiety concerning threat, need to control aspects of their environment and hostility and expect authoritarian leadership to limit options.

The study of normal and abnormal forms of identity (I) has become central in research on the psychopathology of severe personality disorders (Kernberg, 2003). The subjective term "self" with the process of affect regulation in the context of attachment of "Us" relationships has replaced the focus on the concept of identity in general psychoanalytic literatures. A closer examination of the dual concepts of individual and social identity is necessary to grasp the significance of social or "We" identity and its relation to forms of within group violence.

According to Erikson (1956, 1980), the individual personality develops as he/she successfully resolves specific human developmental crises that are distinctly socially expressed (between people) in society but dependent upon the integrity of an internal sense of one's essential psychic identity. Separateness (from primary kin group) with attached relatedness and competence in non-kin groups are important individual goals for survival and success (Kegan, 1982). Normal developmental stages from infancy onward lead to establishing a sense of trust in one's self and others within expanding cultural group configurations, developing a sense of internal identity in family and social groups, and helping the next generation prepare for their future. Kegan (1982) understands this process as an effort to resolve the developmental tensions of the demands for individual differentiation with self-definition and an equally powerful desire to be effectively immersed in the social world with others for intimacy, achievement and rewards.

Although hampered by a Western cultural bias related to the concept of "choice," this "ego" or identity theory is clearly based on a developmental model of psyche-social interaction in modern Western society that favors unique individuality that is rooted in successful social alliances. In totalitarian and primarily religious states choice is often excluded in individual struggles for independence where conformity is enforced or opportunities do not exist.

Emerging adults in every cultural niche form a psychological sense of internal identity and are increasingly required to either adapt to their culture and/or "individualize" their life courses in general and their identities in complex forms of social, economic and intimate relationships (Quinn, 2005; Kegan, 1982). Among these "normal" developmental activities are seeking and working to gain educational or informational competence/credentials and employment experience, searching and then taking the initiative to join self-interest groups for social values and economic security, and to secure safety and intimacy over time. In contrast to individual identity, social identity (we) is described as a sense of inner solidarity with important group ideals, along with the consolidation of psychic elements that have been integrated or one incorporates into one's sense of self from early kin and later non-kin groups. Socially mature identity has sometimes been described as group identity in the social psychological literature requiring flexibility in membership over life span changes. In sum, Erikson's theory seems to straddle the poles between intra-psychic origins of self-knowledge and representation as identity and inter-relational aspects necessary for safe and productive social participation in intimate and larger culture structures without relying on exclusively on sexuality.

Schwartz (2001) argued that Erikson's ideas are metaphorical and rich in description of identity but without precise definitions. Westen (1985, 1992, p. 529), in reviewing the empirical and theoretical literature on self and identity, summarized similar major components of identity adding internal psychic standards of behavior and a continuous awareness of who one is. Westen also added a worldview and a finding of a "place" in it: "a sense of continuity over time; emotional commitment to a set of self-defining representations (beliefs) of self, intimate and social role relationships, and core value and ideal self." These mature elements lead to the development or acceptance of a world view that gives life meaning, and some recognition of one's place in the world by significant others. Marcia (1988) recognized four different general developmental identity dynamic outcomes of normal adolescent stage development: identity confusion, identity foreclosure, identity moratorium and identity achievement. However, there are many individuals who are socially forced to seek "default identification" within non-kin groups because it requires adjustment to external circumstances or limited access, and leads to less goal directed drive and information seeking. It is important to remember that identity formation does not occur in the abstract, it always takes place in a multilevel psychosocial context, within kin and non-kin cultural groups and opportunities. Developmental identity conflicts are implied as the result of fixations or failures to achieve mature functioning. However developmental sequences outside of the opportunities in Western culture call into question the possibility of choice in identity formation. Default identification may be one norm, as choice/searching requires economic/political and kin stability combined with personal freedom and opportunity within an existing safe receptive culture. In non-Western cultures with fewer socio-economic opportunities, solidarity with a large group culture may not be a free choice. In such cultures child development practices will encourage the development of those qualities needed for survival and success in their particular circumstance or niches. Stigmatized groups undermine their perceived group value and struggle with group perception and stereotyping.

While identity may be vulnerable throughout all developmental stages to trauma, contextualizing the concept of adult identity within a broader political and moral framework is clinically necessary to allow a focus on "identity foreclosure." Individuals with foreclosed identities (Marcia, 1988) are described as having a history of exploration with a high degree of searching behavior for social and or economic group membership and often not fitting in to a stable niche or intimacy. At this developmental identity status such adolescents or adults in transitions are not actively trying to determine what is important to them, they are, when free to and not threatened, attempting to resolve an inner quest to join with and ensure survival. People who have foreclosed their identity because of earlier trauma or chaotic attachments, loss or abandonment are not or do not accept or are not able to question the values and beliefs they may be subjected to. Instead, such youth or adults seek to obtain or are vulnerable for their identity to accepting the beliefs and values of an elite or violent leader, often one that is authoritarian, parental and threatening. While they may be compelled to passively accept a group or mass identity assigned to them, some may also be ambitious and creative in implementing their leaders' goals, seeking power or status within their group or taking advantage of a unique talent. Such individuals seek advancement, approval or power in their group matrix that affords them a stronger identity status and meaning. At times of social crises these young men/women likely commit to values and life goals of a political or revolutionary ideal and some accept or seek assigned roles in socio-political groups. Such people usually are acutely sensitive to external cues, and are motivated externally in response to social crises or military leaders. Internally their absence of reflective thinking or capacities for independent judgment combined with identity foreclosure results in a particularly severe form of compliance and negative personal identity that depends on external values and supports.

Individuals who become "foreclosed" are unable to question the results of their actions, nor are they able to consider alternatives (Allen and Fonagy, 2006). People with such an internal deficit of reflective capacity also clinically occur in Western society and their conflicts are intensified when an external group identity dominates or replaces normal individual identity integrity. One individual result of this defensive solution is a dependence upon and psychic fear of the loss of their external directive group identity or leader. In authoritarian societies, or in periods of national group crises, it is important to recognize that there are not the same opportunities to explore the cultural environment to find a generative identity. In such circumstances "role and identity" is frequently forced on individuals without individual choice resulting in the creation of split off hidden selves as in those children who were forced to hide their Jewish identity in the war.

From a clinical perspective certain forms of over-identification with group ideals or roles in non-kin groups with the absence of strong or developmentally achieved individual identity occurred in Nazi Germany (Roth, 2015). This form of "identity" within a hierarchical/military "We" structure may serve as an external defense against painful identity diffusion but likely interacts with a fixed and threatening authoritarian political/social structure: threatening political structures demand compliance and violently threaten non-compliance. Analysis of Adolph Eichmann's Rorschach indicates he likely had that kind of personality structure that was highly dependent on external ideology (Roth, 2015). However, this characteristic of his personality is insufficient in terms of explaining Eichmann's accommodating to his world (Brunner, 2000). He wore masks but it is not possible to determine when he put them on or what they disguised (Brunner 2000, p. 463).

When the non-kin coalitional world is in crises, dangerous and threatening, in varying degrees, the capacity for internal representation of one's own self is threatened, partially absented, suspended or "damaged." Turquet described that a non-kin culture in crises often vacillates between chaos, vulnerable paranoid anxieties and order until a leader or coercive force intervenes to restore order. The society is "felt" to present specific threats to the "We" identity resulting in "a transient experience of depersonalization" (Turquet, 1975, p. 80). When the new leader is authoritarian/military or totalist, he demands or coerces order with force to attain security and often generates a new social identity through enforced idealizing beliefs that often leads to a reorganization of perceived threats. This behavior may initially be a stabilizing factor, helping citizens to feel protected from earlier threats but is a step toward the creation of new "common enemies." This comforting return to order has a price: the quasi delusional, rigid splitting of dangerous and safe offers the predictability of new imaginary beliefs and enemies instead of their earlier uncertainty (Ganzarain, 2000).

As many historians pointed out, this kind of social crises happened in Germany both before and after World War I and resulted in a *Kriegsideologie*: their chaos was at the expense of individual or democratic opportunity and safe individual identity offering an ideology that war and violence enabled political solutions. *Kriegsideologie* as a belief system is likely related to Gerlach's (2010) ideas of the historical pattern and violent punitive behavior of extremely violent societies that embrace war as a solution to social ills. War, or organized state sponsored killing, has its own deeper psychological dynamics according to Fornari (1974). Bessel (2009) saw violence as the essence of a specific form of Nazi politics that was fed by manliness, aggressive nationalism, racial hatred and anti-Marxism that "legitimized" years of violence.

Under Germany's chaotic and collective conditions prior to Hitler's assuming power, individuals unable to forge an independent identity and to maintain self-esteem and identity coherence are more likely to seek and form an absolute "attachment" to a leader for whom violence is an identity solution (Hitler, L. Ron Hubbard, Charles Manson). It follows that when this group identity predominates over individual identity, the capacity for representation of affect, the capacity to empathize with affective experiences of the other, and the capacity to appropriately differentiate between the affective experiences of one's own group and others can remain developmentally undeveloped, absent and damaged in the manner described by Fonagy's extensive research. This combination of deficits results in a dominant cognitive and cultural style in which social reality is rigidly perceived and "negative" projections facilitate a willingness and capacity to malignantly objectify any "other" outside of a primary group. Violence against group "outsiders" is rationalized as politically necessary to protect group boundaries against real, imagined and symbolic threat, to keep identity pure and destroy coalitions against supposed dangerous opposition and change. Individuals in a primarily violent group, to varying degrees, assume a relatively automatic, mindless reactive approach to individual identity formation by becoming who others, particularly authoritarian leaders, expect them to be. Although such an adaptation may present as self-disciplined, conscientious, committed and externally goal-oriented, the individuals possess rigidly organized self-views that must be protected and maintained by shutting themselves off from information that may threaten leader centric values and beliefs. Subjective uncertainty and conflicting information are aversive. However, few individuals had the flexibility to resume "normal relationships" outside of their status based "automatic group identity."

From the perspective of super-ego integrity (the internalized conscience partially derived from early family and schooling disciplinary techniques) authoritarian/elite leaders concretely replaced the internalized cultural value systems. The combination of an existing social threat combined with a leader's future millennial promise replaces earlier concepts of good and bad for their followers. One result of this leader-centric position is that the avowed "enemy of the leaders' enemy is my enemy." This loyalty to Hitler served to enhance his power over his followers and in turn change cultural values, perceptions of internal threats and increased sensitivity to creation of a German social identity with real and imaginary potential paranoid intrusions. When Hitler is seen as a leader who excelled at initiative, describing paranoid threats, fostering terror and was able to inspire followers the simple term "charismatic" is inadequate.

As most totalitarian leaders usually come into political power at a time of social/political crises, they make use of these crises and transform or magnify the real or imagined cultural conflicts and threats. This sensitivity helps capture and direct both obedience and violence in what I referred to as a spreading violent *Kriegsideologie*. The totalist leaders assume ultimate moral judgment concerning who is both "pure" and has the right to life (worth living) replacing earlier moral codes with thanatopolitics.

Earlier attempts by Langer (1972), etc. to psychoanalyze Nazi leaders are extremely speculative as the totalitarian or elite authoritarian leader cannot be understood by individual psychoanalytic theory alone without awareness of their interactive relationship with their followers and their group ideology. Hitler can best be understood in terms of his leadership style and, for my purposes, according to impactful relationship to Jews, and German justice/morality and violence. Public utterance and political speeches previously studied were intended by Hitler, and all such leaders, to send coded messages to radical members and believers: they cannot be any simple basis to understand Hitler's personality but when decoded reveal his collective political ambitions (Gallbraith, 2006). Hitler's aim was to enable a violent retributive society. Hasselbach and Reiss (1996) report that a former neo-Nazi leader remembers that he and his colleagues did not make new members violent but took their inherent violence that was clearly there and channeled it in a politically useful manner. Hitler channeled that violence into political paranoia.

When considering Hitler as a totalist leader (Erikson, 1942) it is important to first consider that he was an outsider in German politics and brought into his new government autocratic structures eventually manipulating most governmental military and judicial functioning under his direct personal control. Any pre-existing structure or sense of justice was slowly replaced in the service of his wished for racist/military-defined empire (Eley, 2013). Opposition real and imagined was silenced or removed by threat and terror. This leads to my describing Hitler's image using insights from Dostoevsky, M. Klein and J.M. Coetzee (Coetzee and Kurtz, 2015). I believe that the image of Hitler as charismatic is faulty. Hitler's ultimate complex motives were "to be admired, if abhorred, as a goal was to be a great criminal" (Coetzee and Kurtz, 2015, p. 39). The figure of the great criminal-conqueror was built on the Napoleonic-Genghis Khan image of great military men.[2] This conqueror image issued a challenge to the Judeo-Christian God and culture, with their models of justice, community and cooperation: Hitler rejected all these moral commandments. He added by his directives to his murderous actions: What does it say about your God that he can allow me to do what I have done; to commit these great crimes? For you to suffer so?

How can his violent criminality be understood? In the twentieth century coding the hidden and conscious motives behind speech and acts followed from both a Freudian (psychoanalytic) and a literary perspective. These understandings made an open claim for social and personal relevance that carried honest (super-ego) and social (interpersonal) components. In any therapeutic discourse lucid self-explanations are possible if ironic and complex. But we cannot assume that Hitler was always saying what he meant and that he was abiding by the same rules of discourse and social relevancy as those usual to leaders of democratic countries. Hitler, among other totalist leaders, rejected the legitimacy of the law under which he was raised and the belief systems to which they belonged. He believed in and established a dual state where the justice system was re-aligned with Nazi goals. Power and violence without moral consequences, according to Bessel (2009), was integrated into the Nazi political movement.

While the outsiders and his enemies questioned too late Hitler's lies and distortions, those imaginary racial and empirical constructs empowered him and his followers to seek greater supreme power over other poly-ethnic lives in Europe. His beliefs in an imaginary superior master race found resonance in Germany and gave him direction and control over German lives, beliefs and military control over the lives of others. The core radical Nazis were people who convinced others of their imperial reasoning and racial beliefs that justified all their violent actions and past events without what is considered normal reflection. It was a *Weltanschauung*: a systematic ideology of a defined purpose. Within this structure Hitler sought to direct the development of youth and choice. Movements for youth were a part of German culture and the Hitler youth (*HitlerJugend*) became central to Hitler's ideology preparing children for sacrifice and military service for his empire. Many entered the war as fanatical boy soldiers with utter contempt for danger: their social identity absorbed in the Nazi ideology of sacrifice and murder. In order to fully comprehend the impact of this Nazi culture on adolescence it must be compared to the open-ended struggle of youth in democratic societies.

If I apply M. Klein's psychoanalytic theory (and her followers), this Hitler/Nazi history in Germany leads to the formation of a paranoid/schizoid national large group formation in which paranoid defenses are collectively brought into formation by the Nazi logic of a constant and expanding internal and external threat and retaliatory violence. That threat required actions by pre-emptive violence, personal sacrifice and obedience. Psychic splitting encouraged in speeches and propaganda maintained the paranoid edge of all good and all dangerous. The German media and military training were used to harden[3] the Germans and rid the national group of ambivalent and shameful feelings concerning their past while locating Hitler's declared enemies and hubris. People and violent goals were structured by simple dichotomies of "us and them" with violent threat or revenge implied. Aryans were imaginatively cast at the top of the new racial order. Expanding circles of devotees surrounded Hitler who owed their authoritarian leader their position and shared his affinities and beliefs. In such a nation he effected a change in which the German society he governed was reconfigured according to his beliefs and a brutal criminal justice, the *Sondergerichte*, the Nazi special courts, were created in his control. Nothing happened without his active or passive approval.

The Nazis openly challenged the emerging idea that the modern universe was good and that governments attempted to be just to all. Hitler and his henchmen transformed the essential nature of social and political crimes such that if the perpetrators could "scientifically" falsify their explanations for what they were doing and why they were doing it, they were not guilty of crimes. He offered a necessary if imaginary military path concordant with the earlier embedded *Kriegsideologie* for creating a community of violence in the service of his ideals by the creation of a racial-genocidal society. This was forged not only by the hatred and paranoia of the Jews and Nazi state coercion, but also by the creation of a new moral and aesthetic exclusive community within the *Volksgemeinschaft*: a people's community that excluded aliens and subjected them to discriminatory laws. Hitler attempted to create an exclusive Aryan community seeking to increase its empire, solidarity and inherited sense of (male) superiority over the law as a political, social and psychological reality (Kuehne, 2010; Bessel, 2009). One vehicle of this violent vision was a nation state in which the Jews were continuously violently excluded from participation until totally eliminated.

From a historical perspective the divine right of dynastic kings was aimed at instilling obedience by explaining why the population were religiously and morally obliged to obey. In contrast, Hitler relied on the coercive powers of all the institutions and instruments of the state in pursuit of racial inequality and strategic objectives with no levels of accountability to a higher power. Hitler reconstituted a lawful predatory state with no separation of the executive from the judiciary so that they did not recognize the fundamental right to life and the rights of property for its citizens. Being a predatory leader of such a violent state leads to a primary strategy that is antagonistic to any generative-protective behavior of the nation: that an elite can maintain political power through the lack of separation between military power and political power creating a collective force to fight imaginary enemies. Loyalty to predatory rulers is based on fear and the prospect of reward, which helps build a predatory coalition around leadership. This collective force aims to control all assets/resources and assume the power of a biocracy through interlocking hallucinotic constructions that created a variety of incentives to act violently. The citizens of countries outside of the ecosystem of Germany were considered "prey" or bacillus while internally German speaking citizens were mostly exempted if they obeyed. The German nation and race were conceived of as a *real* political body suffering from an illness of contamination by a Jewish microorganism that had to be eliminated. Nazism was applied biology.[4]

Notes

1 At one time, then, "identity" will appear to refer to a conscious sense of individual identity; at another to an unconscious striving for a continuity of personal character; at a third, as a criterion for the silent doings of ego synthesis; and finally, as a maintenance of an inner solidarity with a group's ideals and identity. (Erikson, 1980, pp. 109–110, italics added)

2 "Our strength consists in our speed and in our brutality. Genghis Khan led millions of women and children to slaughter—with premeditation and a happy heart. History sees in him solely the founder of a state. It's a matter of indifference to me what a weak western European civilization will say about me. I have issued the command—and I'll have anybody who utters but one word of criticism executed by a firing squad —that our war aim does not consist in reaching certain lines, but in the physical destruction of the enemy. Accordingly, I have placed my death-head formation in readiness—for the present only in the East—with orders to them to send to death mercilessly and without compassion, men, women, and children of Polish derivation and language. Only thus shall we gain the living space (*Lebensraum*) which we need." (Hitler 22 Aug 1939, P. Lochner *What about Germany*)

3 "The weak must be chiseled away. I want young men and women who can suffer pain. A young German must be as swift as a greyhound, as tough as leather, and as hard as Krupp's steel" (Hitler, Nuremberg 1935, published 1938). Pinker (2011) builds a theory of the rise of empathy as counter to violence where the Nazi made a constant demand for "hardness."

4 Attributed to R. Hess speaking at a mass meeting in 1934. Lifton wrote "the entire Nazi regime was built on a biomedical vision that required the kind of racial purification that would progress from sterilization to extensive killing" (1986, p. 24).

4

WAR GROUP DEVELOPMENT AND THE NAZI PATH TO VIOLENCE

How to understand the process of mass murder

> I want once again to be a prophet. If international finance-Jewry inside and outside Europe should succeed in plunging the nations once more into a world war, the result will not be the bolshevization of the earth and thereby the victory of Jewry, but the annihilation of the Jewish race in Europe.
>
> Berlin, Germany. *Hitler speaks before the Reichstag, January 30, 1939*

> The heaviest blow that ever struck humanity was Christianity; Bolshevism is Christianity's illegitimate child. Both are inventions of the Jew.
>
> Hitler, Mein Kampf

> If the hereditary criminal nature of Jewry can be demonstrated, then not only is each people morally justified in exterminating the hereditary criminals, but any people that still keeps and protects Jews is just as guilty of an offence against public safety as someone who cultivates cholera germs without observing the proper precautions.
>
> Von Leer, *The Criminal Nature of the Jews (1937). Copyright 2002 by R. Belser.*

In order to begin to comprehend the path towards state sponsored mass murder it is necessary to understand the profound dynamic issues facing large social human groups. From an evolutionary perspective the avowed intention, or within-group essential self-interest, of any polity, no matter its size and composition, is to nurture and insure the development of its members for the preservation of the group through harmonious within-group integration and generativity, with destructive attacks upon or parasitism on the surrounding milieu, human and non-human. Within this affordance many and varied theories attempt to explain the repeated and seemingly "habitual" emergence of destructive attacks on other coalitions of humans, interpersonal violence or organized acts of group warfare between non-kin polities. Much of that speculation reflects on theories of the evolution of basic human personality that evolved from studies of conflicts between our human ancestors. Between polity and coalition violence is endemic to the history of human societies and there appear to be only a few group defenses or misconceptions that held this violence in check (Girard, 1977). Darwin, among many theorists, viewed war violence in all animals as another important evolutionary process leading to gains in human fitness[1] and survival, whereas Girard (1977) viewed religion as humanizing violence by misinformation that makes wars' origin divine. Peace between states and other varied large group structures, in contrast, appear to be defined as a cessation over time in the history of violent conflicts. Often the search for an explanation for wars leads to the creation of mythologies, rituals and the establishment of the sacred or a civilizing process (Pinker, 2011) as an explanation for peace and forms of "evil" as a supernatural force with a rationale for enemies. Absent is a coherent and truthful understanding of state sponsored violence from a group analytic perspective. What enabled the emergence of warfare among humans was the appearance of non-kin societies with social structures that provided stability and legitimacy to new social roles and complex behaviors. This change required the allegiance to a larger, more varied social entity in addition to the family or clan although clan[2] warfare was common.

Wars are organized violations of established physical group boundaries of another polity or coalition with the use of force or destructive weaponry that violently impacts its members. Wars are a constant throughout human history and they may be generally understood on the surface as the result of an apparent conflict of interest between the elites of non-kin groups or polities. Wars have changed as their weaponry changed and the appearance of weapons of mass destruction has deterred open warfare while increasing deep and genuine anxiety given the consequences of nuclear warfare. Mass murder within an early or modern state or polity, now usually called genocide or ethnic cleansing, can be understood as the outcome of a forceful breakdown of normal group functioning and security with the expressed aim, symbolic and actual, of eliminating specific targeted members of that polity at little or no risk to the perpetrators. The absence of "risk" alters the dynamics of violence and murder described by Athens (1992). Murder and mass murder without risk is not unique among modern or ancient cultures while the voluminous explanations for its occurrence are varied and without psychoanalytic weight or understanding. Mass murders are a Rorschach inkblot onto which explanations are projected onto the varied perpetrators.

Genocide cannot occur without the absence of any affine intervention by a state or government with the power or political influence to intervene on behalf of the potential victims. Midlarsky (2005), from a political perspective, lists several pre-genocidal state conditions that were blocked by affine intervention. The existence of strong potential allies is thought to be of sufficiently powerful or influential importance to deter genocidal activity. The question of affinity raises important unanswered issues regarding the perception and acts against Jews in all of Europe coincident with the absence of "strong" political intervention in pre- and early wartime Germany. In particular the real and imagined connection between Jews and Bolshevism was critical and complex in the existence and nullifying of affinity in Europe. Affinity in the political/sociological realm must be distinguished from "valence" in Bion's (1962) terms that refers to unconscious emotional reaction. Political affinity is defined as a perceived similarity of national interests, beliefs or values but essentially rests on empathy. From the outset the Nazi government used legislation, decrees and threat to ostracize Jews in Germany, in particular Jewish women. Over time other countries enacted laws limiting German Jews from safely entering their country. When the Nazis came to power in 1933 there were roughly 9–10 million Jews in Europe. By the end of the war two out of three of these Jews would be dead (Kaplan, 1999).

The murders committed by the Nazis and their cooperating political partners occurred within a modern psychological context of attacks on a variety of targeted people, best understood as thought to be living "in exile"[3] in Europe. Further, recent historians, survivors and the relatives of the murdered uniquely insist, through differing modern media devices and memorialization, on its horror being remembered, responded to and examined. Anti-Semitism as a belief system and a single unique cause for mass murder is an insufficient explanation for the murders of millions (Falk, 2006). In general the initial source of violence in anti-Semitism is thought to have an unconscious root and to occur with vulnerability of the "nation" to panic or threat. That threat arouses images of an impinging social universe in need of purging the nation of all badness (Stein, 2003) and Jews have historically been designated as different/dangerous. A leader or prophet then appears offering a fusion of defensive or reparative nationalism and a public health-healing fantasy (p. 59) of removing the condensed image of all one rejects. Common to religious and secular forms of anti-Semitism is the persistence of certain fabricated beliefs (myths) that demonized and dehumanized the Jewish people no matter how absurd or delusional these beliefs were. For example, the opponents of nationalism cast Jews as unmovable nationalists, while nationalists such as Hitler saw Jews as internationalists with no allegiance to any country, the root of Marxism and subversion. The violent genocidal solution by the Nazis found a seemingly constant resonance in a sufficient number of citizens to allow violent individual or group action. I believe that anti-Semitism is the external realization of a negative container available for antagonistic religious and political beliefs, hallucinotic beliefs that lack reason and are formed by an energy needed to negatively define an external bad or dangerous entity. First expressed in an accelerating pace of violence is the verbal aggression of public insult, denigration and denunciation or accusation. Then there is physical "reprisal" for imaginary contemporary or historical violations and finally forms of violence, looting and murder.

Concurrent with acts of remembering and mourning of the victims are varied attempts to describe Hitler as a leader of a negative counter-case to democracy and as only a charismatic leader of the genocide. Such attempts fail to account for the Nazis' accelerating pace of political actions and violent horrors inflicted by over 30 thousand multi-national participants and the important role of other than Nazis in carrying out mass murder (Gerlach, 2010).[4] Rees (2012) succinctly believes that Hitler was not simply a charismatic leader; but rather that he systematically controlled and used the German political and willing judicial system, threat, imprisonment, terror and murder to carry out his political and racial imperial agendas. Gerlach recently (2016) argued that violence against Jews was a significant portion of a much wider murderous action against a variety of persecuted groups in a pattern that resembles that of Stalin's purges. Bessel (2009) annotated the central role political violence and elimination played in Hitler's ascension that was followed by Jews becoming a legally targeted category. Importantly, there was acceptance by the German population of a fantasy of a "return to order" intimately related to prior threat and violence that was tacitly accepted in a culture built on duty and security.

Only by understanding the dynamic emergence of the willingness of Nazi leaders to establish an imaginary enemy and their accelerating and multinational exclusionary laws, violence and planned mass organization necessary to establish genocide, can we attempt to understand their violent group dynamics and its appeal. This violent ethnocentric dynamic resulted in prolonged processes of threats of mass murder in many different countries of Europe. These mass murders, systematic and chaotic, gas chambers and starvation, occurred over a time period of two to five years and varied in scope and dynamics in each Nazi controlled country. It is also important to understand the broad multinational cooperation in the conquered countries or their allies (Gerlach, 2010). Unifying concepts as holocaust or Shoah have some appeal but also serve to obscure the dynamic and uncontrolled range of participation of the various polities and personnel over time and place in these unprecedented events that began as Hitler assumed power in 1933. Stanton in 1996 was the first to outline general "stages"[5] that depict the process but his thesis requires greater clarity. Importantly the scope and willingness of countries to "hand over their Jews," with few exceptions, reveals the threatening power and contagion of Hitler's racist ideology and the latent and actual willingness of other countries' leaders and soldiers' compliance with Judaicide. Mass murders over an extended time period and across polities not only changes the psychological status of perpetrators, bystanders and survivors (no matter how ordinary they may be when initiated), it also changes expectancies of safety in the culture as there is a dual absence, of a sufficient opposing preventative armed or an enlightened moral force. Mass murder on the Nazi scale also required extended cooperation and participation of large numbers of people to carry out its mission. This recruitment increased awareness of the violent acts and intentions. Such cooperation was not among equals as German persecutors needed and found cooperation among occupied national elites: particularly for deportation to killing centers and forced labor sites. Under constant threat and subjected to violence the captive Jewish reactive mental reactions were reactive to the fear of and identification with the Nazis' fantasy creating a form of existential hopelessness and social death (Kaplan, 1999).

Systemized and progressive organized long-term political racial discrimination and violence began immediately after Hitler's political ascension to chancellor (Kaplan, 1999). This occurred within a larger socio-historical context of episodic exclusion and historic violence against Jews (Bartov, 2003; Gellately, 2001; Tyrell,

1999; Eley, 2013). Kren and Rappoport (1980) and Davidowicz (1975), among others, illuminate the German socio-historical context of anti-Semitism that played a significant part in how political violence and terror returned with the suppressive Nazi fascism and became an acceptable means of state coercion, exclusionary practices and eventual accelerating mass murders. State organized violent behavior was not new to Europe. However, from a psychoanalytic perspective the social-economic values, hatred and fear of competing ideologies, particularly Bolshevism interlaced with anti-Semitism and Nazified eugenic practices (Kuhl, 2016), were the soil in which multinational group mass persecution and murder accelerated. It is significant that it is not simply that the German version of anti-Semitism and mass murders were unique, as wholesale mass murders of vanquished human beings are found in numerous histories. It was the elaborate scope of the unprecedented wartime Nazi success across polities with the organizational structure built to accomplish this departure from civilized laws that was unique. An ongoing wartime psychology of military power and threat enhanced Nazi murderous destructiveness giving its violent dynamism full opportunity and expression (Bessel, 2009). This was partly because its racialized utopian vision was fused with Hitler's wartime ambitions and hatred of Bolshevism. The privileging of fascist ideology within a violent militarized country solidified that Jews were not only expendable but were the imaginary cause of any German disaster. They belonged to the realm of the "negative" (Sandler, 2009). Under these circumstances discrimination accelerated and became murderously violent drawing upon a deeply rooted apocalyptic mythology for its fuel. The death of Jews was the magical instrument to a utopian future and the destruction of "the negative." What Hitler drew upon was a belief in an amazing magical conversion and transformation of a collective nation through war and purifying violence. Hyper-groupism appearing as patriotism combined with violent xenophobia was inevitably linked with murderous violence. In this violent conversion the Germans become as they were meant to be: pure Aryan lords of Europe and Jews were to be eliminated for their imagined impurity and treachery. The Jews became by hallucinosis immoral, habitually given to lies, impurity, treachery, polluting and every possible crime and danger by splitting, projective evacuation, stereotyping and scapegoating. These murders were inspired by imaginary fears and confused with the primary and residual dangers of defilement, disease and hygiene. At this level of distortion the laws of nature and morality are fused to explain political disloyalty and imagined racial difference to create the existence of an enemy possessing all threats.

From the time Hitler initially took office he embarked on a program of elimination of political opposition by threat, violence and murder (Tyrell, 1999; Wachsmann, 2015). His end goal was to make Germany's goals the same as Hitler's goals (Davidowicz, 1975), and remove any political dissent to his violent plans for order and empire. To these ends he employed all the powers and media of the German state with little open opposition. It is not difficult to see, as Kershaw (1991) suggests, the Nazi aim of global remodeling of German society in accordance with an imposing racial aesthetic, epitomized by repeated de-individuating spectacles and speeches that impacted the minds and everyday behavior of Germans. One key element was the unrestrained undermining of all the protective structures of governance accomplished with the growth of Hitler's autonomy, authority and preoccupation with foreign policy as a pinnacle of achievement (Eley, 2013). Hitler's style of leadership was a personalist dictator as the political life of Germany revolved around his autocratic personality. Although he wore a uniform he was accountable to no other individual or entity and the Nazi ideology was his creation although amplified by his spokespersons. Personalist leaders have limited constraints on their decision-making abilities and are usually held less accountable for policies, including those with negative outcomes. Such leaders require to be surrounded by a loyal group of sycophants who tell the dictator what he wants to hear despite all the leader's excesses, narcissism and paranoia that go with it. His handpicked cadre had huge powers and strong incentives to remain loyal to and uncritical of their leader.

From 1933, as Hitler ascended to power, Davidowicz (1975), Tyrell (1999) and Wachsmann (2015), among others, detail his plans and actions to regain German territory and rid Germany, and later Austria, of Jews and other "threats" while creating a personalist dictatorship. Anti-Jewish legislation striking at professionals, businesses of all types and all forms of livelihood grew in volume and intensity to the effect that "being Jewish" was both taxable and viewed as anti-German (Kaplan, 1999). Both Davidowicz and Bingham and Souza, from vastly different perspectives, view these political acts as not only in the service of Hitler's well-documented personal anti-Semitism but also aimed to extort money from Jews for Hitler's planned retaliatory war efforts. Forced emigration before the mass killings started outside of Germany, following Eichmann's efforts in Austria, were a source of income for Germany as were the resources left behind by those who could afford or were able to leave (Bessel, 2009). Arendt (1951) viewed such enforced statelessness, a recurring outcome following the end of World War I, and the collapse of earlier multidenominational empires, as resulting in a recurring form of political and ethnic vulnerability. New nation states had ethnic minorities and unstable new frontiers along with the rise of a sense of past and future political crises making them unstable and uncertain. The doctrines in behalf of which expulsion, eradication and extermination has been made can be virtually anything that can be defined as impure.

For a moment it is necessary to pause to reflect on the coercive power of Hitler's economic strategy of first passing laws of exclusion as a tactic of coercion in a country where the press, media and opposition was under his control. Jews were systematically deprived of all means of earning money or belonging to a profession; all state benefits and their children were excluded from German schools while there was no effective voice of public opposition. On the surface Hitler was preparing for war of a conventional kind with militarily over matched Poland and to intensify his plan to eliminate or "cleanse" the harmful influence of "alien" populations. Remaking European social and political order along the vague eugenic lines of pure "Volk" was his ultimate utopian goal of a unique German Empire.

He was also augmenting the second and overt stage of his symbolic removal of Jews from any legal protection by the German state while stimulating elaborate scientific and medical combined efforts for liberating Germany from socially deviant or "worthless" *Untermenschen* people. However, there were simultaneous plans for the more ruthless action than the fantasy of a Jewish state elsewhere, i.e. Madagascar. While all non-Germans were to be expelled, Hitler's plan for racial cleansing began in earnest with his augmenting plans to build a war machine and invade Poland. Prior to the actual invasion, anti-Jewish belligerence was instigated in various small Polish villages while during the invasion (Gross, 2001) the *Einsatzgruppen* were unleashed against Polish leaders, Jews and gypsies followed. This was prelude to ghettoization and later his planned brutal "Final Solution" (*Endlösung*). Without legal or military constraint violent racial and territorial Germanization spread in Europe without any real opposition. The Nazi war machine forced people from their homes, factories and created a dislodged unprotected mass of people without leaders and protection. These Nazi behaviors enhanced the "foreignness" of Jews as the basic sense of self is tied to a sense of place: those places that are comforting (and safe) and those places that are menacing (Stein, 2003, p. 60).

From a kin perspective of "Us" versus "Them" (Berreby, 2005), Hitler's speeches ratcheted up German ethnocentrism and xenophobia as his new elite Nazi group intensified aggrandizement of the vague conceptual symbols of Volk and Aryan in ethnocentric preparation for war and the required national sacrifice. When one kin group is elevated as superior as the Nazis did, the other kin or affinity groups are denigrated and a fixed social boundary is established to create enemies or degenerates. Enemies and degenerates are the outcomes of negative psychic processes of psychic evacuations of danger and threat. Denigrating war opponents, Poles or Russians, as worthless is not new to warfare but the Nazis began killing unarmed Jews, intellectuals and Polish officers on any pretense as soon as the war started. Coupled with the earlier exclusionary Nazi verbal and legal practices such violence was also a totalitarian attack on diversity and complexity to maintain Nazis' simple notions of an imaginary boundary in which they possessed racial authority to murder and attack any oppositional being and source of antagonistic ideology. This was rationalized as a genetic "pruning" of inferior others at a historical time when "race" was considered a biologically fixed character attribute immutable to change and education. Importantly race became an additional code that distinguished the fixed boundaries of the different moral values of various human groups. In medicine, Jews were denigrated to the status of research animals (Spitz, 2005). However, the acute sense of racial difference and value was embedded in a Nazi ideology that disregarded reality and individuality inventing an imaginary back-story for the "race" of Aryans and false science and anthropology to prove their illusions of superiority. To that end they established the "Reich Institute for Ancestry Research" and "Research about Enemies" department and collected Jewish skeletons and skulls for "anthropological studies" and lectured on alien races and the absolute necessity of the separation of Germans and Jews. Most of these researchers were tried after the war for exploiting the notorious opportunities provided by death and labor camps.

At the same time Hitler's history of anti-Semitism rhetoric was sparked beyond exclusion to lethal action by the formation of the RSHA (Reich Main Security Office) as an action arm. Lethal behavior by armies at war cannot be considered a new military practice. Turse's (2013) vivid account of American soldiers in Vietnam ignoring the rules of war and killing civilians indiscriminately as potential enemy has a remarkable similarity to the behavior of the SS in Poland and then Russia. What was unique was the number of persons and resources employed by the often-murderous effort and the obliteration of a former social-cultural reality by wanton killing based on a conspiracy theory of contagion and "blood" descent. The armed perpetrator groups under the auspices of the RSHA and its individual members were supplied with threatening Nazi symbols (Death's Head) granting them "special treatment" in the service of hidden racial and pseudo scientific explanations. This encouraged the start of the Nazi murderous "final solution" to an imaginary human contagion. Hitler's propaganda and behavior was aimed to galvanize "action from below," to bring his bloody vision of Europe as a Nazi Empire into reality. Obedience and loyalty to the authoritarian Fuhrer and the resurrection of Germany, in a literal and direct manner, may have contributed to a lack of full emotional realizations of what Hitler's empirical obsessions embodied and recognizing the real threats to their success (Eley, 2013). However Bessel (2009) argues that most Germans supported the political culture of violence against Jews and accepted its by-products.

For Hitler simply going to war with the German armies was not as ideologically true to his racist mission as was the SS under the control of Himmler and Heydrich. The invasion of Poland began with a persisting splitting of the German armed force at war: a traditional army exerting exceptional military power and an ideological ruthless racist force sent to eliminate newly defined anti-German humans under the control of the RSHA (Wildt, 2010). In addition, special agents incited local violence against Jews (Gross, 2001). Over time, Hitler tried successfully to ideologically challenge the army generals to adopt his eliminest biological/contagion racial political strategy with erratic success. What form of coercion he employed was not reported as he used his personal authority to exhort obedience from his generals. For example the SS recruits was required daily to swear allegiance to the Chancellor, Hitler (Kershaw, 1991), supporting the idea of Hitler and Germany being one and the same. However, the common soldiers justified their violent actions and generally expressed indifference to Jews (Neitzel and Welzer, 2012).

War with Poland served to increase and intensify the already active euthanasia program of mentally and physically ill into a destructive laboratory preparing for mass murder and deportation. Medical doctors were usually employed by the government and generally sought to discard the values of the earlier Weimar government. From the corridors of power of Heydrich and Himmler, radicalized social and medical policies were applied to the killing fields of Europe. Judaicide in

Poland required an active network of social, local and military support among various Nazi groups. As the prison camps expanded, with Sachsenhausen (1936), Buchenwald (1937), Flossenbürg and Mauthausen (both 1938) and Ravensbrück (1939) joining the original Dachau (1933), they were filled less with the regime's earlier political opponents than with those deemed harmful to the *Volksgemeinschaft*—that is, anyone whose hereditary racial, moral, social, mental or physical negative characteristics deviated from evolving Nazi definitions of the Nazi normal, desirable and pure. This was where the exterminating practice of the racial state became punitively concrete (Eley, 2013, pp. 5113–5117). R. Hoess, deputy director of the Nazi Party, employed a popular Nazi expression: "National Socialism in nothing but applied biology." However, the reality of the Nazis' killing unarmed people was not simply governed by a directive racial ideology but by deeper unconscious beliefs of a culture of impunity that allowed them to remove moral obstacles to murderous violence and medical research. It was a transition from bio-politics to thanatopolitics: assuming the state's right to control and deny the rights to life that included euthanasia, medical experiments on live inmates and masses of slave labor. In addition to this power, the imagined Aryan superior racial type became a false narrative against which all races were to be judged inferior and expendable (Enoch, 2004).[6] Under the Nazis the usual care of life sciences (bio-politics) became the administration of death by marking the deviant to be eliminated as below human.

From a group psychoanalytic perspective eliminest racism in Germany was enhanced by the almost immediate creation of a threatening autocratic police state whose aim was to violently create an imaginary "scientific biologized" object of eugenic inferiority and ridicule as a threatening enemy. By depriving Jews and undesirables of the ability to participate in social safety through false science and the space to organize any expressions of injustice other than in letters and newspaper reports, the Nazis preached an exclusive resurrection of a pure German speaking race.[7] The constantly repeated threatening dynamic of Nazi rhetoric can be understood in Bion's terms as attacking normal learning links (emotional knowing, Bion 1962) impairing the ability to make rational decisions and deal with alternative possibilities in the persistent presence of terror, social threat and fictions (Arendt, 1951). Lifting all restrictions of the Nazi government courts and secret police (Gestapo) to imprison and interrogate "offenders" enhanced the level of social terror and exclusion dehumanizing the Jews in the German culture. The combination of persistent threat and the millennial vision of the Third Reich illusion of superiority inhibited social/emotional learning from experience. Limiting any contact outside of Germany restricted perspective and enhanced social isolation, compliance and anomie. The focused rhetoric of pseudo racial and historical explanations delivered repeatedly by Hitler further demonstrated the centrality of his regime's intentions and coerced acceptance of its message while finding co-believers. Hitler repeatedly used simple threatening racial metaphors with unique bravado exonerating historical failures to further his aims and vision of a new racial empire. This was built upon an imaginary hierarchy of competing races to create a momentum towards a reparative war with ideological and empirical enemies. His rhetoric of extreme otherization and dehumanization not only helped establish a world-shaping bio-political belief system for Germans with Hitler as its agitated magical author; it established the perception of the Jews' criminality and impurity responsibility for past and present failures. This combination stripped most German citizens of their civilizing veneer and granted permission for the emergence of a police state. At the same time Hitler's growing autocratic power reduced the political power and status of the individual in relation to the state. Hitler's speeches to large groups offered a message that unified and gave purpose to a group of disparate followers supplying a sizable plurality with an omnipotent prophet-father, *Führer*, as strongman: a populist new leader to stand above past political disharmonies and the failures of the earlier Weimar state. It also gave hints and demonstrated threats and punishments for all those that did not heed its message by pointing out the violence and "re-education" of those already judged guilty or degenerate. With Hitler's force and racial definitions individual moral judgment was co-opted by the totalist state. The repeated forceful connection between degenerate, sexual deviance, disease and Jews inevitably collapsed into Jew as disease, infection and criminal in German minds prepared for this message (Enoch, 2004). However, in most nation states criminals have some recognition and a protective legal system. People deprived of their nation state by laws, made stateless, are represented by no country or protective power; the Jewish infection was based on the imagined purity of blood and the German physician was elevated to "racial warden." Blood became the hidden marker of pathological difference. The prime minister of the Polish state in exile captured the international response in a letter written in 1943: "By other countries looking passively upon the murder of defenseless millions ... they have become partners to the responsibility" (Friedlander, 2007, p. 598).

Historically the juridical power of dynastic sovereign leaders under threat was the right to decide life and death. The Nazis first legally claimed power over "the degenerate and diseased" at the level of mass murder as a scientific illusion to cull the Germans to make them safe, stronger and purer. The Nazi hierarchy claimed the sovereign "right" to kill with the power of a predatory state and willingness to define the real and imaginary danger as the dangerous "non-German other." This kind of thinking aims to alleviate the perpetrator of moral responsibility for their violent actions by substituting the leaders or scientific judgment for the individuals' responsibility.[8] Even as the war turned against Germany, Hitler continued to externalize responsibility for the allied bombings and losses to "The Criminal Jew" (Friedlander, 2007).

The Nazi party's bio-ideology was a magical illusion yet it slowly gained momentum and presence among the German population through euthanasia and the repetition of the presence of an internal and external threat by non-German enemies. The Jew was re-constructed as a biological, criminal, greedy and infectious threat. For example the planned violence of *Kristallnacht*, to coincide with M. Luther's birthday, is a primary example of hidden authorized Nazi violence aimed to demonstrate a shift in social criminal values by not punishing widespread violence against the outsider Jews. The widened arc of destruction of synagogues and business elicited none of the expected forceful international condemnations and Hitler ratcheted up his rhetoric of false polarization issuing his infamous prophecy[9] of impending war and murders. While designating Jews, despite their minority in Germany, as both the real and fabricated enemies of Germany through Bolshevism and racial threats, Hitler fostered extralegal possibilities to concretely remove anyone who deviated from evolving Nazi definitions of Aryan Germans. This included anyone not physically normal and racially desirable. Under Himmler's control, correctional medical and social killing purification policies were then expanded to include work, re-education camps that later were transformed into forced labor and death camps (Katz, 1994). Scientific panels were created to determine those who were biological Jews or were tainted, staffed by physicians who were tasked as bio-political protectors. Hitler's rhetoric and the growing lack of legal protection for Jews created polarized status in Germany and served to take attention away from his growing tyranny and the formation of a racist authoritarian culture primed to employ eliminest violence in wars. At the same time he sent repeated coded messages approving the destructive use of murderous force against Jews outside of Germany as part of his foreign policy. This was all in the service of his vision of a racially pure empire "free of Jews" (*Judenfrei*) by killing human pestilence as a form of healing. This is an illusion common to some forms of murder. Lifton (1986) restricted this dynamic to Nazi doctors who rationalized that they were curing a sick society in killing Jews (Falk, 2006) I believe this is a core issue in culture in which there are strong beliefs in *Kreigsideologie*: killing as a solution to remove the negative.

During and following the military successes in Poland of his barbaric ethic and political cleansing, Goebbels, Himmler, Heydrich and Eichmann sought a "comprehensive solution of the (German) Jewish question a 'final solution'" (Roseman, 2002). The movement from brutal occupation and barbaric ghetto policies to recognized and organized genocidal measures took place seemingly without a comprehensive set of direct commands from Hitler. Jews had been gassed at Chelmno since December 1941 and other extermination camps were under construction. Full-scale state genocide was a step away and, by then, planned for by the RSHA. Cumulative radicalization of violence and murder was at the center of the paths to mass murders supported by a core body of well-educated believers instigating plans for massed murders. Hitler established an educated inner circle that shared the Nazi racist belief system (Roseman, 2002) and acted to further their Fuhrer's bespoken goals in the occupied countries.

During the 18 months after the occupation of Poland in fall 1939, faced with Poland's large numbers of displaced and unwanted unarmed Eastern Jews, resettlement, mass expulsion, ghettoization and random murder were implemented in roughly overlapping and destructive sequences. What spontaneously followed was violent disorder and resulting problems of managing the conquered, including mass starvation, appalling hardships, generalized brutality and indiscriminate killing. The planned invasion of the Soviet Union moved the killing from sporadic localized mass murder to the pan European imperial project of organized and systematized killing studied by Roseman (2002) and Gerlach (2016). As the Nazi movement to war with Russia became realized, the Nazis concurrently crossed a psychological threshold of killing (Roseman, 2002) and a new psychopathic union was formed within the RHSA to plan and carry out mass extermination (see also Alexander, 1948; Schmitt, 1996).

Having tested the German citizen's capacity for increasing coercive predatory violence against Jews that elicited little internal or international response, the Nazis unleashed murderous predatory violence along with the escalating violence of war against Poland then Russia. Violence against Jews, wherever found outside of Germany, was essential to the core purification ideals of the Nazi movement against all racial differences as *Untermenschen*. The power of the SS was then widely known, feared and understood: most Germans realized the effects of eliminest anti-Semitism without embarrassment and adapted or benefitted from it. Eley (2013) rightfully believes that while Gellately, the major historian of Germany, never hid the coercive power of Nazi rule (re-education or concentration camps, Gestapo, work camps, near public executions), he downplayed its impact horrendousness, power and wide coercive social reach. Importantly, the Nazis found and attracted willing converts to fill the personnel for the ongoing bloody tasks and growing support outside of Germany (Wachsmann, 2015; Gerlach, 2016; Bessel, 2009).

With the ongoing violence of war, a Nazi growing preoccupation with predatory killing (at little or no risk) surfaced as an important and unconsidered psychical prerequisite of mass murder. In the Nazi mass murders there was little risk. Predatory killing among mammals occurs when exploitable victims are surrounded and weakened, and defensively form groups of reduced size offering little resistance and are usually physically confined. Among socially cooperative carnivores killing occurs when an individual is surrounded by a group of aggressive individuals. In contrast individual members of confined groups through combined alertness are less vulnerable to attack: although there is a risk of toxic immobility the domain of danger is reduced. Mimicry of the aggressor or what is referred to as identification with the aggressor may also occur. Genocidal murders differed from war battles as they were opportunistic massacres of the vulnerable by any means and at the other extreme were deliberate raids that aimed at ethnic cleansing. One common thread was that the killers were at low risk of being hurt. According to these dynamics the rewards for killing safely are favored by natural selection and likely have neural rewards for men (Taylor, 2009).

Planned killing of the mentally ill and retarded, castration laws thought to prevent criminals fathering offspring, while justified by pseudo-scientific racist ideology, may also be viewed as eliminating the weakest within a predatory society i.e. "free-loaders" for obvious psychological reasons. The biologically weak and the stigmatized were not to share the spoils of the ideal Nazi empire. In warfare, in contrast to predatory killing, the outcome of conflict requires risk to the participants and the outcome is in doubt. A predator-prey model of Nazi and Jew explains some elements that other models cannot: in particular, earlier cycles of prosperity and violence. Growth and visible success among the prey group can be understood to stimulate predation based on envy as powerfully as weakness. The two populations may grow together at first, but when the balance of power shifts toward the predator state or a new leader seeks violent power there is violence as well as when the prey numbers grow too large. When Hitler's dictatorial powers were aimed at the Jews in Germany and Austria he shifted the balance of legal and militarized power to the Nazified German national state's racist elite and the coercion of Jews moves increasingly toward murderous violence against unarmed Jews as prey. It is important to recognize that in a predatory regime, nothing is done (or stated) for publically stated reasons. Indeed, the men in charge of a predatory regime do not recognize that "public purposes" or public welfare exists. The usual or prior social rules in a predatory regime are meant to be broken and the public coerced to follow by threat or lies (Galbraith, 2006, p. 31). Predatory states often emerge when a new ideologically based political elite controls all access to the capacity to kill and has long time horizons with real or imagined competition or threat. Pol Pot in Cambodia killed educated people and those who wore glasses: an example of predatory killing of the strong to be able to have greater force over the weaker.

Hitler's public and written verbal statements recorded and analyzed by historians and erroneously by some psychoanalysts were not simply revealing of his personality as Galbraith suggested (2006, p. 31). His speeches and Nazi rhetoric were meant to coerce the Germany people to accept a dynamic Nazi ideology, support his foreign policies and justify the separation of Jews from the protection of the German state. In addition, Hitler also sought to explain, recruit and exonerate the numbers of people carrying out his brutal predatory policies within a police state. As the war turned against Germany and as the Allies advanced, he continued to offer sanctuary to persecutors of Jews from other countries. In predatory states and groups violent speeches and acts are not meant to simply communicate the personality of the leader but to inform and keep the ruler's bias, maintain his power over life (thanatopolitics) and take control of resources and stand against threat (Kohl, 1933, quoted in Lemke, 2011; Adorno, 1973). In this context Hitler blamed "Jewish agitators" for the bombing of Munich as if to continue to incite reprisals against Jews.

The increasing RHSA wartime role in Poland then understandingly follows an escalating predatory pattern. First violent racist paranoia emerged with their needed earlier laboratory for mass murder, to the quickening flashes of local genocidal fury in Poland, into murderous chaos. Paranoia? Under the conditions of war-threat and scarcity it becomes a necessity to be hyper-alert and be able to recognize one's own, aggregate and bond among temporary allies excluding others. The politics of Nazi racism, that began with economic coercion and racial laws unleashed without opposition, reached its full violent and heightened paranoia by globally defining enemies of the state. After *Kristallnacht* anti-Jewish behavior became ruthless functional violent paranoia. Through Himmler's apt "warriors with a cause"

(*Weltanschuungskrieger*) in the SS, the dehumanization of Jews became routine and was made internally legitimate. Far from being desk-perpetrators, the RHSA was driven by finding a rhythm and means for eliminating the masses of prey called "undesirables," first through political, ideological and racial misinformation and threat: an escalating predatory war mentality. Nazi victory is Poland led essentially to successive preparation for harnessed indiscriminate human predatory violence against masses: persecution, expulsion and elimination. Classified as asocial, unfit, being a Jew or other enemy of the Aryan race, with no recourse under the imaginative dynamism of the Nazi rule, Europe was deformed. Even as most of the Jews in Europe were already dead, Friedlander (2007) recognized the shrill intensity of the Anti-Jewish belief when in one of Hitler's last speeches after the allied bombing of Hamburg, he grotesquely attributed the German demise as "this entire bestiality has been organized by the Jews." Hitler continued to warn of the fate of all Germans in Jewish and Bolshevik hands. While this may appear as standard "fight to the death exhortation" the continued centrality of threat in "Jews and Bolsheviks" is astounding.

Research on genocide must move beyond viewing mass murder as an abhorrent act. The dynamics of mass murder may shed some additional light on these terrible events that are viewed as a unified processes—yet they unfold over time and in different locations: mass murder was a joined group process whose meaning continued after the events. For example, Hopper (2003) originally described a large group response to massive external threat and trauma in group analytic terms as "massification." This "basic assumption" (Bion, 1961) he argued is a massed interpersonal defense against the psychotic anxieties associated with a powerful threatening real possibility of social and personal annihilation. Following severe traumatic experiences in which the group members continually fear or were actually attacked, unarmed, the threatened people physically retreat for safety into a human mass within which individual identity was unsupported and discarded. Faced with the immediate and real omnipresent threat of total annihilation by the Nazis, without effective leaders, the "conquered" Jews likely adopted such a massification in prey-like behavior in fear of annihilation. Individuals within such violently enforced group masses regressed into a merged mass, with some seeking means of survival, with shell-like defenses against terror and awful knowing and group mourning. For some survival needs predominated or for others a form of total psychic surrender occurred called "walking dead". In addition, the ensuing interactive deprivation effect of helpless massification likely stimulated Nazi predators to ratchet up their efforts to find and use cost effective elimination of their unarmed massed racial enemies. According to this psychological model group surrender and helplessness in mass are a conspicuous signal to a malignant military that arouses increases in predation, random violence or exploitation. Predatory-prey relationships, group perpetrator group victim relationships are interactive and influenced by time and were based on state induced and state protected practices of open predation, theft, exploitation and mass killings. The trapped, coerced, oppressed or massified were simply viewed and signaled as an object of thanatopolitics signaling for the assassins. While it is normal to believe that life and death are biological phenomena, the Nazis made "certain" that the right to life became a political decision based on the creation of false beliefs. The easier the unarmed prey are to capture and mass, in ghettos, concentration camps and ravines, the more the human predators will perfect their abilities to kill their prey and justify their surplus killing without limits. When prey is easily available, plentiful and cannot escape predators can kill without risk. Surplus killing is killing beyond immediate needs. It may be important to consider that there seems no reason to believe that violence against a prey is the same as violence against another predator and are part of the same motivational system. Predators in mass murders may be driven by a different motivation than soldiers on a battlefield.

The Nazis embarked on deliberate callous bio-political eliminest policies with no or little risk against them, justifying mass murder by their mythic explanations and mind set of being superior without restraint against an imaginary negated enemy. Such violent behavior bonded the Nazis groups in what the psychiatrist Alexander (1948) at the Nuremburg Trials called a criminal "blood knit" to their murderous groups, ideological leaders and modes of ideological justification and explanation. Had Alexander been able to interview the same people Wachsmann (2015) did in the death camps who were lower and bloodier in the Nazi hierarchy, he might have recognized lethal mass annihilation on a grand continuing scale of a seeming unending stream of Russian soldiers, Polish and other Jews, and slave laborers. Once killing started, this was not a predatory blood lust that could be satisfied and continued as the Nazi retreated. "The Jew" became an active central force and negative entity in Nazi minds, independent of the concrete fate of the Jews who had been murdered.

One result of this mass destruction of human lives was the enormous production of cadavers that posed public and medical health hazards. The Nazi responded to this by the implementation of crematoriums and mass un-ceremonial burial. The cultural meaning of this mass disposal, after scavenging the bodies, added to the Nazi declaration of the meaninglessness of the murdered lives: not only were they insignificant but worthless residue that was without individuality. Predators respond to prey as meaningless[10] and without individuality but a necessary source of sustenance and motivation. The term " negative" and "minus" in Bion's formulations, while inseparable from the positive, create a realm of not-me, not human falsely believed to be extinguished (Sandler, 2015).

Notes

1 Fitness refers to the capacity to produce offspring.
2 A clan is a collective that traces its origin to a single ancestor who may be a real person, a mythical hero or a deity. These groups were often in conflict with other similar groupings.
3 Statelessness following the fall of the Empires prior to World War I was a profound problem according to Arendt (1951). The relationship between statelessness and Jews is a complex one beyond the scope of this book; however the idea of a nation state is discussed in the final chapter.

4 Gerlach (2010) points out that after the annexation of Austria many European countries passed laws barring fleeing Jews from entering. This essentially confined most Jews to areas controlled by the Nazis.
5 Stanton (1996) outlined eight stages: Classification, Symbolization, Discrimination, Dehumanization Organization, Polarization, Persecution, Preparation, Extermination and Denial.
6 Obviously, the construction of a diseased and degenerate identity foisted upon the real and conceptual Jew was a matter of life and death. Many authors speculate about the common use of these fears in genocide.
7 Friedlander (2007) describes attempts to "purchase" Jews in danger in 1943, protests and ritual mourning in Tel Aviv, and failed efforts in the United States Congress to act.
8 This is not the same dynamic as the notorious "following orders" but the leader's judgment replacing the peoples. See Arendt (1951).
9 On January 21, 1939, Hitler told the Czechoslovak Foreign Minister "The Jews here will be annihilated." Nine days later, on the sixth anniversary of the seizure of power, he issued his infamous "prophecy," repeated intermittently during the war: "if international finance-Jewry inside and outside Europe should succeed in plunging the nations once more into a world war, the result will not be the bolshevization of the earth and thereby the victory of Jewry, but the annihilation of the Jewish race in Europe!"
10 In 1989–1990 there was an intense international debate that followed the discovery of body parts from "euthanasia" victims used for anatomical teaching and research in Europe. A formula emerged in that all specimens for which provenance were uncertain, were buried while a controversy raged over the recognition of the victims as persons. The actual extent of medical involvement with the Nazis was ignored.

5

THE NAZI PLATFORM OF GROUP HALLUCINOSIS

> The Jew can take the credit for having corrupted the Greco-Roman world. We shall regain our health only by eliminating the Jews.
>
> *Adolf Hitler, February 22, 1942*

> The receptivity of large masses is very limited. Their capacity to understand things is slight whereas their forgetfulness is great. Given this, effective propaganda must restrict itself to a handful of points, which it repeats as slogans as long as it takes for the dumbest member of the audience to get an idea.
>
> *Adolf Hitler*, Mein Kampf

In order to further understand the power and appeal of Nazi propaganda that communicated false beliefs throughout Germany and Europe, it is necessary to develop a platform of understanding from individual clinical psychoanalytic theory and then apply this understanding to Nazi group dynamic behavior. First it is necessary to understand the significant psychic difference between the concepts of belief or faith that stands in contrast to fact and perception. Faith concerns the degree of internal commitment to a cognitive or emotional belief that may be either true, deceptive or an illusion. In order to understand "faith," as compared to "fact" from a psychoanalytic perspective, it is necessary to initially start with some of Bion's ideas regarding attacks on truth and psychic meaning that emerge from his psychoanalytic theories of disturbed thinking (Bion, 1962b; Meltzer, 1968). Following that clarification distinctions between individual beliefs and group belief will be explored.

In his later papers Bion described a psychic process in the representation of disturbed thinking and his understanding of that process. He theorized that disturbed thinking was the end product of an internal (psychic) unconscious attack on or nullification of meaning, devaluing, distorting and attacking actual accurate internal mental representations, perceptions and images of persons, experiences, symbols or ideas. In his theoretical numerical shorthand he called this destructive transformative process Minus K (Knowledge). This negative or minus in thought or knowledge he believed to be the internal or psychic source of cynicism, lies, false beliefs and psychic delusions: the negative of a necessary search for truth and/or meaning in Bion's system. Bion's description is different from Money-Kyrle's (2015) concept of innocent, unintentional misunderstanding growing out of early developmental distortions of experience (p. 255). Bion's unconscious process, Minus K (Knowledge), is not explained by a regression to primitive thinking; in this model it is a psychic violation of normal adaptive reality testing by undigested psychic elements. Bion's idea has not previously been applied to group conflict, group cohesion or the Nazi system of propaganda and violence (Roth, 2013). From this current perspective violent war conflicts between large groups are often the result of conflicts in beliefs or faith in ideas while group cohesion can be understood as large numbers of people sharing or having faith in certain ideas as true and meaningful.

The dynamics of group beliefs present a different and more complex dynamic than individual beliefs. Engagement and acceptance of a belief on a group level is not the same as on an individual level. The dynamics of a shared belief distinguishes a group as different from an aggregate. The psychic act of "identifying" oneself as a group member changes the individual's identity and increases their vulnerability to the emergent pressures of conforming to the groups' leader, beliefs and mission. If the group leader is a charismatic leader capable of finding and engendering anxiety and/or fear and its solution in the group, psychological mechanisms emerge that limit logical thinking and pressures emerge to accept a solution to that fear. If adherents believe they posses the true order of the world and meaning of history they will likely act to make this order come into being. Indoctrination to a true or false group belief usually occurs in stages: proselytizing, recruitment, compliance, internalization and consolidation although zealots may appear. Early normal exposure to a belief system by children may resolve forms of anxiety and enable a "family" set of beliefs to identify with that provides a framework for meaning and values. In both cases an "us" and "them" is facilitated and there is a tendency, with employment of true and false beliefs, to cast nonbelievers as the "other," unenlightened or enemy. This transformation becomes evident in the psychical tensions of ethnocentrism and otherization occurring in "hot" and "cold" wars. Hitler was able to generate such extreme measures of persuasion and threat by restricting information and constant repetition of his emotional messages such that his followers were impervious to other influences: they were transformed into "true believers." The so-called charismatic effect the leader has with his or her followers, and why the followers " identify" with the leader, is determined by a) the leader justifying the mission by appealing to moral issues of "right" and "wrong," b) communicating in symbolic language that makes the message clear and vivid that carries the moral unity of the collective, c) demonstrating conviction and passion for the mission (Antonakis, 2012). The extent that the content of the message resonates with the collective, the leader will appear as ideal to the collective or, in contrast, loathed by those who do not resonate with the message. Social preconditions of threat and anxiety aid the acceptance of the leader's magical promise of relief.

Hitler seemed to posses an excitable form of non-directed thinking that forms lateral solutions and a sense that he was speaking with a divine sermon (Redles, 2008). This primitive form of prophecy was a mixture of apocalyptic beliefs and paranoid threats with a messianic promise of redemption. He created a revitalization movement for Germans arousing hope for Germany and love for him, and compliance with his new perceptions and order. A great new violent mission and future was inflicted on Germans for better or worse.

"True believers" in a hierarchical group structure process information differently and perceive reality in accordance with their faith in ideas, the leader and his beliefs. Most group members develop cognitive "techniques to process" messages of appeals and information attending to the language of the emotional appeals, threats and end goal rewards (Gass and Seiter, 2013). Such cognitive and emotional processes contribute to an individual social confirmation bias, attending to what one believes to be true, coerced by group process into believing and ignoring contradictory messages or information as irrelevant. Often this bias leads to disparagement of "alternate" perspectives or believers in favor of the leader's elite beliefs and the appeal of predictions of a new world order that reverses prior status. This often appears as closed mindedness.

Bion widened the psychoanalytic field of inquiry focusing attention of events that might otherwise be overlooked. For Bion, hallucinosis is that event that occurs when a perception of a portion of reality becomes interdicted by elements of fantasy (beta elements): the distinction between reality and fantasy collapses in the direction of fantasy so that perception and meaning is transformed. This accounts for the elements of experience taking on or being subjected to an intrusion that reconstructs them and their meaning. It represents, in Bion's (1984a) description, a failure in normal symbol formation in which something in reality is transformed by an internal process to be powerful, dangerous or gratifying. In this psychic process a bizarrely reconstituted scenario can coexist with a normal external world of perceptions.

Bion's process presupposes a greater degree of unconscious functioning in thinking that creates prejudicial transformations. As a function of this automatic projective transformation, when the perceived object is distorted the perceiver may or may not be aware of this process of distortion. To a greater or lesser extent the potential for a hallucinotic experience is always present as part of thinking. Bion pointed out that, in any group transformations, to a greater or lesser extent, the hallucinatory phenomenon is always present, since he considers this one of the mind's functions and occurs more often than recognized. Often overlooked is that the self is also transformed in the hallucinosis while the realness of people has its significance changed. He also maintained rivalry, envy, greed, thieving, violence, together with his sense of being blameless, deserve consideration as invariants of hallucinosis (Sandler, 2009, pp. 132–133).

Building on Bion's original ideas Meltzer (1968) contributed an important idea that any member of a family who has a personal sense of present internal terror might serve as a central focus or matrix for this emotion by projecting it into the environment and terrorizing the weaker of the family individuals as a reaction to the felt belief of a threat. Although Meltzer was not a family or group therapist this contagious and destructive dynamic is applicable to the leaders of large groups or nations who are unable to contain and spread a threatening internal fantasy. Such leaders seek to ameliorate their and their nation's terror or disillusionment through construction of a real or false belief matrix or ideological faith into which their followers are able to identity with and discharge strong emotions. This joint dynamic may be at the core of the receptivity of what is called charisma. Faith is then in a dynamic system of filtered perception that confirms certain values, images and guiding beliefs without proof. Under such conditions of terror and group disharmony or "disarroy" (Turquet, 1975) in certain large groups, the positive functions of normal healthy search for accurate knowing (K) and symbolization can become (violently) suppressed, split off or delegated to a superior leader often seen as a genius or mystic. In place of accurate learning a negative anti-reality delusional belief may be constructed by a leader that attracts a shared (group) projective delusional processes. This dual projective process generates a false emotional belief or faith that allows some mastery over the feared and hated object and a discharge of emotion. Other like-minded believers find elements (mythic, intuitive, universal) to identity with, follow and act upon joining with the prophetic leader. When such conditions occur leader-centric group processes (Bion, 1961) emerge that interact with other people's psyche seeking relief from any threat or seeking to identify with a real or imaginary cause or leader. Often a community of believers or spokespersons is formed that acquires a compelling power and willingness to act violently or as missionaries. When this shared illusion occurs there is a suspension of doubt and individuals increasingly believe in their leader's false perspective (prophecy) freeing them of the influence of reason, the anxiety of thinking or an inner emptiness. An emotionally powerful, coercive and threatening leader (Hitler, Pol Pot) re-enforces the lack of separation of truth and faith, and by shared delusion, repetition or fantasy, the oracles' fiction is given the sanctioned appearance of truth that dominates reason. With extreme fears of a group threat often the concept of a safe "We" is also fractured by archetypes and artificial social boundaries between real and other imaginary coalitions are redrawn. For example, Jews who had been citizens could suddenly not be Germans and their civil rights were taken away and their homes looted.

Hitler's repeated used manipulative "double messages" in his speeches reconstructed social/political boundaries and threats: an example of the paradoxical message is "Aryans are superior but are in danger." This message creates a mixture of narcissistic status and simultaneous threat. For this to be accepted, the large group's (Germany) morality or national and personal identity and faith must have been previously undermined by widespread dysphoria and fear (of collapse) so that imaginary apocalyptic dangers were able to convey an imaginary threat as described by Meltzer (1968). A pre-genocidal dynamic of imaginary threat, betrayal or contamination occurs in all organized genocides in which earlier ethical norms and values were devalidated and replaced by mythological archetypes and threats. The Nazis also promised a return to an older form of military order and purification, a combination that is not unique to mass violence and murder while also reappearing in different forms of new salvatory movements (Barkun, 1996). This combination of violence and salvation frequently forms particularly dangerous types of charismatic authority that leads to group violence.

Feared earlier dangers of national collapse in Germany appeared potential, remained and were reimagined in the Nazi ideology or faith as being caused by Jews. The specific dangers emanating from Hitler's core threatening Anti-Jewish rhetoric found sufficient resonance in the German people's psyche (Rees, 2012) and dominated the propositional logic of cognition (Bytwerk, 2004; Gonen, 2000; Weiss, 1996). Propositional logic is when two statements are joined together with "and," the complex statement formed by them is true if and only if *both* the component statements are true. The end result in Germany was a mass conversion experience to new Nazi authority established by public displays of shocking force, terror and accusation. Such violent displays of authorized violence likely caused otherwise unaffected others to seek psychological protection in various ways by serving the persecutors making the concept of "bystander" or "ordinary" questionable (Gerlach 2010; Kuhl, 2016).

Outsiders are puzzled by the power of Hitler's belief system to change behavior because they are outside that historical matrix and not vulnerable to a conversion experience in which the power of these false beliefs emerged and attracted followers. Often this conversion is erroneously ascribed as Hitler's charismatic leader effect rather than understood as a prophetic threatening, independent of reality, ameliorative and cumulative group messenger (Baron-Cohen et al., 2008; Weiss, 1996). The group experience may involve a complex psychic surrender to the leader and finding "truth" in the message that changes evaluation of the self and judgments of value. This is a transcendent conversion rather that a regression.

Applying the dynamics of threat and conversion to the power of beliefs of the Nazis is revealing. Real and mythic political, social and medical dangers threatening Germany were repeatedly exaggerated and amalgamated by the Nazis in their propaganda and co-constructed with Jews. In turn these threats were cannily contrasted to and helped rebuild a new imaginative but clarifying belief in Aryan superiority and Jewish dangerous threat. Not only were Jews dehumanized and de-Germanized by forms of propaganda and laws, a Nazi representational system was imposed in which persecutory anxiety was dynamized in terms of infection. Hyatt-Williams discovered that persecutory anxiety and felt betrayal were essential to individual violent murderers (1998, p. 45). On a group level such threats were converted into an active death threat constellation. Violence as distinct from power, force or strength requires implements for harm and a rational for its exercise. The death threat is a constellation of fears of these implements or infections, fantasies and preoccupations with violent harm and death that are usually in a balance with constructive forces in individuals and collectives. A combination of constitutional and environmental traumas can create a large group dynamic imbalance in the proportions in a social or psychic death threat: that tension in certain violent prone societies must be resolved by a destructive attack on "diseased" life processes or their inanimate representations. This is one of the unconscious underpinnings of a cultural *Kriegsideologie*. When the imbalance between destructive and generative forces coalesces into a character trait in an individual or value and intention in a culture, the person(s) or group has to violently act to kill off in reality whatever is or is thought or imagined to be the painful or infectious cause. In other words societies may vary along a dimension of potential violence that includes finding causes for strategic bombing, forced imprisonment or expulsion, starvation, lynching, etc. as an expression of a remedy to this dangerous threat.

Based on the false proposition or repeated illusion that Jews posed a past and present intrusive death threat against the Germans, the death threat (ideology) of the Nazis was heightened and it followed in dynamic false logic that Jews must be eliminated. In order for this to occur there must have been widespread social support for this dynamic form of state authorized eliminest solution that was initially initiated with the German euthanasia movement of purification.

This powerful imaginary political threat of destruction of lives also requires a real or imaginary target for contrast: one pure and the other lethal, Aryan and Jew, Hutu and Tutsi, resulting in a splitting of core social structures and beliefs. This psychic splitting of safe/pure and lethal reduces immediate anxiety, guilt and shame by a false explanation, and then requires a discharge of violent action. Once such a violent process starts, the elite leadership responds as if the violence demonstrates and reinforces their power and/or supremacy as a cure for the repeated mythic falsifications (propaganda). An external balance in the mass retaliatory violence was in their minds "necessary" to maintain by intuitively keeping the death constellation externalized in an enemy in reality and subdued in the German psyche. Bold and clever use of the political and media systems placed a premium on the Nazi capacity to turn imaginative fictions and illusions (false beliefs and science) into racial myths of mortal danger. In the guise of logic, science and historical facts (Adorno, 1973; Welch, 2002) Jews became "mortal" enemies in reality. This was, according to Bion's group ideas, a basic assumption group rhetoric distorting reality in a concrete binary of superior and morally dangerous. From the perspective of Hyatt-Williams' (1998) theory of violence, Nazi propaganda was a psychic concretization of mortal danger threat symbols directing violent action at others. Baron-Cohen, from a different vantage (Baron-Cohen et al., 2008), describes this kind of concrete thinking as propositional logic that serves varying emotional and directional purposes for the various members in the large group. In accord with this violent basic assumption mentality leader, murder raids upon other polities were required to increase terror that made the other dangerous, discharge violent energy and importantly to prove that enemies exist in reality while justifying the external source of the lethal threats. Actual destruction of lives was also necessary to magically reverse national and individual psychic histories of helplessness, internal threat and fear. Mass murder demonstrated uncaring violent power over the now made "weaker" enemy/threat as originally described by Meltzer. Through externalizing projective processes a lethal enemy was made of helpless unarmed people. In addition to a necessary discharge of violence are the further complex needs to organize and continually revitalize the Nazi beliefs that emerged in World War I around a unique German destructive capability (hubris) over discernable often-unarmed enemies (Gerlach, 2010). An enemy in reality takes years to define by propaganda, double-dealing and secret alliances but it is easier to construct than a valid (generative) cause or hallucinotic purpose. The psychic possibility of repair, generativity or normal mourning between enemy combatants in this delusional system was distorted and replaced by an ideology that created a reversal of status. This reversal included a delusional system of projective processes that constructed the enemy-victim as malignant and inferior lives or enemies not worth living: Russians, Bolsheviks and Jews. As (Minus K) external dangerous objects they served as negative worthless containers (Meltzer, 1968; Weiss, 1996) necessary to be eliminated to save Germany. The historical absence of true generative or reparative tasks in the Nazi Germany era from the start of World War I to World War II and the emergent search and preoccupation with weapons, militarization and *Untermenschen* in the Nazi military society (social, etc.) can be understood as an early ideological construction of what is a predatory basic assumption group mentality. This is based on a dynamic of inclusion within (Arendt, 1951) and violent exclusion with threats of extreme annihilation. In sum, there is a deep inter-fueling between violent societies and the emergence of predatory behavior seeking interlocking false beliefs in a search for victims who are in various ways malignant to eliminate in some manner. How this occurs varies in different forms of violent societies with different values.

There is an additional possible profound group perspective that emerged from a recent extension of Bion's original work on hallucinosis by Sandler (2009). While Russia was a political threat in reality to Germany and rival to Hitler's Nazi Empire building fantasies, the paranoid delusion of a racial Jewish infection required building ongoing elements of large-scale group "hallucinosis" (Meltzer, 1986; Sandler, 2009). This belief was used to falsely explain prior betrayals and continuing mortal threats to Germans. Hallucinosis describes an emotional environment or belief in a normal mind or group collective that is unreal yet escapes judgment and passes for real: a collusive group belief that depends on what Baron-Cohen called propositional logic (Baron-Cohen et al., 2008). Propositional logic constructs causality as when (A) happened (B) caused it. Social leaders, or prophets as replacements to leaders, in whom the hallucinosis and delusion are endowed, foster a false belief in place of a testable group reality. For example it is true that Germany lost the war (A) but the Jews did not cause the loss (B). The Nazi jointly held false belief provided an equilibrating psychic function for the individual and group by containing or falsely explaining the intolerable, disillusioning and threatening danger as being outside or external to the German people. This proposition transforms the reality of us/them beliefs by a paranoid and/or redemptive process that included a duality of group superiority and life or soul threatening enemies (Sandler, 2009). The definition of the imagined Jewish threat by projective processes was located on the outside of the individual (Green, 1999) or group and contained all forms of malignancy. In this manner the individual's capacity to normally perceive reality was transformed (Bion, 1962) in a fixed manner. The transforming agents attain status, power, followers and a bond creating a reverberating circuit of reinforcement for the false belief by its variety and repetition. Hitler assumed the position of a visionary prophetic national leader offering an explanation for the distresses of Germans and a transforming solution. He identified Germans as superior and the cause of their plight as Jews. He maintained leadership through the creation of a persecutory violence against real and imaginary enemies inside and outside of Germany that required retaliatory and protective violence and a return to a purer racial Germany.

Hitler revived a hallucinotic process regarding German history regarding Jews and became the forceful psychic magnet of delusional belief and justification for the Nazis' right to annihilate and scavenge. Mass murder as a lawless racial redemptive act against a fictive (delusional) infected enemy allowed normal guilt to be bypassed revealing a horrifying indifference to humanity. The Nazi Basic Assumption thought system within the hallucinosis transformed cause and effect by all-blaming Jews and constructing a belief system that elimination of Jews would enable a safe Nazi fascist ordered world: both a national Nazi redemptive cure and safety (Hinton, 2002). This co-construction of a murderous basic assumption group and leader(s) enabled an intense affective upwelling in admiration and support of the rescuing leader with a spewing of justifiable violence in the hallucinotic belief of additionally being on a rescue mission to prevent the disintegration of Germany by Jews and Bolsheviks. Coincident with the German war with Russia, the destructive power of the hallucinosis intensified by the construction of Jew/Bolshevik image such that unarmed commissars (officers) were demonized and murdered without concern as Bolshevik threats, while the murders of unarmed Jews and others spread and accelerated. In summary, the German Fascist hallucinotic solution sought to reverse, transform and eliminate both Bolsheviks and the Judeo-Christian presence and mores in Europe with the propositional myths of German Fascism, Aryan superiority and rightful murderous violence.[1] Here the Nazi hallucinotic dream of world mastery went catastrophically awry.

The concept of a Nazi hallucinotic negative basic assumption makes a more direct psychoanalytic link to Sofsky's understandings of the Nazi concentration camps' raw brutal power over human life. The Nazi power over life was extended beyond the camps into warfare and the treatment of prisoners. Bartov's (1996) and others' notion of psychic motivation originating from an abstract ideology as sole Nazi motive fails to confront and fathom the multiple origin of the delusional hallucinotic quality and wide psychic appeal of Nazi eliminest anti-Semitic rhetoric. The release of violence with delusional minus K thinking was directed outward, although restricted to only a psychic level in Bion's original theory, and became a violent cohesive force in the Nazi group's ideological cohesion and violence. This murderous force contributed to a blood knit and an emerging medical science devoted to killing; a bonding together of medical and military killers in cleansing Germany of impurity (Alexander, 1948).

It is traditionally thought that in acts of perverse or sadistic violence that conscious violent fantasies are present and in various ways contribute to the conscious actions of the perpetrator. Within a group sadistically prone individuals more easily disarm the normal internal resistances to violent murderous actions and supply targets and models to follow. The actions and beliefs of Hitler as a revered transcendent or omnipotent group leader with an empirical delusional cause repeatedly suggested that Germans reject their inner inhibitions to violent action. This process was more dynamically complicated in Germany because of the accelerating nature of Nazi propagandizing of a mythical Jewish threat, creating work and death camps that served to represent a "death constellation": a society with an indigestible preoccupation with death (Hyatt-Williams, 1998, p. 45) out of which euthanasia and mass murder became accepted solutions in Germany. Hyatt-Williams suggested that the psychological contributions to this constellation are a predisposition to excessive envy, the lack of an object or system that contains or deters violence, exposure to trauma brutalization and long painful illness, and a failure in symbolization as preparatory for prime perpetrators. I believe that there is also a failure in attaining independent mature symbolization and a reliance on propositional logic with the absence of healthy containing social punishments for violence. In addition, motivation for violence and some form of a justification after the event as a self-explanation may be quite different in criminogenic environments then in nation states at war.

Certainly almost all humans have some death anxiety that is part of our existence and is usually socially managed by rituals and beliefs. The human group into whom the death constellation has found deep roots and flourished is felt to be under the sway of its painful power and is psychically changed by its absorption. It is possible that the survivors of strategic bombing and of the atomic bombs suffer from this as an existential-depressive affect. A death threat that has been transformed into action by perpetrators through state sponsored murder is psychically experienced as possessing the potential power to "boomerang" and destroy both the victims and perpetrator and their group if they do not violently act. This is often expressed in perpetrators as a fantasy of "revenge" or retaliation that serves to keep a violent self destructive society energized. The perpetrator is often compelled to continue to act to remove these internal and external causes to avoid its return establishing a path of violence. This psychic relationship to the return of violent threat limits symbolic thinking and the dynamism of the projections are taken in as concrete ideograms. Once group violent expression occurs there is an escalating tendency for it to occur again although continuing to murder does not remove the psychic threat. This group struggle with a predatory violent death constellation in the Nazi group members generated a genocidal basic assumption that continued to be acted upon, spread and became lawless mass murder. To varying degrees within individuals the genocidal basic need became a psychic structuring phantasy of feeling infiltrated by unmanageable mentally indigestible threatening experiences and memories, with no possible relief or containment possible, other than to continue to remove its sponsored or targeted false external source. In some cases the psychic splitting process of murdering under hallucinosis within individuals' psyche was so mentally complete, the perpetrator was able to appear as ordinary and without apparent remorse or shame when not under its influence. It is important to understand that this reversal of threat dynamic can turn so-called "ordinary" people into serial murders as they are only "ordinary" before the first murder.

Given the Nazi organizational structure and its embedded and continuous destructive threat, it became the most powerful group engine to spread a mass movement of constructed hallucinotic denigrating hatred with permission and direction to act murderously: without fear of external punishment. The Nazi messianic destruction of the Jews found its engine and energy in this complex hallucinotic group mentality.

What is now possible, building on Sandler's theoretical extension of Bion's ideas, is a new understanding of a hallucinotic leader who imaginatively transforms reality for a majority of the nation/group with a variety of thought transformations of the normal safe ordering of social non-kin reality. The range of Nazi/Hitler false belief utterances (propaganda) served organizing and empowering functions throughout the German population that included a state justified sense of righteous well-being in which there was no need for curiosity or examination of their leaders or Hitler's murder driven messages. One result of this conversion/unconscious process was the emergence of concreteness of thought, sharp racial contrasts and rigidity in thinking, with intolerance for dissent along with a massed release of a spectrum of violent projective identifications necessary to define and eliminate imagined dangers for an imaginative cause. The full knowledge of what people did to each other was unrecognized until the war was over.

This kind of dehumanizing hallucinotic dynamic cannily used by Hitler is repeatedly found in destructive groups of all kinds and sizes. More commonly found in religious groups than political ones, the examples are many: for example Aum Shinrikyo, the Japanese cult that released sarin nerve gas in the Tokyo subways: the Peoples Temple founder Jim Jones; the Manson group, etc. Upon analysis hallucinotic thinking may also be found in the dynamics of all forms of warfare and the social construction of political enemies and threats.

In contrast to Friedlander (1995) who viewed the Nazi murderous events as almost outside of human history, it is more accurate to describe that hallucinotic thinking as a group body of ideas of false belief that appears around us in various combinations. Further, that the Nazi behavior is but one extreme occasion when violent murder has been the result of such thinking.

There are not only numerous examples of hallucinotic group behaviors, their outcomes bear a remarkable similarity to Lifton's criteria for thought reform but fundamentally all ideologies make a claim based on an irrational belief: i.e. Noah and the great floods. What are essential to be dynamically understood are the variations in individual psychological attraction to hallucinotic ideas that likely depend on the psychological structures of individual identity, their relations to groups and the residue of unconscious anxiety and rage. The appeal of millennial/violent group actions depends on the interaction between beliefs and identity structure of the individual, the openness and closed-ness of individual thinking and individual and cultural potential sadistic/predatory behaviors.

Every form of ideologically driven group movements can be understood as fueled by a conversion through hallucinotic basic assumptions. As Bion and Sandler, 2009) suggested these include conversions that psychically reverse personal or national anxiety and annihilation fears by crusade like redemptive ideology. Without doubt there are huge psychological differences between various ideologies that serve psychic needs as containers for aims, anxiety, identity or ambitions. Hitler envisioned his leaders' mission as oracle of "truths" and purity, saving Germany and replacing a corrupt and doomed heterogeneous world with its imagined rightful heroic heirs. He found adequate converts to his imaginary beliefs to collude with him. Basic-assumption thinking, murderous violence and violent dreams spread by the Nazis over the vastness of poly-ethnic Europe until stopped by a counter belief and force.

Note

1 Gerlach (2010) argues that physical closeness to Russia was an important physical determinant for the intensity of the murderous violence.

6
HALLUCINOSIS AND PERVERSIONS

In the earlier chapters I have established a relationship between state-sponsored group murderous violence and the creation and manipulation of "false beliefs." Bion (1962b) made the important observation that certain forms of faulty or hallucinotic thinking is that mental occasion in which something(s) unreal or falsified is transformed into or confused with something real to avoid an internal painful awareness or that which is a threat or is negative (Green, 1999). A transformed hallucinotic core idea or image can exist in an otherwise normal individual and direct a portion of their perception, excitement, behavior and thinking. This proves to be a remarkably versatile and productive concept when describing the dynamics of "false beliefs" particularly when they occur in large groups. The clinical utility of this concept occurs when the hallucinotic content for believing about reality is unrecognized and others do not accept its delusion as real or factual. Often the perceived transformed relationships in reality are interlocked and arranged either as superior and inferior (Sandler, 2009, p. 173) or believers and non-believers. Hallucinations are objectless perception where hallucinosis is the presence of a hallucination in an otherwise preserved personality. There is a greater tendency for hallucinotic collusions or hysterias (Bion, 1965, p. 133) in a group as the distortions are embedded in conscious and unconscious communications that exert pressures on the individual to give up curiosity to conform to the group's fears and beliefs. The social psychologist Solomon Asch was the first to demonstrate the powerful influence of group conformity. When mainstream cultural coherence declines or has been threatened, anomie and identity confusion become far more common, and vulnerability to an imaginary solution that reduces psychic pain becomes more attractive. When a prophetic leader is the source of the hallucinotic distortion in a collectivist culture, forms of projective identification become excessive and have a massive influence on the behavior of the group members often producing powerful identifications and a variety of emotional and muscular discharges. The deluded or hallucinated construction of elements of reality is shared among the group members for a spectrum of conscious and unconscious reasons and often becomes unexaminable when combined with hidden anxieties or unconscious threats. Not only can group beliefs fill a psychic void and become imperative, all hallucinosis transform a group and/or individual basic anxiety into actions or excited beliefs. The group anchored by a hallucinotic idea may then become a refuge and restores imaginary beliefs and serves as a source of continuous reinforcement of adoration, hate, envy and idealization of the leader. This false belief can inform a highly specific way of knowing and of seeing the world. When the need to belong to a nation is exceedingly strong out of fear, guilt and threats there is no recognition of the "rest of the world" (Kris and Speir, 1944, pp. 285–286) but in reality governments are ill equipped to be "good parents" and resolve identity difficulties with an integrated ethical orientation. The Nazi murderous phenomenon is one of the most notorious and significant group occasions for this form of hallucinotic behavior leading to organized murderous violence. This chapter is focused on the pathological effects of hallucinotic ideas that lead to sexualized excitement, violence and abuse.

Interpersonal violence as a psychological event has mostly remained outside of psychoanalytic investigation. Only in recent years has there been any attempt to explore individual violence and murder from a psychoanalytic perspective. Hyatt-Williams (1998) and Cartwright (2002) are the rare exceptions engaged with and studying actual people (male) who committed violent attacks and murders. In so doing they have contributed to our understanding of the dynamics of human violence while contributing to a clinical dilemma as they were studying individuals after they had been legally detained for their actions and in some form of protective capacity. Thus confined, punishment and apprehension likely changed the dynamic nature of their internal mental life and the healthier aspects of their personality were likely striving for expression and safety while obscuring or minimalizing the destructive elements. Glasser (1979, 1986) initially speculated that perversion and violence shared a common early origin in psychological development that affects the course of later development. At the center of his view is a core complex, an internal constellation made up of the inter-related ingredients in a fluid state of the longing for intimate gratification and security, the anxieties of annihilation and abandonment, with the attendant depression, and the aggression and sado-masochism of self-preservative violence. This early oscillating core complex is thought to redirect development and to violently respond to threat. The internal oscillation of its conflict reappears in adults in two distinct or hybrid self-presentations: a violated, humiliated in-danger position and a violent, cruel, triumphant position. The oscillation between these positions may also account for certain aspects of impostoring.

On an individual basis, the theoretical psychoanalytical relationship between the dynamics of violence and perversion are subtle yet extensive. As distinct each apparently involves instinctive and narcissistic demands that compromise moral inhibitions, deficits in inhibition of actions and splitting of the ego as a defense. Both the psychology of a perversion and interpersonal violence are different from each other as they serve significantly differing sources of "pleasure" indicating the likelihood of different neural pathways, engage other people in different social outcomes and represent a psychic maneuver to alter the subject's psyche or body and his or her interpersonal environment or integrity and often occur in a sequence of acts. The actual manifestations of violence and perversions are extremely varied and numerous while having certain dynamic psychic and relational configurations in common for the perpetrators: 1) sadistic acts in which there is a fantasy of reversing earlier humiliations; 2) self-preservative acts based on a perception of real or imagined threat and danger; 3) self-protective acts that are thought to protect from bodily or mental intrusion (threat) and humiliation. I will not attend to the devastating impact on individuals and families of the victims of violent acts that can be life changing for the victims. It is assumed, from an analytic perspective, that these acts provide arousal and gratification of hidden and dormant impulses or offer security from a real or imagined perceived threat.

To understand perversions I believe it is important to note what Bion believed. Bion believed that sexuality was erroneously given a preeminent place in psychoanalytic thinking because of it being stimulated by the analytic pair (Abel-Hirsch 2015). The nature of human development he postulated was based on other emotions as Love (L), Hate (H) and knowledge (K) (Bion 1962a). Bion's idea allows a different perspective on perversions that may contain elements of L, H and K. Glasser (1978) reduced the origin of perversions to the existence of an early oscillating "core complex" that leaves the individual vulnerable and affects the internalization of a stable or safe self-representation while distorting further developmental stages. The vulnerable pre-existing "core complex" is thought to be responsible for the perverse individual's early terror of both annihilation through being abandoned or equally engulfed that results in the fusion or a lack of differentiation of sexual and violent impulses.

Bion cautioned about abstractly making assumptions about development and drew attention to the primary pairing couple in his basic assumption of the pair in group theory. He believed this "yearning" to pair was fundamental to sexuality and contained a precursor of sexuality and a premonition of sex (1962a). Greenacre (1987), following the notion that trauma in early stages of development impinges on later ego development and body image, also noted a tendency toward severe misrepresentation of self or other in reality testing. Chasseguet-Smirgel (1984), in a manner similar to Glasser, focused on the existence of a latent perverse core in development that affects all impulses, thoughts and mental and emotional processes and can be activated by trauma or social conflict. It seems a short distance from these "core" perspectives to an understanding of a transforming hallucinotic process in which contradictory beliefs can be simultaneously held about the self and the other that permits some sort of illusory perception that is usually followed by a form of recovery. The early and continuing vulnerability of these infantile psychic structures to this transforming influence likely depends on the adequacy of the early normal splitting processes and the nature of the idealization of the self and primary other as Meltzer (2008) described.

The achievement of the stability of a self-representation and internal ethical/moral core is believed to protect against vulnerability to such forms of psychic threats. Unstable self-representations are a product of significant developmentally destructive failures of introjection and paternal containment during development that also leads to the kinds of cognitive distortions described by Bion and Money-Kyrle (2015). Steiner (2011) argued that it was essential to understand these distortions and misrepresentation of self and other as they play a role in the maintaining of confusions between the self and the external world. Some degree of splitting, evacuative projection and bisexual identity may be "normal" in mainstream development; in perversions it is the varying degrees of organization that includes hate or antagonism toward the other that intermingles with erotic desire to debase the other. This extreme psychic constellation acts like or is experienced as a foreign object in the personality that seeks a physical erotic experience intermingling reality and fiction. Stoller (1975; 1986) emphasized hostility as the motor force of excitement in all other erotic scenarios.

O'Shaughnessy (1990) approached closer to a description of the extreme dynamics in perversion in describing a deficit in early primal relationship in her analysis of chronic lying (falsification). She hypothesizes the presence of a strong uncontained and hidden or obvious destructive instinct in some patients during development and a history of delight in violent or perverse acts either in reality or fantasy. The key word is delight that has an emotional and sensory component. Although fantasies are highly varied along a spectrum for every individual, in their fundamental form perverse fantasies are usually repetitive and somewhat fixed with a wished for narcissistic or omnipotent control of the external reality or an individual in an encounter. When patients' perverse and violent fantasies are closely examined it is possible to place these dynamics along a rough continuum. At one end are located fantasies seeking authentication or praise from a significant other or a search for a real or imagined positive end goal; at the other bifurcated end are found malicious deception of sexuality symbolically described on one vane, and at the other, a relationship between a helpless individual and an annihilating violent one. In this vane a violent or sexualized force are intermingled in the violent/erotic event. I believe that violence against a participant is commonly found in the bifurcated end that confirms Stoller's (1975) idea of erotic hatred. In summary at the one end of the continuum is the seeking of narcissistic supplies or gratification and on the other impaired or exaggerated aspects of "normal" sexuality and arousal.

Central to understanding the expression of and dynamics of perversion and violence is their dependence on the use of harsher more primitive defenses that blend violence and sexual impulses accompanied by distortions of perception of both bodies. One result is that the perverse idea of what arouses desire and constitutes sex for such persons likely carries elements that have been produced by more primitive distortions cemented together. In particular projective expulsion, splitting and dissociation allow neurotic and benign regression to be evaded as the hallucinatory or "foreign" activity suddenly infiltrates perception and leads to a transformative physical act in reality. This kind of rapid transformation indicates a psychic structure that has possibly been defined by early splitting and projective evacuation in the personality in question. From a developmental perspective along with early splitting there was a "premature or precocious closure" (Grotstein, 1985, p. 193) that limits adaptation and results in a lack of participation in further stages of normal differentiation, particularly the organization inherent in the Oedipal period. Or, there is a threat of diffusion of identity that occurs with sexual excitement. A precocious split off mental part, the foreign internal object, I believe, is the site of or agent of either the hallucinosis or perverse core, a part of the self that is in distinction to the good parts of the self. The split off part of the self violates the usual social norms of sexual intimacy and integrity.

In the early history of psychoanalytic models the concept of regression played a primary role in major disorders.[1] The historical use of the concept of regression in describing sexual perversions exposes one of the limitations of Freudian libidinal theory while revealing one of its major flaws in dealing with a psychic "structure" of individuals called perverse. A complete review of the theory of perversions/regressions is beyond the scope of this effort and so highlights or a review will have to suffice. For Anna Freud regression was first in her delineation of defenses and suggested that acting out contained elements from earlier stages of fixated development expressed through action. Balint (1968), among others, sought to distinguish types of regression (Akhtar, 2009, p. 215) so many theorists assumed that perverse acts represented a regression to an earlier stage of psychosexual development. I believe there is sufficient clinical evidence to support another explanation based on psychic splitting as Hinshelwood (2008) suggested that does not require appealing to a model of regression. The fundamental issue concerning splitting is the nature of the elements formed by the early splitting process;[2] the model is of the creation of a hallucinotic core that is responsible for changes in perception, defends against being drawn into the sphere of the normal "contained" object relations and remains split-off (Bion, 1962a; Grotstein, 1985). This core appears in "the tricks of interpersonal relations (not of object relations for they are highly narcissistic in their organization) of psychopaths: the liar, the cheat the poseur, confidence man, 'prostitute' (Meltzer's tramp), professional gambler, dope pusher, committed pervert and dedicated anarchist" (Meltzer, 2008, p. 97): these characters all imply a fundamental attack on the values of a safe intact-shared psychic space within normal Oedipal triangular structures. The psychopathic aim and fundamental method in perverse acts is the creation of basic persecutory violent, manipulative, sexualized confusion or crises in psychic reality regarding the basic integrity of "the Law of the father" as described by Lacan (1955–1956). For Lacan this "Law" is a symbolic (internal) acceptance of the cultural, linguistic and family norms of a moral patriarchy that emerges when there are actual mediator/barriers between the child and the mother pair that are identified with. The perverse person is understood as unconsciously craving a restoration of the early danger of psychic chaos or catastrophe from which they may or may not survive. Bion used the term catastrophe (Sandler, 2009) to depict a sudden and destructive perturbation in a given real or hallucinated status quo that will lead to a potential dreaded psychic calamity and the expression of a prohibited or uncontainable bodily excitement and pleasure. The result of such an act is that split-off aspects of the self reappear and one person transposes himself or herself mentally and physically overcomes the other person in the pair violently, sexually or parasitically.

I believe that the strong connection between the sexually perverse and violent acts suggested originally by Glasser (1979) and Bion is found in the following projective process: that person unconsciously identifies with or seeks to eliminate that which is an unprocessed part of the self that will be projected by evacuation into the "victim" or partner in the pairing. The victim has knowingly or unknowingly attracted this re-exposure creating what is an external (perverse) phantasy object that cannot be discriminated from the aggressor's projected unprocessed elements. The exciting erotic attraction and finale consists of transformed self and other with a suspension of assessment of any consequences and danger. This Bion (1984a) called a transformation in action[3] that may be followed by a period of re-introjection or re-internalization of what has been psychically expelled,[4] creating a cycle of behavior that resists normal psychic mentalization or symbolization. Cartwright (2002) and Hyatt-Williams (1998) have described a similar cycle in violent attacks.

Reducing perverse psychosexuality exclusively to an expression of early object relationship desexualizes it altogether (Fonagy, 2008) and cuts it off from its roots. Bion also cautioned against the use of mechanistic models to understand sexual behavior (Abel-Hirsch, 2015). Fonagy (2008) importantly suggests that sexuality (both aim and drive) belongs to a part of the mind that is simultaneously owned and not owned and is "pre-mentalistic" making it vulnerable or available to the intrusion of forms of fantasy and unresolved developmental conflicts. Bion referred to this mental component as "proto-mental." The proto-mental system is the earliest mind in which the physical and psychical is undifferentiated and according to Meltzer (1986) holds the most primitive automatic elements of the self. This nascent mode of pre-symbolic mental life is dependent on and responsive to good-enough mothering and in this pre-linguistic mode of pre-mentalistic experiencing the intentions of the other and the self is sensed by their observable behavior and observable intentions. This mental state is more attuned to body stimulation and is considered the location of reverie. Physical demonstrations of adult affection or love suggest pre- or proto-mentalistic ideation or transformations in action that may contain unusual beliefs, preconceptions or myths about the body, what is exciting and the most primitive images of the primary couple. Where the trauma of discovery of the "primal scene" has had some dominance in classical psychoanalytic theory, I believe that in perversions there is a creation of a primary couple by projective evacuation that misuses or misdirects psychic and body pleasures when aroused. The primary or primal couple may contain early mother and child elements as well as a variety of sensorial distortions of parental intercourse. In Bion's (1961) pairing basic assumption the primary couple is a complex idea about the parental couple as a proto-mental configuration of the pair. Central to its being subjectively experienced is often the child's intuited sense of being absented from the primary couple. This proto-mental image of "twosomes" is modified by experience and conflict over time. The healthy unity of psyche and soma has as its basic element the productive biological function of generativity of the Oedipal couple that is vulnerable to attack. This attack is likely related to the reports in the analytic literature that people with perversions create a quasi-analytic pair pretending to be in an analytic or generative pair while enslaved by a hallucinosis that prevents a therapeutic exchange.

A developmental psychoanalytical model usually is employed to explain perversions. The dynamic process leading to perversion is thought to begin very early in development. It is assumed that if the child between the ages of 2 and 4 experiences a threat of sufficient strength (from inside or outside) they have to resort to massive or excessive projective processes of both normal and expulsive nature (Bion, 1962a, p. 157): that stage is set for the child to sacrifice a part of their mental apparatus in order to reduce their psychic threat. This splitting and expulsion occurs before clear distinction of mind and body in the child and often is either a phallus[5] or a powerful negative and threatening element (Grotstein, 1996). A perverse internal nucleus is established based in a hallucinotic core as a split-off or separate psychic cluster. This cluster is what will become the perverse part or core of the personality that remains differentiated from the psychotic or neurotic part of the personality. This distinction is important for the sexually perverse hallucinosis reconfigures body images and functions of self and other in reality by the influence of defective projective processes. This differentiation of a hallucinotic core is an attempt to protect the integrity of the self from further assault while simultaneously having pleasure while producing a mental attack on the biological or cultural truth of the physical differences between the sexes. The body images of both self and other are mentally reconfigured much in the manner that Picasso reconfigures bodies out of fragments in his art.

When considering a psychoanalytic model of perversion it is important to recognize that masculine and feminine have a surplus of theoretical bias but maintain a template of adult genital sexuality. Internalized gender identity, excitement and sexual behavior are always an amalgamation of biological reality, fantasy, familial and cultural folklore within what constitutes a preliminary human framing structure of reference (Ogden, 1988). From a cultural perspective the perverse act is valued according to social norms and deviance and is defined by the diversion from the usual normal joint use of the reproductive organs. Although someone with a perversion derives enjoyment from these acts "they" appear to have destroyed either by their actions, imaginations or dreams what is biologically viewed as normal, often along with the real differences between the sexes (Lacan, 1955–1956). The active perverse individual, as well as the violent one, may be unable to feel authentic guilt or remorse and often appear hopeless: "from which the good parts of their self will crave release at any cost, even of the abandonment of the real world" (Meltzer, 1973, p. 96). What is the origin of this perverse sub-organization or state of mind?

Everyone is assumed to have a unique structure of desire while there are certain acts that deviate from that structure. The internal perverse structure (Baranger and

Goldstein, 1980) is best considered as a structure having various psychic levels that further distort the process of introjective identification and internal construction of self and body images, inside and outside reality. This distortion depends on a physical equivalent to Bion's Minus K link in which as development continues the biological-cultural truth perception of the primary couple is attacked and another idiosyncratic truth is created. For example the normal internal penis-as-link identification and introjection that usually allows recognition of difference and the full or ongoing internal Oedipal situation that includes the child in relation to the (primal) parental relationship (and mental bisexuality) (personal communication, Birksted-Breen 2016) is distorted. These early perverse negative distortions misconstruct ongoing developmental progressions and change (skewing) the nature of the emerging internalized parental link (Birksted-Breen, 1996) that also distorts affect regulation. The later development of an ongoing internal Oedipal structure based on the primary pair is also distorted.[6] One early result is that the paternal link, similar in function to Lacan's law of the father (Birksted-Breen, 1996), develops a perverse structuring function and promotes a distorted and erotically charged self-state and mental space for thinking. Without that normal "triangular link" manipulation or attack on the perception of external and internal "truth" is made credible and the normal projective and introjective identification in interpersonal dialogue becomes distorted. The distorted perverse projections misperceive reality for its exciting gain that can possibly lead to forms of deceptions, excitement and falsehoods. In this activity massive projections and fragmentation as in psychosis is avoided. Immature infantile polymorphism has to be distinguished from the residue of innocent lies of children that are without perverse intent (Meltzer, 1973).

Certain mother's bi-sexual mental functioning and mirroring can mitigate the child's psychological movement toward perversion. Her bisexual mental function supplies a thinking couple and the structuring linking function of the father alongside her maternal preoccupation creating a sound primary pair. If the mother is capable of "reflection," high quality mirroring and containing the child's destructive fantasy life in productive arenas, she may serve to help establish calming, adaptive and productive links for symbolic thinking. Helping to establish a mental space as described by Britton (2004) and Fonagy et al. (2007) can be facilitated by this complex maternal capacity to reflect, think and metabolize anxiety and threat. This "space" is a psychic platform more secure from fusion and the symbolic claustro-agoraphobic dilemma described by Glasser (1979) and Rey (1986), while it permits the lively capacity for true communication and symbolic exchanges. An exchange of thoughts that is dependent upon both the achievement of separateness and a safe internal link between the observing self (I) and other as a pair. The secure primary pair is the precursor to love, hate, jealousy and aggression in the Oedipal structuring of the psyche and the manner in which the primary objects come together in reality and fantasy to gratify each other. In perversion the primary couple is attacked because it has been "experienced" as cruelly excluding. Often the patient with perversion will test the analytic pair by exposing it to extreme relational configurations that disguise sexual excitement. In this kind of analytic pairing true and false communication is always present.

This unassimilated internal perverse basic core can emerge with various levels of character structures as described by Meltzer (1973) who distinguishes three. These three are habitual perversion, addictive perversion and criminal perversion, each with different clinical manifestation but using the same type of internal organization and dynamics. Importantly the three levels may not have discrete boundaries in an individual and they may resort to mixing more than one type. I believe there is a fourth non-sexual type of manipulation; the liar who derives gain and excitement from his manipulative actions against the truth and perverts communication between people (O'Shaughnessy, 1990; Akhtar and Parens, 2009). The dynamics of a projective expulsion altering process can be applied to many human activities creating a perverse pair (Meltzer, 1973, pp. 132–133) that weakens or distorts elements of reality. How then does this come to be?

There is psychoanalytic theoretical agreement that in all male perversions the dramatized or ritualized denial of male castration fear is also acted out through the "revival" of the fantasy of the existence of a maternal or female phallus (Ogden, 1986, p. 16). According to Green's (2000) developmental model this fantasy does not occur prior to the onset of castration fantasy but exists through that stage. I believe this discovery usually occurs in either of two ways. At the age (2½–3½) of the recognition of the differences between the sexes and the early start of the emerging clarity of the child's gender recognition, a primitive projection occurs in which the child fails to move on to recognize gender "differences" and gives up his mental penis as a link (or other body part) by projective expulsion. I believe that the mental organization of the perversion is internally initiated during and after this projective expulsion of the idea of female bodily penis. If this idea becomes fixed (hallucinotic) there is a great risk of confusion among the ongoing stages of development and individual primary sexual identity. The resolution of this confusion in turn requires a primitive thought transformation (Bion, 1984b) producing an attack on the location and nature and appearance of the genitals and the difference between generations that fosters a redirection of sexual excitement, identity and pleasure. A fundamental aspect of the representation of biological gender reality, the primary pair (Abel-Hirsch 2015), eventually the nexus of the Oedipal structured family (Kaes, 1993) and the primal scene, is transformed. This psychic attack appears to an analyst that the perverse person denies the differences between the sexes, between the father and the son, between the pre-genital and the genital, thus denying usual biological reality. The patient may or may not be aware of this as an attack on the biological truth necessary for certain forms of mental representations as the distortion (distortion in -K) is the negative of the biological truth.

The core of basic identity within the perverse core does not function with the same dynamics as either the split-off part of the self or the normal mind. Perverse distortions can be isolated within the hallucinotic space and serve as a false-self weakening the sense of self-identity allowing it to be vulnerable to and to seek erotic physical stimulation in fantasy. This solution is not the result of a neurotic or creative regression to another stage (Chasseques-Smirgel, 1974) but the result of an earlier creation of a separate fluid alternative unassimilated mental reality expressed almost in its original form by radical splitting (Money-Kyrle, 2015, p. 32). In other words analysts as observers are viewing the origin of the sexual behavior from a radically different psychic vantage than the perverse person: the perverse individual can function within this split-off internal core perversion while the analyst is an observer with a different biological model of what constitutes sex (Abel-Hirsch, 2015). In that perverse core a wide selection of mental mechanisms and fantasies are potential, all of which may deny the sexual mystery, or the outside world of social rules, and seek to sustain its own behavior and excitement. It is an erotic triumph converted from the catastrophe of developmentally early splitting, precursors of identity and projective expulsion in which a source for pleasure and excitement is preserved and mastered (Stoller, 1975). As Grotstein (1996) recognized, splitting and projective evacuation caused by psychic pain forfeits normal developmental progressions.

This separate (split off) perceptual-mental structure is the result of a radical splitting of the ego, that results in what Bion called "reversal of function," others called longitudinal splitting of the ego and Meltzer (2008) called projection of an internal organization (p. 118): all have elements in common. The perception has already been changed by the return of internal (psychic) bits that haven't been discharged into the unconscious. What is constant in perversion is the intrusion of rigid and exciting misperception of some symbolic part of the body or its function most of us assume to exist as a matter of truth and fact that is reorganized as sexually arousing. I believe that the perverse core is the source and origin of the body distortion. In perversions these altered body parts elicit differing degrees of sensual excitation and body arousal: it is a virtual reality often in someone who might otherwise seem quite normal.

The expansion of the theory of hallucinosis recently put forward by Sandler (2009) and Meltzer (1986) establishes an important conceptual base upon which misrepresentations of reality in perversions, as a thinking-emotional body process, can be examined and understood. Thinking as a psychic act was for Freud the essential mode of identification and representation and is considered essential to the psyche. Bion repeatedly took up this concept and analytically expanded it to include forms of or levels of thought and the causes for their misrepresentations. Fonagy (2008) cautions not to forget that arousal and excitement occur with and without thought and require body discharge making a fragile bridge between thoughts and sexual excitement. Sexual excitement lies in the content of what is seen and imagined and in the subjective mental processing of what is looked at by the viewer. The relationship between viewer and sexual excitement is always one of fracture, partial identification, pleasure, expectancy and distrust.

When considering thinking as a psychic process, misrepresentations of reality are an overlooked aspect of a wide number of group and individual behaviors that range from holding and acting on beliefs and imaginary ideologies with absolute certainty, fighting wars of conflict, and sexual excitements and perversions. All of these behaviors are founded on a spectrum of disordered misrepresentations of self, other and reality: on hallucinotic thinking or transformations in hallucinosis with psychosomatic innervation (Harris, 2010).

An understanding of the process of misrepresentation starts with Bion's (1962a) early and basic attempt to understand severe distortions of thinking and the loss of the capacity to think. Within his theoretical system, thinking arises out of the transformation of sensory and emotional contents into mental data (beta elements). Fonagy, in a series of papers, describes a similar process as "mentalization" and he understands this process to emerge in the early developmental interactive caretaking of the infant through intricate responsive processes. Mentalizing is defined as an "imaginative mental activity, namely, perceiving and interpreting human behavior in terms of intentional mental states (e.g., needs, desires, feelings, beliefs, goals, and reasons)" (Fonagy et al., 2007, p. 288). Mentalization is a process that includes both the interpretation of others' behavior in terms of mental states, and the awareness or understanding of one's own mental states. In addition, this process develops into the ability to differentiate one's own and others' mental states, and to differentiate mental states from external reality. One essential difference between Bion and Fonagy's approach is that Bion's inborn process is neutral and may include times when the body and mind are undifferentiated in a proto-mental state and constructs a general assumption of stimulation made psychic that requires psychic links to external aspects of reality. In general Fonagy is operating within the realm of early interactive development of the child's mind and protective attachment dynamics that does not emphasize but acknowledges bodily sensations (Fonagy, 2008). Bion abstractly elaborated the unique role the mother's mental state played in protecting and containing the infant's ego. However, Fonagy makes stronger claims that disruption of this internal process by trauma, abuse and impinging environmental factors leads to mental dysfunction and problematic mentalization.

Both Bion and Fonagy describe the mind's basic task as the conversion of internal and external raw experience into thinkable internal mental objects that includes understanding behavior, intentions, and emotional states, states of mind and body arousal. For healthy individuals the process of registering an experience with the special quality of giving the experience meaning creates an object of thought that is representable in the mind. With this representation meaning and emotion (psychosomatic) are linked and this combination is called an object representation and the construction process mentalization (Allen and Fonagy, 2006). The capacity to conceive of the contents of one's own mind, as well as the others' mind is an essential prerequisite for normal object relations (Baron-Cohen, 2011). The failure or distortion of this process is thought to be a consequence of the poor quality of early relations and the incapacity to process new information (stimulation) and modify earlier representations. Many theorists have observed the vulnerability of thinking under stress and excitement and there are many mental hazards that occur in early development or social reality that can disrupt this vulnerable capacity for thinking.

Within this psychoanalytic model distortions or failure in the capacity to think or misrepresentations of reality are understood as caused by the influence of psychic mechanisms that impact and distort the perception of reality or of the self in various personal ways (Allen and Fonagy, 2006). Traumatic impingements alter representations and affect reality testing of self and the perception, meaning and intentions of others embedded in or separated from social reality. The mentalization process possesses both a self-reflective and an interpersonal component. Brown (2005) provided a clinical example of distortions in the organization of psychic representations following trauma that focuses on Bion's model of thinking. Traditionally this form of clinical case study reveals that less attention has been paid to the shifting representations of the body, the biological marker of our identity, than to thought. Ruptures in developmental milestones as those that are revealed in the therapeutic treatment of perversions directly affect the regulation of sexuality, perception of the physical self interacting with its mental representation and the perception and communication with the receiving partner.

Freud emphasized that psychoanalysis had to do with sexuality and thoughts but reducing psychosexuality to an expression of hallucinosis not only desexualizes it but also makes it only a product of mind. Psychic sexual life depends on the erotic stimulation of the physical body and the mystery of the source and mechanisms of excitement as an autobiography of physical and mental illusions and memories (Stoller, 1986). The selection of partners and relational peers are not only on the basis of psychic states but are bodily grounded and mentally body aware.

A distorting false personal belief (a hallucinosis) or a perverse arousal does not create an object that is not in reality, it constructs or distorts or makes a transformed inference about something existing and exciting in external reality. This belief may be firmly sustained despite what almost everyone else believes and despite what constitutes incontrovertible and obvious proof or evidence to the contrary. That false belief is often not one ordinarily accepted by other members outside of the person's culture or subculture or is idiosyncratic and becomes a mask for disguising hatred and threat in sexual excitement. One positive basic assumption of this hypothesis about thinking is that human beings are innately predisposed to seek the truth, and to seek to understand and negotiate their environmental reality; an idea advanced by theorists of many different orientations. However reality is not always benign and secure for survival and thinking must adapt to threat and stimulation from social reality and the negative as envisioned by Bion. The negative is "violent, greedy and envious, ruthless, murderous and predatory without respect for the truth, persons or things" (1984b, p. 102).

From a psychoanalytic perspective rapid attributions of a threat in a neutral situation have significance. Bentell and Kaney (2005), as one example, argue that attributions are made in order to prevent internal negative self-esteem dynamics becoming conscious. From that vantage it is necessary to distinguish attributions of threat from innocent "misconceptions," defined as unintentional misunderstandings growing out of early developmental experiences, ignorance or anxiety (Money-Kyrle, 2015, p. 255). Other forms of misconceptions are embedded in developmental stages on the path to "mature" capacities that effect the capacity for representation and meaning. In considering hallucinosis as described by Sandler (2009), in contrast, there is a disruption of the mentalization process and that results in confusion of the relationship between the self and the perceived object evoking a misconception. When a misconception is formed, perception of the external object world is also changed or corrupted in the mind of the perceiver. Bion believed, along with many other psychoanalytic theorists (Meltzer, 1979, p. 107), that traumatic early emotional experiences potentially distort the mechanisms of perception into a "bizarre object" and they are bizarre because the perceiver projected something (negative) into them that has changed their status from their original state. Once changed they may mentally exist as a symbol,[7] thought, belief or meaning that arouses strong internal emotional or physical experiences that were originally thought by Bion to be discharged in either of three forms. Into an unconscious group experience, into a somatic experience or into a reversal of function that facilitates the formation of a bizarre object (Sandler, 2009, p. 198; Meltzer, 1986, p. 114): all of these solutions represent the perceiver's incapacity to "mentalize" inner emotional pain that then corrupts self-esteem and forms misconception (external) and disorientation (internal) (Money-Kyrle, 2015). In reversal of function, rather than mentally ingesting new information, that internalization process is over-ridden by projective defenses that results in an inability to learn with catastrophic fear produced (Bion 1970, p. 107–108). With psychic splitting of the normal process of mentalization some individuals may remain quite able to formulate and articulate coherent statements that contain a transmittable form of misrepresentation of meaning, representation or self-identity. Such split-off thinking processes are commonly represented in fixed ideas, conspiracy theories, sexual excitement and prejudice: literally defined as an opinion or belief formed (internally) before the (outside) facts are known or in spite of new and observable facts.

Significantly when considering the process of hallucinosis, in Bion's original theoretical formulations he omitted any form of discharge aimed to violently remove or damage the dangerous bizarre object (Roth, 2013). Any act of violence may then be an attempt to create a mental space in relation to a confusing internal fantasy transformed into an actual belief of danger and threat as described by Perelberg (1999b).

A current reformation of Bion's theory that includes acts of violence in reality will facilitate connections between the group experience of genocide and violent murder of an individual that is dependent on distorted perceptions turned into beliefs and ideologies. It also establishes a basis for understanding the distortions of perception that accompany sexual excitement in perversions. There are other psychological events that have in common distortion of perception of the self and another in reality through a distortion of mental process. These are expressed in varied and different forms ranging from phobias, delusions, and prejudices and include sexual perversions and fetishes. For Bion, a lie is also an intended transformation of the truth into a distortion of reality. Among such distortions are myths, confabulations, social lies, "little white lies," compassionate lies, hypocrisy, lying to oneself, defensive lies (sometimes used to save one's life). Included are those related to perversions and those due to omniscience (an omnipotent mental state which also generates a vast large number of lies) although those who sustain this mental attitude would swear by the "truth" of their prejudices (De Bianchedi et al., 2000).

Here is one relevant formulation. Anti-Semitism as an idea or percept appears to be held in different degrees: from being a simple misconception (Money-Kyrle, 2015) to making Jews bizarre[8] objects that must be eliminated for some imagined reason. This process can be explained, as Ogden (1988) argues, that internal bizarre objects can be conceptualized as objects that are unacknowledged aspects of the ego/self that have been mutilated by splitting/fragmentation and "evacuative projection" into mental representations and are then evacuated externally into reality. In prejudice thinking and perception usually becomes protectively fixed. One end result of prejudice is that a group constructs a "bizarre object" that is mis-seen and misperceived as dangerous by an over-endowment of internal affective linked evacuative processes. These misperception processes can be and have been exacerbated by group dynamics particularly if the groups share a belief in sanctioned destructiveness or alterity. It is possible to see a commonality of mental processes in the exclusionary dynamics regarding Armenians, Tutsi, Chinese in Indonesia, Vietnamese in Cambodia, etc.

While examining other forms of distortion is compelling I wish to first examine various forms of genocide to determine if the ideas of misperception in hallucinosis help form a psychodynamic explanation of other mass murderous events and perversions. In violent genocide there seems to be a passage from a composite of "proto-mental phantasy" to an illusory system (hallucinosis) in response to an authorizing leader and harmonizing or arousing group dynamics leading to violence. One significant difference is that in genocide the actions are murderously violent and criminal while in perversions the externally constructed other or part of the other is eroticized and the individual is physically aroused to act.

Notes

1 Theorists question the very idea that primary process precedes secondary process; they point out that it makes more sense to assume an ongoing developmental integration of the two, with maturation developing both processes into forms that are more complex and more informed by experience and safety. Harsh trauma interferes with this integrations and a negative meaning or emotional element is disavowed.
2 Four kinds of splitting can be defined: a coherent split in the object, a coherent split in the ego, a fragmentation of the object and a fragmentation of the ego.
3 In Bion's theory there are transformations of mental imagery into thinking or transformation into action in reality.
4 Fonagy (2008) uses the term "mirroring stage" for this process.
5 Birksted-Breen (1996) theoretically distinguishes between a phallus and a penis. What she refers to as penis-as-link is part of the position in which the vagina is known allowing for a tripartite world of the self in relation to the parents as different and linked to each other. It involves the knowledge of difference and the recognition of incompleteness and need for the object (p. 650). Meltzer (1973) makes a similar claim while noting distortions of the body organs.

6 The internal image of a parental couple linked in pleasure, care for the child or care for the man's children is enormously helpful in working with men who have been abused by one or both parents.
7 It seems important to distinguish "representations," which can be restricted to "things" in the mind, from symbols. Symbols are clearly related to representations. But they are more than representations—symbols are the conversion of representations into something that is abstract and communicable to other minds as a concept rather than a thing.
8 The formation of Jews as a bizarre object is a process by which the mind of the perceiver created the sensation that they are threatened or entrapped by the presence of the Jews. This hallucinosis can remain split off in the mind as a separate agency maintaining its own dynamic structure. Explanations for the beliefs are mythic.

7

THE HISTORICAL RANGE OF MASS MURDER AND THE UNIQUENESS OF THE HOLOCAUST IMAGINARY THREATS AND VIOLENT SOLUTIONS

> If ever we are constrained to lift the hatchet against any tribe, we shall never lay it down till that tribe is exterminated, or driven beyond the Mississippi.
>
> *Thomas Jefferson (from Mann, 1995, p. 70)*

There is a wide range of theoretical attempts to understand genocide and specifically to comprehend the causes or preconditions of the infamous mass murders in World War II. I believe these efforts offer inadequate or partial explanations for the mass killing and forced displacements that occurred. Still conspicuously absent is a set of integrative concepts or causal process from a group psychoanalytic perspective. Why and how could it appear rational and necessary for a state regime to engage in the costly activity of eliminating a portion of their non-kin population? One answer is that the holocaust occurred because of the conjunction of numerous different large group dynamics and the rise of violent beliefs about the rights of nations to eliminate designated others imagined as a threat or dangerous. It is not simply that a large group of people hated Jews, Gypsies, Armenians or Hutus and killed them.

All of the recent genocides occurred with nation state sponsorship with varying degrees of citizen support and participation. It is important to understand from a psychological perspective how a nation state comes to believe it is necessary to carry out this murderous process when the nation state was constructed to offer security under a form of constitutional law. The nation state appears psychologically as an imagined community or coalition of non-kin within an arbitrary physical boundary comparable to religious communities. Collective national identity is a constructed conjoined fantasy employing unique symbolic signs that are learned and presented as a shared entity in reality. Nation state meaning rests on transforming dynamics of individual experiences and group history to the realm of shared beliefs, language and ideas resulting in a fantasy of collective sameness[1] out of which a large co-operative "we" identity is mentally formed. A complex network of true believers, wishes, beliefs, acts and relationships among a subgroup of members holds these fantasy national coalitions together under a political proper name which may provide a variety of adaptive and legislative consequences. One consequence of these ideas is the designation "foreigner" (someone from another place) who is believed not to hold or share these beliefs and as different threatens a subversion of identity and elicits various defense mechanisms to safeguard "we" identity (Bohleber, 1992). The manner in which this primary fear, xenophobia, is perceived and managed within a fantasy of "unity," purity and sameness in authoritarian national states is significantly important to the emergence of state sponsored group identity and violence.

In Mann's (1995) related description of this process nationalism emerged from below and was related to the public's demand for democratic representation in conflict with the increasingly interventionalist military state. The perception by the dominant military or elite group that another coalition threatens or is dangerous to them is not necessarily linked to their citizens' interests and experience. The appointed or elected guardians of the dynamic "We" identity announce the psychic source of the perceived threat although all individuals in that coalition are vulnerable. Perceived threats that another group will harm the dominant group or its legitimacy are understood as a profound threat to the existence of the primary "We" coalition while groups that posses different values are perceived as a threat to the belief systems of the primary group. Political beliefs are similar to religious beliefs in the respect that they are measurably part of the person's self-representation (identity) and what a social group is identified with (Kaplan, Gimbel and Harris, 2016).

Concern or fantasies about physical harm or a loss of access to resources is perceived as a realistic threat and responded to with protective violence by nation states: concern about the integrity or validity of the in-group's meaning and belief system is a symbolic threat and usually responded to with forms of censorship or threats of exclusion. From this perspective the Nazi elite constructed a false belief system (hallucinosis) in which the Jews were combined into a single racial entity destroying their individuality while serving as a realistic and symbolic agent of betrayal and contamination. Perceived threats in Germany became a resource enabling collective action. Perceived threats also intensified support for the primary political or religious beliefs heightening group bonds in which members shared a common imaginary descent. In Germany these relational changes lead to punishing economic and legal strategies that included exclusion, expulsion from the state and then violent escalating murders. Punishing strategies are usually constructed from the coercive power of the state and are believed to establish and maintain safety, pacification of the population and dominance as the method of national (racial) survival.

Nazi escalating mass killings of civilians was usually carefully or chaotically planned for large numbers of victims, random for small numbers and independent of any actual military goals or crimes. While other forms of inter-state conflicts or competitions are usually designed to win a "prize" where fatalities are a by-product of confiscation, the mass murder of Jews and civilians were designed to violently eliminate their presence. This is usually accomplished in stages of civic predation. The predatory society is the inverse of the ideal democratic community. Behavior in the predatory society is opportunistic and violent in a "steeply hierarchical structure." Vertical bonds of violence and inter-dependence are established to prey on the weak or undefended. Usually the prey has no strategy. Wealth is extracted, labor is exploited and real ethnic tensions are mobilized. Criticism is silenced and opponents eliminated by legal manipulation, arrest or murder. The line between the police (Gestapo) and the criminal is erased. Corruption becomes the additional energy for violence and the means of government activity. The existence of the prey has no meaningful status.

While the Holocaust or Shoah is still considered unique it is necessary to determine the common and unique dynamics in the process of genocidal mass killings to confirm its uniqueness by comparing it with other genocides. By no means is the comparison meant to diminish any significance. Since World War II some 50 episodes of mass murder have led to between 12 and 25 million civilian casualties.

Although mass murder of unarmed groups of people is an ancient technique (Katz, 1994) of violent militarized empires and nation states, it was first turned to by modern national states with the start of colonial expansion in the nineteenth century in which conquest and nation building was a goal. However, it was in the twentieth century that biologistic or explicit racism came into play with mass murder in ethnically polarized nation states. While there is significantly more collected evidence and studies of the German Nazi behavior than other killing groups, genocides differ in sociopolitical context and dynamics. While the psychological motivations and triggers for mass murders remain a "mystery" (Gross, 2001) it is my task to try and specify some of the psychological conditions and group dynamics common to systemic genocides. As there seems no simple explanation of the reasons individual people gave up the integrated standing of safe non-kin relatedness for mass murder and violence, I have searched for hidden group dynamics in this violent one-sided group process. This is done keeping in mind that "never before (did) a state set out, as a matter of intentional principle and actualized policy to annihilate very man, woman and child belonging to a specific people" (Katz, 1994, p. 28). And, this Nazi attempt was transnational and international (Gerlach, 2016). In addition, unique circumstances play a part in Genocide as Arendt pointed out:

> If Gandhi's enormously powerful and successful strategy of non-violent resistance had met with a different enemy—Stalin's Russia, Hitler's Germany, even pre-war Japan, instead of England—the outcome would not have been decolonization but massacre and submission.
>
> *(Arendt, 2014)*

To begin: despite the controversies over the definitions of genocide and its participants, all agree that the genocidal nation state commands the resources and organization to make possible the seeming arbitrary and purposeful termination of the right to exist of a specifically defined segment of their population in mass and in individual cases. These violent acts bear no resemblance to war games, as its goal is not victory or a prize but elimination of life. This violence occurs regardless of the surrender or lack of threat (in reality) by the collective victims. Threats can be constructed out of perceived and real differences in race, beliefs, history, imagination or affiliation. From a realistic perspective genocides differ in their scope and extent regardless of the number killed and must be considered multi-causal: with leader, race, ideology, weaponry and social-economic conditions as contributions. In that regard analysis of the dynamics of other mass murders establishes the holocaust's uniqueness through the multinational basis of the cooperation of other governments, particularly of dictatorships.

Harff and Gurr's (1988) research on genocide risk describes the following categories of genocide:

- **Hegemonial genocide:** The racial, ethnic, national or religious groups are being forced to submit to the authority of the state.
- **Xenophobic genocide:** Murder campaigns are part of a state policy of national protection or social purification where victims are defined as alien or threatening.
- **Retributive politicide:** Mass murders target groups that formerly held power or were dominant within the state. Members of the once powerful group are targeted out of resentment for past privileges or abuses.
- **Repressive politicide:** Mass murder targets groups engaged in some sort of oppositional activity against the state. This may include members of political parties, factions or (populist) movements.
- **Revolutionary politicide:** Mass murder targets the political enemies of a state that is pursuing revolutionary ideologies. Also called autogenocide.
- **Repressive/hegemonial politicide:** The victim group is an ethnically or nationally distinct group, but is targeted because of some form of (real or imagined) oppositional activity (rather than because of their ethnicity or nationality per se). So, it is considered politicide since the policy of the state is to repress opposition to the state, but because the opposition group (or groups) shares some communal trait, it has genocidal characteristics.

All reported historical genocides contain three basic group dynamic components in common: (1) "group-selective" forms of murderous violence, that is, violence that targets specific groups and individuals for their perceived membership (identity) in certain non-dominant national groups; (2) "extensive" violence, meaning deliberate and random murderous violence that is of a large or organized scale, that is sustained over time and across space, is public, systematic and often indiscriminate; and (3) violent means that is under the exclusive control of a perpetrator group whose purposive logic is predatory about depriving a group of the ability to survive in a specific territory (Strauss, 2016). It also seems evident from this perspective (Harff and Gurr, 1988) that the Holocaust started as a movement of eugenic culling with a "repressive ethnic politicide" that converted into a violent xenophobic genocide that was co-energized by the increasing accelerated violence of continued war making and the construction of a Jew/Bolshevik merged identity. In contrast, the Cambodian revolution started with a limited genocide that became a violent politicide. Importantly, Harff and Gurr (1988) reveal that the greater the resources any government devotes to the development and technology of warfare the more likely violence or a genocide will appear as an irrational solution to an imaginary threat. In contrast, the more ethnically fragmented the population is the less likely genocide will occur (Bae and Ott, 2008). The former confirms Gerlach's (2010) idea that violent societies or nation states are more likely to engage in massed killings as sanctioned state actions. Yet another variable to consider in within state violence is the degree of ethnic polarization within a nation state. Group identity is very often based on an ability to perceive others in a contrasting and/or pejorative sense contributing to ethnocentric belief systems. Polarization then appears as a form of non-kin tension and conflict that serves as early precedents to formal warfare, civil unrest and mass killing (Esteban et al., 2012). Ethnic polarization is related to the underlying emotional and economic alienation that individuals and groups feel from one another that skew social communication and social and economic relationships. Such alienation is also fuelled by notions of within-group sense of self-esteem and other differences in income, status, trust, opportunity and citizenship. The language of otherization and belonging is shown to be a key to revealing the potential for intergroup prejudice and violence. Language like "malevolent," "treacherous" and "cunning" is often replaced by "deadly" and contaminating forces that destroy unthinkingly. The language of atrocity and revenge employs both forms of otherization (Taylor, 2009, p. 13). This use of language would be less important if it did not accompany a call for violent action and obedience that required a "disguise" (Hirsch, 1995) of its true goals in reality. Genocides often rely on an Orwellian falsification and negation of evil and of reality (Levi, 1986, pp. 28–32) as in the falsification of death certificates by Nazi doctors. In this Nazi reality Jews were not killed, they were "cleaned up." Lifton (1986) pointed out this falsification of language was particularly true of the Nazi doctors who employed "responsible military-medical killing behavior" or euthanasia to camouflage mass murder and brutal medical experiments. However the infamous Nazi term "Final Solution" carries a hidden menace and may have roots in German medicine.

Dynamically, once mass killing begins, the individual and group incentives to continue killing as a "solution" become stronger. This dynamic suggests that group killing has its own rewards and that new incentives for violence occur spontaneously and are inner directed rather than totally ideological. The various studies quoted earlier that seek to clarify genocide proneness within a polity focus primarily on economic incentives and make no serious attempt to describe underlying psychodynamic group variables that contribute to those forms of violent dynamics.

The description of genocidal proneness from a within nation conflict perspective reveals eight additional complex factors:

- Prior genocides and politicides: a dichotomous indicator of whether a genocide or politicide has occurred in the country (since 1945); Gerlach (2010) describes these polities as violent societies.[2]
- Political upheaval: the magnitude of political upheaval (ethnic and revolutionary conflict and wars plus regime crises) in the country during the previous 15 years, excluding the magnitude of prior genocides.
- Ethnic characteristics of the ruling elite: a dichotomous indicator of whether the ruling elite represents a minority communal group, such as the Tigrean dominated regime of Ethiopia.
- Ideological characteristics of the ruling elite: a belief system that identifies some overriding purpose or principle that justifies efforts to restrict, persecute or eliminate certain categories of (other) people as inferior or dangerous.
- Type of regime: autocratic (military and non-democratic) regimes are more likely to engage in severe repression of oppositional groups and have the means to do so.
- Ethnic or religious polarization and discrimination increases the risk of mass killings.
- Mostly groups with potentially large resources holdings and low productivity and weaponry are targets to be victimized.
- Trade openness (export + imports as % of GDP): openness to trade indicates state and elite willingness to maintain the rule of law and fair practices in the economic sphere with other states.

These critical organizational indicators of proneness to mass murder reveal an elite group's predisposition based on three dynamic socio/political variables: a history of punitive laws and critical behavior aimed at affirming a dichotomous polarity of an elite "us" and a lower status "them" in the dynamics or rigid otherness (alterity): an exclusionary or narcissistic ideology seeking unity or purity coupled with a history of violent ideological or ethnic conflict (Chalk and Jonassohn, 1990); a death ideology or constellation (thanatopolitics) expressed through the idea that war and/or predatory violence is necessary as a preventative solution or a necessity for order (i.e. lynching and vigilantism) to enforce racial and class hierarchies with political/economic advantages. These potentials for violence also can be understood as basic assumption behavior in group formation (Bion, 1961) and confirm Jacques' (1955) assertion that all organizations are the repository of disavowed destructive process that are disguised as "policy." From Bion's and Jacques' analytic perspective large group public and psychological identity emerges partly through "chosen" traumas and glories that are ritualized and often used politically to manipulate the populace and foster both identification and violence against dissenters. One benefit of violent atrocity performed in a group setting is that the horror of the events causes the impending victims and their affiliates to respond with passivity, shock and hopelessness while the bystanders may likely feel justified or deny the meaning of the activity. Violent coercion fails if it only destroys those whose compliance is desired. For example the use of unpredictable lists and "Elders" at Thereienstadt created the aura of choice in powerlessness and conformity. While in the south of America public lynching for minor social transgressions served to terrorize and traumatize while affirming the mobs' right to take life and violate the body of victims for trophies. In addition, lynching was a community event with no opposing force to prevent its occurrence. Southern states often rewrote their constitutions to maintain legal white supremacy.

Reviewing the history of genocide creates the impression that the right to life and the power to end life has regularly been coopted by the nation state. The power of the state was often converted into thanatopolitics. Foucault (2000) argued that biopolitics had a powerful negative dimension that effected the judicial composition of the community or the "We" expressed in the dynamics of exclusion in colonialism, racism and genocide. The modern state seeking safety, security, health and protection is, at the same time, capable of being at odds with the universal rights of individualization. The power of the nation state is frequently expressed in a negative manner as one that forbids rather than authorizes what is best. One result is that there has been "an explosion of techniques for the subjugation of bodies and populations" (Foucault, 1978). The modern state as an entity may also be subject to trauma and states of emergency in which it seeks to protect itself from real or imagined threats. Bion's (1961) original idea of basic assumptions in groups is of a collective unconscious force that suspended the positive aims of the group when threatened. The Nazi German state strategically replaced civic safety with the particularly German historical traditions and experience of domination, exclusion and empire building. This trajectory contained a residual predatory genocidal impulse of "take life or let live" (Foucault, 1978). Such a predatory trajectory required an absolute dangerous "Other" as an enemy that harvested and directed murderous violence as a guiding right of the state making every other European a potential target. Ultimately every one in the Nazi state had the power over the life and death of his neighbors, if only by informing (Foucault, 2003). This was so because the Nazi national state organizations became the repository of disavowed destructive process that were disguised as "policy" and an instrument of judgment without concern for truth that greatly extended its power over life.

Lifton's (1987, 1999) exploration of a theory explaining terrorism includes a clear example of the conversion to a predatory death ideology. This negative ideology was expressed through a group led apocalyptic fantasy that included the necessary destruction of those designated impure to create a fantasied purified society. As with earlier findings individual identity becomes fused with the group collective identity and goals. The terrorist may be considered as a triumphant human self-sacrificing predator who intensifies his behavior if there are by-standing audiences of innocents by increasing the indignity of the humiliation and sense of mission as a group event with an audience. Terrorists also believe they are in a battle to redeem the world (from an imaginary threat) through forms of destructive acts directed against symbols or lives. The technology of destruction is available for that use. A common theme motivating warfare is self-sacrifice to protect the imagined future. A mythology of sacrificial heroic death for an emperor, country or ideology also politicizes the sacrificial death mythology. This mythology was also found in Bushido, the Japanese warrior ethic that requires the person to have an intimate relationship with "death" and completely separate him or herself from the realm of "compassion." This separation results in a state of heroic nihilism in which there is both a mythic core of belief in a heroic mission of redemption and a readiness to commit acts of extreme violence in that cause. Himmler's speeches carried a similar message. As Griffin (2012) points out, this heroic/suicidal mission is an archetypal fantasy encountered in many epic cycles of fundamentalist religious and mythic wars that sanctify death, making it for an imaginary sacred or pure cause. At the root of the sacrificial mission are the conversions to a true "believer," a new man perfected through conversion, faith, and devotion and willingness to self-sacrifice or kill for a belief. For example, Himmler repeatedly spoke of the SS as the new higher moral order as an extension to the history of German Teutonic knights defending Jerusalem with the moral right to kill invaders. German bravery was proof of national virility, manhood and honor.

Absent in most of the historical analysis of the elements of genocides is that the state governmental body has almost exclusive access to superior weaponry (the capacity and means to kill) and uses superior violent forms of coercion against a real or imaginary threat (Bingham and Souza, 2009) against a non-kin group. In addition, in actual genocide, the violence is one sided by a perpetrator defined by an imaginary group threat or inferiority that in reality posses no real violent threat and usually is unarmed. However, the very existence of the imaginary idea of a threat establishes and fortifies the basis of a violent cure.

Embedded in these descriptions is one additional important group dynamic question. Why would a perpetrator elite invent a pseudo threat from another group, as the Nazis did with the Jews, and the Hutu did with the Tutsi, when other real group threats were at hand?

Larner (2000) offers a partial dynamic answer from her studies of the history and dynamics of earlier real "witch hunts." She suggested that the creation of a pseudo-group for a pseudo conspiracy serves to legitimize a new regime trying to impose a new moral ideology. This psychoanalytically oriented group dynamic does not meet the original standard of a powerful group misperception based on a perception of threat. Katz (1994, p. 435) comes closer to psychoanalytic thinking when he described witch-hunts as genderized mass murder in which a perennial imaginary attribution of secret, bountiful, malicious "power" was collectively made in an environment experiencing internal social, moral or ideological conflicts of power. The stigmatizing, victimizing and murdering of accused "witches" is more accurately seen as a pseudo protective collaborative paranoiac enterprise. He suggests that both men and women found it easiest to fix some fantasies (misperceptions of witchcraft) attached to women and turn them into horrible reality to be violently acted upon.

Katz (1994) further suggests that some unknown fantasy tension present in that society leads to organizing a group misperception with paranoid/violent features of an imaginary and potent danger. Along with that tension the social or legal bodies within that society came into actual agreement in reality as to how that imaginary "danger" was or has to be eliminated. Legal or moral authority is subverted by the same tension to find the imaginary accused guilty. In a like manner Nazi science and anthropology imaginatively "confirmed" Hitler's beliefs about race yielding punishment by a compliant judiciary. Importantly, such witch danger occurred when the monotheistic religions in that society were deeply intolerant and repressive and may have sought to establish their ultimate political power. Within a similar authoritarian state control, as with intolerant religions, there is only one right way of doing things, every alternative way was more than wrong or alien: it was dangerous. In this rigid social dichotomy a Manichean ideology of hatred was easily constructed containing beliefs that we are good, sacred and pure; others are evil, witches, devils or Jews. There is a direct linking here to Midlarsky's (2005) argument that an imaginary dichotomous moral belief coupled with a search for unity (exclusive kinship) is a powerful fantasy substratum upon which genocidal and criminal thinking can be built (p. 179). If a new intolerant authority is seeking unity or has been imperiled by a real or imagined alien (other) presence such as a witch or a Jew, then national identity or basic society was constructed to appear vulnerable and threatened. Resources for violence became a sacred protective obligation as an option to eliminate any constructed "collective enemy" (Schmitt, 1996) and reduce imagined vulnerability. This is a violent public transition from being threatened to becoming a vengeful victim (Twemlow, 2003) protecting family, country or belief. Twemlow (2003) believed this reversal from victim to violent avenger is an essential dynamic in violent paranoia. Cartwright (2002) found a similar rapid dynamic in rage type murders when individual self-esteem was threatened. Semelin (2009) summarizes this dynamic as the death of the evil "them" makes possible the omnipotence of "us" in the world of the imaginaire (p. 17).

Even a cursory review of literature, popular entertainment, religious and legal writings, and the history of nation states, suggests that vengeance in thought or action is a pervasive and perhaps inevitable response to real or imagined injustices. Revenge can be sought for an imaginary insult regardless of whether the individuals making the inference are the perpetrators themselves, the injured parties or outsiders. While revenge implies a prior hurt, insult or transgression, people and states, such as the Nazi state, were less likely to harm individuals, groups or nations who possessed the power and means to retaliate (Schulman and Ross, 2010) until they attacked Russia. Another variable found in violent retaliation is the allocation of existing predatory forces (Bae and Ott, 2008): clearly those with resident predatory forces are primed to seek revenge. Whatever the state dynamics of revenge and nation state politics they must also be considered to exist outside the realm of normal communicative projective identification and in the realm of intrusive projection as described by Harris (2010). Projective identification and introjective identification are part of complimentary psychic exchanges between individuals that enable shared communication. Intrusive projective identification is a feature of paranoid behavior that was important to Fornari's (1974) description of the causes for war suggesting that nations engage in various communicative exchanges. This paranoid psychic intrusive process seeks to control the external others through the psychic evacuation of unwanted parts of the individual or collective self. This dynamic results in an attempted interpersonal tyranny and a conflict situation subject to other forms of violent exchanges in which perception supports the paranoid illusions. Group-supported violence easily occurs.

The categorical descriptions of genocide by Harff and Gurr (1988) remain at some external distance regarding the process of making enemies and the violent upheaval that was embedded in the murderous group violence. For example, the Holocaust can be seen over time, according to their categories, as moving from an unopposed politicide to an extended incendiary genocide (Gerlach, 2016). Its chaotic growth included a special interest in the involvement and recruitment of locals as violent agents, Jew, Poles and Russians as slave labor but also in the participation of local governments and an expanding Nazi new governing elite led by Himmler and Hitler. The motives and atrocities of pro-Nazi auxiliaries and state authorities caught up in predatory "blood fever" and criminal acts are grossly under-researched (Gerlach, 2016) for their motives and rewards: such as Browning's so-called "Ordinary Men" (1992). In many cases other than Germans perpetrators were working under a Nazi umbrella of protection and becoming a heterogeneous force in imaginary avenging violence with unknown motivations.

In addition, selective violence against Jews occurred in a European and Asian atmosphere of post-colonial politicide that emerged following World War I in which ethnic cultural identities and state violence came into conflict with each other and pro-national loyalists.[3] The opportunities for political and economic participation and graft created ongoing ethnic tensions, popular racism, civil unrest and casual violence. The most obvious outcome was the retaliatory and often long-term "violence" against former guerrillas, rivals and loyalists through informal killings, imprisonment, reeducation, trials and execution or exile creating massive social uncertainty of national identity dynamics. In addition, there were contributions from rapidly shifting expectancies of personal safety (Gerlach, 2010), realigned nation state boundaries and legal rights granted by national governments. With politicide and its aftermath, long-term social changes directly affected the role and status of women, as more men then women were killed in earlier state wars, threatening the cohesion of families and undermining the role of men as protectors: sometimes later restored through a domestic beating, rape and criminal activity (Gerlach, 2010). It seemed to Gerlach that violence between the wars was always present. And with the shifting tides of war covering wide territories of Europe, friend, foe and dominating ideology shifted with those tides. Gross (2011) offers insight into the effects of rapidly shifting occupying forces in one Polish village.

Genocide, whatever its geo-political understructure in time, place and duration, leaves an open breach in the culture and the sense of an underlying shift to the perception of a dangerous or predatory national legal authority, that results in a primal fear of the "violent" fanatic or paranoid government. Such ongoing fears were common in many survivors and bystanders often leading to enduring anxieties and distrust of governments' intentions. A fanatic or fanaticism is a follower of an ideology who has strongly and rigidly developed beliefs in the ideology he/she serves and a readiness to act to achieve the ideological instrumental goals. He or she is intolerant of doubt and a narrowing down of consciousness along with a transferring of responsibility to an external cause or system. Often tolerance of criminal actions co-occurs with uncritical idealization of the source of the ideology. A fanatic is insensitive to and unaffected by new information, or counter-information, appeals to reason and the values and sensitivities to other (non-kin) human beings (Haynal et al., 1983). Ideologically driven fanatical groups encourage the cognitive splitting of a society into Manichean dichotomies of a narcissistic "Us" and a negative "Them" while attracting a range of people with a psychic need for such an absolute dichotomy, fixed categories and inspiring leaders: eliminating any need for interpretative reflection or open doubt (Erikson, 1980). Semelin's (2009) descriptions of the dynamics of "massacres" start with such a negative characterization of perpetrators and adds a willingness to violently obliterate the imaginary worthless "them." Both from a historical and everyday life perspective, we are often exposed to varieties of fanaticism in which categorical "beliefs" are presented as facts and undeniable truths but are psychologically attempts to use intrusive mechanisms that seek to destroy (Harris, 2010).

The core common element of genocide in Harff and Gurr's (1988) categories is an ideology of immediate threat calling for one-sided violence to destroy an imaginary danger: this threat I understand in Bion's terms to be created by a shared group hallucinotic disturbance. The large group acceptance of a false belief of a threat leads to a disturbance in the perception of social reality authored by the governmental elite within governance they control. This false belief must resonate with a latent belief in a prior real or imaginary threat in individuals for whom "protective" action against that threat was required. How this shift to designating an evil or dangerous polluting one occurs is open to speculation but I believe this to be a paranoiac group dynamic that is inherent in all genocides defined by a present or future threat: paranoiac in the general sense of vulnerability to a threat. For example when Hitler's propaganda is examined in comparison with the remarks of the Hutu military (Gerlach, 2010) it becomes strikingly evident that there is some constancy concerning the designation of a pestilent evil or "threat to be eliminated" within a political context of a posed real or imaginary war. War as an actual national state event or as a threat arouses group bonding, definition and ethnocentrism, which provide the necessary ingredients for justifying violence and murder. In war killing is self-preservation (Glasser, 1986) or a reversal of the threat of being a potential victim by becoming an avenging killer (Twemlow, 2003). Avenging self-preservative violence, against an individual and group, aims to not only eliminate the perceived immediate danger but to establish a violent reversal of roles: from imagined victim to avenging killer. This should not be confused with the conversion from passive to active but a psychic and behavioral transformation from having been a potential victim to being perpetrator. This theme of rising up against a threat of being a victim has great currency in myths, history, movies, fiction and legal cases.

The seeming logic required of motivating state sponsored mass killing seems quite different from warfare and is proceeded by emotional appeals for the removal of the designated real or imagined threat with either retributive justice or self-protection as motive and rationale. As the imaginary threat or fantasy enemy is being removed, a punitive (re-)establishment of a "closed" social/punitive morality enforcing unity and purity often continues (Lifton and Markusem, 1988; Lifton, 1999). The creation of a real or fantasy enemy in a violence prone society does not satisfy completely the internal individual or group origin of the threat: the violent energy responsible for mass annihilation of the enemy continues to insure the governing body's readiness to threaten and eliminate non-believers and maintain a readiness for violence. This potential for violence persists as the primary false belief in a victorious closed social order is considered an enlightened state, the highest state of communal ethics and meaning. With a newly imposed communal morality of threat the states' monopolistic use of violence becomes governed by their false beliefs with a heightened vigilance to threat. Continued preferences for violent action in successful genocidal coalitions contribute to ongoing tensions and a continuation of violence and menace. One result is that the violent treatment of others is seen as a natural feature of predatory social life rather than of war.

It is in war, revolution and genocide that mass group violence in the political realm becomes violently real and communal in its aims. Individual rights cannot provide a reasonable justification for sacrificing oneself for a political state or taking another's life (Schmitt, 1996).[4] Schmitt introduced the central distinction between friend and enemy in politics; Schmitt explained the political distinction as between *hostis* (a collective or public enemy) and *inimicus* (a individual or private enemy). The political is founded on the distinction between those on one's side and those on the other side. Any friend-enemy polar distinction is always connected (link) with the abiding potential for preservative violence. The tension of the possibility of group conflicts of interest produces the political dimensions leading to war. Here Schmitt advances a theory of the constant tension between friend and enemy that is beyond current political theory in that Schmitt believed that the inclusion of violence in which people are murdered is a constant inherent fact of the political life of nations. The political life of nation relationships is different from all other relationships as the state is different from the individual and often indifferent to the individual. The friend, enemy and combat concepts receive their real meaning precisely because they refer to the real possibility exercising the rights of killing (p. 33). To articulate the reality *of the political enemy is the capacity of human groups to take their differences so seriously that they will physically kill or die for them* (Schmitt, 1996). From this theory of political dynamics, difference or stranger (us/them, kin/non-kin, brother/enemy) must be created by boundaries in the state between polities as if friends or enemies: it is not reducible to the moral distinction between values of good and evil. All individual and group differences in this dialectical system have the potential to become political and change to a new reality. Schmitt's analysis not only supports the idea that war is when the sovereign tells you who the enemy is but that all relationships within a state have the potential to become political and therefore violent. Schmitt also insisted that a commitment to the maintenance of the state's constitution was to the maintenance of stability.

Schmitt's complex political theory permits both clarity of the realm of the political and concrete examples of the seeming natural tension between real and imagined human dichotomies in the paranoid realization of difference: "us-them" Aryan-Jew, Hutu-Tutsi and most recently in a completely distinctive way in Cambodia.

The core motivation of Pol Pot in Cambodia was the purge of the educated or the belief of the low probability of revolutionary re-education of certain categories of Cambodians. This idea stands in contrast to the unyielding governmental decision based on "race" to massacre all Jews, Armenians and Tutsi as being different, alien and consequently made dangerous. Basically people were persecuted in Cambodia for what they believed or were thought to believe, because of family links with those suspected of holding beliefs detrimental to the state or being "corrupted" by foreign learning or religion. People were executed for what others thought they were thinking. Killings based on racial hatred in Cambodia involved a small number of Vietnamese and some murdered not for their racial origin but as traders (middlemen) and capitalists. Here was a new form of dangerous pollutants beliefs as "microbes" of potential opposition and real opponents within Pol Pot's party that were exterminated. Pol Pot, a mysterious communist leader, was to return Cambodia to a primitive purified society that included a form of political witch-hunt within a revolutionary ideology that made Stalin notorious. In Cambodia the ideal of communist reform collectivism was not only applied to the destruction of the cities creating a communal peasantry, but was used to cull the people according to an imaginary dimension of purity that led to eliminating the functional educated elite, money and individual possessions as pollutants (Jackson, 1992).

In the complex ongoing Cambodian genocide/politicide the state again assumed absolute power over life and death that was assumed from the individual's perceived state of mind, education and beliefs. Individuals were being deprived of their quality of being unique, irreplaceable and entitled to their own thoughts. The start of the political Cambodian revolution may have initially carried with it a message of positive (altruistic) hope for cultural reform that was fragmented by the supreme fantasy of absolute reform to collective farming and a collective or unitary pure agrarian population. Having discerned the supreme truth and the root cause of evil, the true believers (fanatics) believed the elimination of its human and structural carriers of evil and its byproducts must be assured. Political states have regularly employed murderous violence fueled by real or imaginary perception of danger that threatened their fanatical utopian vision of political communal unity and regeneration. This is a paranoiac's crusade to remove imagined beliefs as "pollutants."

In all the researched examples of genocide the consequences of the ideological construction of an imaginary polarity that becomes an enemy to murder in mass asserts the state's sovereign power over life and death. Most genocidal intentions are subsumed to cleanse or purify the polity of real or imagined pollution and then restore or create order or unity. To borrow from Katz's description of genocide

(1994), the imaginary idea of the corrupted vileness of the perceived other was immutable: only overcome by mass murder. From this violent premise everything else flows. Mass eliminist murder as an *idea* found concrete recurring expression in different forms in the political life of national (political) groups prone to didactical thinking. Fostered by a fanatical leader, a widespread violent group hallucinosis emerged that the creation of an imaginary utopian reality, as Sandler (2009, pp. 200–201) describes, depended on an anti-reality or minus alpha as a building block in the phantasy of protective elimination. That newly constructed and perceived concrete reality was confirmed by propaganda, imaginary science or anthropology, or thought reform. From that core hallucinotic idea, "true believers" and "just following orders" are ancillary but necessary concrete explanations confirming that systematic distortion of reality for mass murder. The efficiency of the perpetrators, the cooperation of the bureaucrats and judges, the venal participation of the looters and business owners were and are consequences of, and subordinate to, this moral overriding and empowering idea based on misperception of a pre-constructed reality; a group "hallucinosis."

Communism, National Socialism, the violent maintenance of political hegemony, cultural genocide (the intent to destroy ethnic, political, religious, social or class identity of a group) are all founded on cognitive and emotively distorted belief systems: hallucinosis. False beliefs are a controlling, omnipotent, superior, exciting, sadistic triumph over an existing and prior reality. Accordingly, if there were an effort made to assert another version of this pre-determined reality this would threaten to crush the perpetrators' psychic reality. To varying degrees violent ideologies of dangerous difference not only "protect the group against imaginary threats" they fit complex individual motivations to "belong," to be "pure," sacred and eliminate imaginary enemies by violent acts of obedience.

Notes

1 This fantasy involves the wish to be understood and accepted embedded in the idea of sharing some important experiences and beliefs.
2 The participatory character of violence is crucial in defining a potential extremely violent society in which mass murder was seen as in accord with the will of the government.
3 Military defeat and downfall following the First World War resulted in unprecedented chaos. The prior empires that offered some protection to minorities vanished. The transformation to a continent of poly-ethnic nation states led to calls for ethnic cleansing and mass murders.
4 A controversial political jurist.

8

SUMMARY AND THE IMAGINARY NATION

> I want to also mention a very difficult subject … before you, with complete candor. It should be discussed amongst us, yet nevertheless, we will never speak about it in public. Just as we did not hesitate on June 30 to carry out our duty as ordered, and stand comrades who had failed against the wall and shoot them—about which we have never spoken, and never will speak. That was, thank God, a kind of tact natural to us, a foregone conclusion of that tact, that we have never conversed about it amongst ourselves, never spoken about it, everyone … shuddered, and everyone was clear that the next time, he would do the same thing again, if it were commanded and necessary. I am talking about the evacuation of the Jews, the extermination of the Jewish people.
>
> H. Himmler at Posen, 1943

The intimate and emotional process of writing this book has been a significant and challenging journey of grappling with essential ideas about how we humans live together in groups and how human groups become untrustworthy, dangerous or violent. In response to this effort I experienced an increased sense of personal vulnerability.

My interest in mass killing of unarmed civilians started during the aftermath of the World Trade Center attack in which unarmed people were killed. I was a blind man looking for answers in the wreckage and lethal dust of that tragedy. I asked what I thought was a limiting and limited question: How was it possible to motivate groups of humans to kill other unarmed humans? Asking that question was the first step in a painful learning process. I believed then that an answer was to be found in psychoanalytic group dynamics. Recent shootings in schools and public events in the United States raise other notions about the dynamics of finding victims and killing them.

Group and individual psychoanalytic theory, although predominantly preoccupied with the male psyche, had nevertheless avoided grappling with violence in general and specifically with state-sponsored violence by armed groups. There was one notable exception, found in the early work of Hyatt-Williams (1998), who focused on the psychoanalytic treatment of murderers. I specifically refer to the male psyche because I believe that the gender-limiting concept of fight-flight reactions and the derivatives of Freud's group theory were formulated from a faulty understanding of male neuropsychological responses. It is well established that it is men who make war. The usual female response to threat tends to be entirely different: to protect the family offspring and the family nest, and to try to befriend the threatening party and plead for safety. As group leaders, women are likely to reduce overt competition and external expressions of anger, and to encourage cooperation while competing in different ways.

I turned my attention to study the mass killing of unarmed people during World War II. I found enormous collections of factual material generated by historians and very little of substance by psychoanalysts, who were preoccupied with survivor trauma and other effects of war. This failure of psychoanalytic theorists to grapple with the Nazi phenomenon, as reported by Pick (2012), now seems inevitable since Freud's Oedipal-oriented group theory offered psychoanalysts no suitable platform for understanding either their own fearful, avoidant group behavior and silence regarding violence in general or state-sponsored genocide in particular. Freudian analytic group theory remains an artifact of eighteenth-century models of science, which needs to be drastically re-evaluated to accommodate the complexity of current psychoanalytic thinking, as well as the rise of nationalistic and authoritarian states that have replaced dynastic empires. Bion's (1961) attempt to correct analytic assumptions regarding male-oriented group dynamics, derived in part from his traumatic military experiences, led to a cognitive blind spot at the entrance to the death camps as he focused on psychic violence. Other psychoanalysts' early and futile attempts at explanations of individual Nazi psychopathology confused the correlation of symptoms (i.e., monochordism) with causality, offering fantastic explanations or seeking traumas in perpetrators' past history to account for the psychic origins of anti-Semitism. There is a remarkable absence of any study or understanding of the group formations that emerged within the death and labor camps and controlled basic existence among Jews and Nazis, turning men into predators and lives into ashes.

Slowly, with great internal struggle, I sought to understand Bion's psychological inability to be able to think beyond his own traumatic war experiences (Roth 2011). Yet I remained dependent on aspects of his theory of thinking and disruptions in thinking. The next piece in the emerging puzzle was finding Bingham and Souza's (2009) work, which unblocked my understanding of the social and cultural impact, the structuring and the inhibiting function of technologically advancing weapons that "killed at an increasing distance." Bartov (1996), a historian, refers to this aspect of genocide within the conceptual frame of "modernity" as the mechanized, rational, impersonal mass destruction of human beings sanctioned by states, scientists, jurists, academics and intellectuals. Whereas Freud conceived of the political state as having the exclusive capacity and authority for war (weapons),

Bingham and Souza (2009) offered a more complex understanding of the importance of advances in weaponry in warfare and their secondary use as coercive guardians. Bingham also personally pointed me in the direction of the importance of the non-kin dynamic in murder (Daly and Wilson, 1988). The historical growth of military weaponry also coincided with the rise of interventionist, militarized solutions by political entities. The use of weapons to enforce policing, protection, threat and codes of justice has become culturally embedded in almost every society. Human societies have found justifications to "legally" convert weapons and means to kill fellow humans under a constructed umbrella of beliefs, codes and laws for centuries. Yet, human societies are also capable of forms of authoritative self-policing at low cost to the group, although this capacity is subject to its own essential dynamics. One dynamic force ignored in most studies of genocidal murder is that the perpetrators have exclusive control of the capacity to kill, and they often murder widely, excessively and with a variety of devices. The second important ignored element is the significance of non-kin violence. For much of our evolutionary history, to venture outside the network of kin and affines has meant almost certain death. Kinship can also be a disruptive force but the modern absence of or discontinuity of kin networks may also contribute to alienation and violence. In addition, violence appears to have a strong effect in fostering ties and cooperation in violence-prone males (Campana and Varese, 2013).

In an effort to understand the impact of Hitler and National Socialism on the German people that led to the deaths of millions I realized that theories of individual psychological identity have ignored an important cultural and social aspect of psychological identity. It is generally accepted in developmental theory that individuals move from early primitive core attachment states into evolving forms of partial physical and emotional independence from kin. There are many early stages in infant developmental processes, ranging from the early emergence of a unique kin identity, to non-kin affiliation (friend) and social or safe non-kin engagements. Eventually dynamic varieties of interdependence from kin are established, including social and work coalitions in which there is some form of interactive reciprocity. As individual achievement occurs within varying cultural opportunities, individual development continues within a variety of emerging "we" identities, each with unique values and intentionalities (Marcia, 1988). This human ability to develop and adapt to a variety of non-kin "we" identities is testimony to the inner plasticity of human identifactory capacities, which adapt within and among differently structured ideological and emotional affiliations. The failure to construct a working and mature reciprocal "we" identity is often the outcome of disruptions of early development milestones and achievements (Szanto and Moran, 2015; Zahavi, 2015). One important result of such a disruption in the internal capacity to distinguish between "you" and "me" and deficits in "we" intentionality is implied by the developmental failures of the theory of mind[1] (Baron-Cohen, 2011). Individuals who fail to safely "feel for another person" or develop a capacity for concern (Winnicott, 1965) may become vulnerable to manipulation by external "we" intentionality, such as deceptive propaganda, imaginary threats and untested conspiracy theories. This vulnerability to deception depends on the continued existence of a group hystero-paranoid syndrome (Carveth and Carveth, 2003): an anxious vulnerable state characterized by projective processes used to secure the protective boundaries of the group.[2] In a large group, the individual dynamics of vulnerability and the energy of self-directed persecutory thoughts can be emancipated from the individual and psychically expelled at an external object (other), resulting in massive destructive energy. Members of such protective "we" groups morally define themselves in righteous opposition to such projectively constructed enemies and gain a sense of purpose and meaning from their beliefs (Barkun, 1996). Often such groups also require absolute submission to a leader's punitive or benevolent ideology in order to earn the leader's "love." This dynamic often replaces the group members' internal moral structures with a two level morality: the exalted leader and an external enemy to pour projections into. Athens (1992) captures a part of this dynamics in his concept of "internal community" in violence prone individuals.

The psychological and developmental importance of a "we" identity becomes evident as modern state-sponsored violence usually occurs between different extended imaginary "we" coalitions called nations. Developing independent, mature "I" and "we" identities is a significant developmental achievement. The modern concept of nationalism rather than a kin or religious "we" contributes a recent component of identity by creating a specific named place and native language of origin in the reality of other created political states. The failure or the absence of the specific capacity to construct an independent "we" identity leaves the individual without a community and vulnerable to isolation in non-kin groups. Jews were a historically vulnerable group made increasingly vulnerable when they were made "stateless" in Germany. Statelessness (apatride) is a political condition with psychological consequences. The UN refuge agency reported that being stateless takes a serious psychological toll on children who describe themselves as "invisible," "alien," "living in a shadow," "like a street dog" and "worthless."

The imagining of a nation state also created a distinctive set of complex social/political constructs that contributed to the withdrawal of recognition and empathy for other non-kin individuals and their coalitions. The "modern" construction of discrete nations has resulted in grids of affinity, an enhanced "we" identity and vulnerability of individuals to the impact of external authoritarian false beliefs and justifications for various forms of state violence.

Central to the mass murders in World War II was the construction of a false belief of a racially elite German nation state combined with the radical racial politics of national identity. Millions of people were killed, became killers or were willing to die for the imaginary belief systems of nations. Arendt (2014) argued that no breakthrough in understanding state-sponsored violence is possible without the capacity to understand its false rationalizations: in other words, to attain the capacity to think independently and decipher the messages and purposes of a nation's "false" beliefs and accusations.

The significant achievement of attaining an inner sense of personal identity, in its diverse forms of attainment, may be based solely on internal cognitive structures and abilities. Significantly, such psychic structures continually require the ongoing discrimination of an "I" and a "we" and the possibility of a nonthreatening alterity (not me). However, unique inner subjectivity and individuality grow in some free and spontaneously occurring interiority or is a uniquely achieved social and mental product. Zahavi (2015; Zahavi and Michael, 2016) points out we are dealing with internal ideological categories constructed in an expanding system of socially embedded, unique achievements and human cognitive organizations. Selves are not simply born but arise in complex interactive processes of ongoing social experiences and patterns of verbal and nonverbal individual and group interchanges (Zahavi and Michael, 2016, p. 11) within a culture. As a result of this interactive complexity, the formation of a mature stable self is vulnerable through development to external and internal influences. Many current theorists consider the individual self, due to its social embeddedness, to be more a matter of politics and culture than of science and psychology. This is significant when considering that both individual (I) and cultural (we) identities are constructions of nominative inner-cognitive categories within a variety of hierarchical cultural organizations, which require both self-definition and the recognition of individual and group differences. The vulnerability of the constructions of an individual self (identity) play a significant role in the capacity for the continuing experiencing of reality, the resiliency of the self and the degree to which a self is defined by external values and intentions. Although fears of intimacy are related to the integrity of the self, individual fears, beliefs and defense mechanisms also affect the nature of the affective bonding to and rejection of "we" groups. Complex internal dynamics of projection, splitting into good and bad external objects, disavowal and the idealization of leaders also play a significant role in the individual vulnerability and receptivity to imaginary ideas and false rationalizations. Usually the forms of imaginary or false ideas convey a simplistic "moral" dichotomy along with varying degrees of imagined differences and threat. All of these interactive dynamics are aimed at changing the meanings of the raw data of experience (beta elements)[3] and affecting the basic group process of identification with the "we" while negatively defining people outside the "we" group. The designation of an outsider, alien, "other" may be based on any human attribute or belief.

An important perspective on the power of the concept of "we" identity may be achieved by expanding the well-known psychoanalytic notion of Winnicott's (1965) holding environment.[4] Winnicott's affirmation that there is no mother without a baby extends the concept that individual (self) identity emerges as a unique interpersonal entity and as such is dependent upon ongoing social interactions with significant others. Bion (1961) referred to this as a primary pair that was the bedrock for all later pairs. Early bonding social interactions in normal human development also leads to the primary capacity to discriminate between "me" and "not me." Kegan (1982) argued for extending Winnicott's idea of a primary holding environment to all stages of the life cycle; in his view, this idea of social containment is intrinsic to human evolution, not just individual development. Humans did not develop as isolated individuals but as members of highly variable and complex forms of adaptive social coalitions influencing their behaviors and beliefs. This is the inherent basis of our "groupishness."

Building on Kegan's perspective, it is possible to conceive that there is not only one primary holding environment early in life, there is also a highly variable succession of interactive animate holding environments on a cultural level. Most humans have a life history of social embeddedness, containment and potentially shared beliefs, language and concepts. These external containers are the psychosocial and ideological constructions that actively yet permeably contain us and enable the idea of "we" (as a form of interactive entities) that can be distinguished from "I." Such constructed social entities supply the cognitive ingredients of belief essential to an identity. From Kegan's perspective, it is then possible to describe varieties of holding environments that miscarry because of social trauma, such as war, famine, military intervention, etc. Social traumas contribute to a traumatic disruption in individual affiliation and the capacity for mentalization. Such trauma also results in individual disorganization and a psychic readiness to perceive, re-experience or imagine threat and loss. Failures of the social holding environment may more accurately be described by attachment dynamics, such as early secure, fixated and chaotic attachments, as well as destructive or disorganized core-holding attachments. Applying Kegan's idea as a longitudinal model of Winnicott's primary holding environment potentially reveals patterns of attachment during development. A person may have early chaotic attachment and then actively seek dependent, intimate, friendly "we" or "us" attachments that may be dynamically in reaction to that early disruptive attachment. Perceptions of the social world and the people in that environment are organized within each attachment container of social or intimate relations as either safe or unsafe. For example, Erikson (1953) maintained that certain vulnerable persons are drawn to movements in which external moral and ideological principles are absolute as a compensation for earlier anxious or unstable family experiences. Involvement with such an authoritarian holding environment with a charismatic or prophetic leader supplies an authority figure to idealize and an unquestionable, dichotomous ideology that inhibits surface doubt and anxiety. In other words, in a totalitarian holding environment, a compensating "mental compromise" may be found in which conformity replaces searching for truth or safe learning and curiosity does not usually occur. Large-scale holding environments can also become dangerous due to the destructive capacities of conflicts between kin coalitions, seemingly antagonistic belief systems and nations that seek redefinitions of non-kin status.

The nation state as a holding or containing group can be understood as replacing earlier ideologies of religion in providing a broad collective foundation of group identity (we). An examination of European and Asian history reveals that such religious identities often became militarized in a manner similar to that of the Nazi national effort and sought to violently remove non-believers. Religious and linguistic transnational wars were usually longer and bloodier than other types of clashes; they are also twice as likely to recur and twice as deadly to noncombatants.

These conflicts may be dynamically understood as the establishment over time of a particularly intolerant and sensitive "we" identity and culture of beliefs that seek to establish authoritarian conformity, purity, the superiority of a myth (false information), the contrasting alterity of non-believers and the inferiority of all others. In Nazi Germany the imaginary Aryan "We" also contained a fantasy of reparation for real and imagined insults, aiming to change perception of the social reality and history of Germans and Germany. In the early 1900s there was also a growing awareness of the significance of anthropology and the Nazis aimed to reinvent themselves the first and primary progenitor of Europe. German anthropologists constructed an Aryan myth that was dependent on an elaborated false anthropology of invented Aryan superiority, essentially different from the imagined democratic American identity of the time, and the British or Russian "We."

Such an active construction of a national and scientific false origins could not dynamically arise from a limited kin or "dynastic royal family" fantasy. National mythology was a cognitive method of restructuring the beliefs within the German social-political context of racial superiority. Claiming divine origins implies close contact with great spirits and a potential for miraculous victory over other competitors. National identities in Germany were formed by the state-sponsored definitions of pure Aryan, linguistic and other symbols, with parental and schooling cues to young children, guiding their perception of an imaginary "national state" as an enlightened alloparental holding environment. Unique ideas of German values and concepts of right and wrong behavior were articulated in a particular Aryanized culture, which internalized the idea that while Germany was exalted, Germany had profound enemies. This Nazi identity was also constructed with this heightened sense of imagined threat to the nation's existence from both inside and outside of the imagined boundaries of Germans and Germany. While elements of the myth were therapeutic, along with the threat was willing violence that altered the status and perception of the "good German." The state supported violence was necessary and accelerated to a nearly perpetual state of war against "state enemies and inferiors," creating legal, state-supported murder and an extremely violent Nazi society (Gerlach, 2010). The aim of the Nazification of Europe sought to rightfully bind all German-speaking people together, eliminate racial inferiors and establish German governess of conquered areas through violence (Bessel, 2009). Language also plays an important role in national identity and culture (and deserves separate study). B. Anderson (2016), among others, explains the importance of the unifying processes of a national *lingua* in forming and serving cohesion of a national identity. In addition, the symbolism of the swastika flag, one of the earliest forms of the cross, also played a role in the Nazi national identity: the red represented the social idea of the Nazi movement; the white disk represented the idea of the nation; and the black swastika, used in Aryan cultures for millennia, represented "the mission of the struggle for the victory of the Aryan man, and, by the same token, the victory of the idea of creative work," as declared by Hitler in *Mein Kampf*. That idea of creative work was turned into the concept of *Blitzkrieg* (lightning war), the mobile rapid and forceful destruction of rivals. The military tactic of *Blitzkrieg* was part of the Nazi risky belief that the whole of a human society was an organism that could be shocked and manipulated by politicized social engineering in which murder, enslavement and genocide were viewed as entirely conscious and rational strategies, chosen to achieve a certain racial empirical aim. Hitler sought to convince Germans of his aims of a Great German military Empire.

With the legalized violence of Hitler's Aryanization of Germany, Jews were increasingly designated by the state as German imposters and perceived as "bizarre objects"; they were bizarre because the Nazis projected something dangerously negative onto them that changed them from their original human state. Once transformed, they were perceived, no matter their earlier status, as a composite of dangerous, bizarre, murderous, polluting or corrupting objects (Sandler, 2009, p. 198); it was deemed necessary for them to be isolated, then removed without remorse to ensure Germany's pure identity and prophesized future. This is a central dynamic in a monstrous violent transformation, in which the mechanisms of the state redefined the status and viability of a portion of its own population as stateless, less than human and dangerous that was previously accepted as citizens. The social identity of Jews as a "racial" entity was externally transformed in Germany by rhetoric, law, threat and visible violence: state-wide violentization. These historic events raise important questions regarding the vulnerability of any human group, of any size, with a distinct "identity" within a nation state when a safe state-as-container is transformed by the creation of false beliefs of a pure national identity and its threats. The effects of mass projective expulsion as a group dynamic are evident when the leaders of any political state decide to denigrate, expel or carry out the destruction of a defined group of people believed to be alien, dangerous, invading or polluting. Such negative and dangerous attributions imply that the polluting danger is in their very being and must be removed violently.

The dynamic differences between culturally shared belief systems and unique individual belief systems, and their respective roles in identity formation, led me into the unbounded world of perversions as a belief system. Gender identity, its mode of sexual expression and its choice appear to originate with and contain fundamental "beliefs" and excitements that may or may not depend on physical-biological differences in anatomy. Here Britton's (1998) ideas about beliefs are significant, due to their unique attention to normal and pathological beliefs having an unconscious derivative, and to his cautious mode of presentation. Caution is required because psychoanalysis itself is embedded in a number of unmistakable and remarkable "beliefs" about human development, individual mental functioning and group dynamics.

Writing this chapter on perversions was extremely challenging. Also challenging, at least initially, was translating Bion's (Sandler, 2009) perspective on the psychic results of false beliefs from the individual to group disruptions of collective cognitive and identity processes. False beliefs are powerful forces that promote changes in identity and the projective expulsion of elements of the self into others in reality. I struggled to understand the complex, individual, subjective inner space or deep emergent beliefs generated about one's basic gender and body excitement and its relationship to the reality of biological neuro-anatomy. It was difficult to find a developmental psychoanalytic space between these distinct types of experience: inner belief and external biological anatomy. That struggle was productive; I turned to an editor for help and had to sort out my own understanding. I concluded from my clinical work that an important cognitive-emotional foundation in humans is to generate beliefs about the world, the others in it and the self as objects[5] in that world. Internalized gender identity may be best understood as an accrued amalgamation of constructed and "perceived" biological reality, personal fantasy, familial response, and cultural ideas and folklore within a preliminary human framing structure of references (Ogden, 1988). Among these contributing factors, there is a normal developmental history of true, experimental, false and imaginary beliefs, in which one's subjective experience of self is transformed into a composed experience of identity ("I") that includes or shapes an internal conception of gender and sexual identity, excitement and aim. These real and imaginary phenomena have pervasive importance to the human experience of gender and exert influence in a potentially unique disregulated or experiential form (Fonagy, 2008) in the human psyche. Most liberating was accepting that psychopathology was not limited to psychosexual development as originally constructed by individual psychoanalytic theory (Abel-Hirsch, 2015). Sexuality was recognized as being important because it was part of the dynamics of pairing (Basic assumption) in the analytic dyad. "It is as if there could be no other reason for two people coming together except sex" (Bion, 1961, p. 62). This important observation captures the complexity of the levels of interaction possible between two people. Theories of perversion attribute its origin to early phases of development and tend to ignore the role of the body and excitement in its expression of sexuality.

From the divine rights of emperors, to the religion and mythology of various cultures, to believing one is an orphan or the son of a king, or of a particular caste or nobility, people have invented imaginary or culturally bound explanations, much as children construct imaginary friends: to soothe themselves and to explain experience and sensation. Every human culture has invented and invested in beliefs, and humans have "fallen in love" with their constructed beliefs that "explained" reality and governed social status and behavior. These constructions range from dangerous imaginations of "facts" and outright deceptions, to imaginative play and simple evasive/defensive imaginations that reflect unselfconscious beliefs. These beliefs arise from the root or deep structure of mental organization: the vulnerable self as object and interpreter of experience. For an extreme example, in schizophrenia delusions are not simply individual observations about the external world but reports of altered psychic structures of experiencing and believing. All humans continually endeavor to make sense of the stimulating world around them and the people in it. We naturally attribute meaning to our perception-based experience. We attribute meaning and beliefs about our bodies and gender, our dreams and other people's intentions. We attribute meaning to the groups we belong to and what pleasures us. For example, a nomadic group might believe that they are the "chosen people" or the guardian of democracy, that vaccinations are dangerous or global warming is a fantasy: all of these are examples of individual and group imaginary beliefs that may or may not be subject to verification. In the psychoanalytic theories of perversions almost all the theorists rely on the concept of imaginary or fantasy regarding the idiosyncratic beliefs about sexual excitement. I wondered whether "fantasy" or "imaginary" is the right term for ideas, perceptions and body states of stimulation that are so real to the people who hold them that they incite sexual excitement.

I believe "the imaginary" originates in the deregulated or proto-mental area of the psyche (Fonagy, 2008) where the biological and body processes are malleable and may diverge from their seeming normal course and are vulnerable to illusory ideas or hallucinosis. While sexuality as identity in its complexity is in the mind–body realm, beliefs, touch and psychosexual imagining influence and define its subjective state. Sexual fantasy refers to consciously experienced imagery associated with feelings and mind–body states that are explicitly associated with erotic sensations and lust. I believe that a core imagined sexual identity is a belief and its recruited variations in perversions are essentially hallucinotic and resolve early proto-mental dynamics of threat, excitement, suffering or trauma. The psychic issue is not that sexual gender and excitement is imagined or created but that erotic sexuality is uniquely created.

Once the nature of the power of imaginary beliefs is recognized it is evident that humans are ingenious in the creation of a variety of imaginary beliefs, such as inherited nobility, serfdom and castes. One of the most recent and common imaginary inventions is the idea of the sovereign, territorial nation state (B. Anderson, 2016). That the idea of nation state is imaginary does not make it less powerful or variable. The nation state was imagined as sovereign because the concept was born in an age in which the Enlightenment and political revolutions (French, Russian) were destroying the legitimacy of the imagined divinely ordained, hierarchical, dynastic monarchies and empires. The very notion of a nation state was revolutionary yet imaginary: a political community of homogeneous uniform or believing citizens within an arbitrary, elastic, physical boundary beyond which existed other (different) nations or states. Regardless of the variations in the status of the inhabitants, and the degree to which they were exploited or exalted on the basis of that status, the nation state was to be viewed as one entity with each inhabitant a citizen. The recent nation state appears to have arisen when the colonies of North and South America sought independence from their colonial parents. This separation depended on the French Revolution for its model of ideology, and the term "citizen" became important and protected. Citizenship is a state of bonding beyond kinship to unite people of different genetic backgrounds in relation to a particular political entity that enables certain rights. It was then in the nation state's interest to use whatever means necessary to promote the idea of uniformity among its citizens, even when it was not true, and often at the expense of indigenous people. This usually included the construction of representative symbols, the use of a unique uniform, official language in newspapers and schools, and a myth of origin that narrated a sacred history, which was often taught as factual history (B. Anderson,

2016). Immediately what come to mind are the Nazis burning sacred Jewish objects, ISIS destroying historic mosques and jihadists destroying ancient shrines in Timbuktu for their being sacred sites of origin of offending groups. For a new nation state to construct a new illusory reality, it seemed necessary to create an imagined origin to create a righteous imagined trajectory to the present (in other words, a sense of national destiny) as well as to destroy the legitimate domains of its rivals and predecessors. Violent acts, declarative texts or documents and accusations usually accomplished these aims.

The myth of origin of a nation state is imaginatively elaborated as needed, prompted by surface events, conflicts and designations of heroes, villains and traumas. In this manner it duplicates or borrows from the construction of an individual history or identity. There is an embedded grandiose fantasy at the nucleus of national myths, requiring that ideas of inferiority be split off and projected onto alternative others outside or inside that imagined state. In national rituals and anthems, citizens identify with the symbols and meaning of that myth, which replicates the splitting process of us versus them and reaffirms in righteous language and symbols the exalted status and origin of the imagined communality. Hirsch (1995) argued that the origin myths of nations or other tribes and religions frequently define other split-off people as outside of the "universe of obligation," establishing an imaginary essentialism of real or imaginary differences. This often included imagined transgressions and real or imagined exposure to threat or trauma, requiring physical sacrifice for the new state. Performing military service and dying on a battlefield or for spiritual reasons for one's country became an honored sign of sacrificial patriotism for an emerging modern nation state. The only honorable alternative imagined in this scenario was the destruction of others as a means of preventing one's own annihilation or exposure of the sanctuary of "home" to threat. This primary dynamic represents a characteristic defense in which a fear of being destroyed is transformed into acts to destroy others. An imagined pre-emptive invasion or catastrophe of some kind avoided by a verbal or physical attack is very different from a "fight-flight response."

The essential irrationality of this common pre-emptive "attack" defense obscures the centrality of its repeated political and personal occurrence. For example, the imaginary threat posed by Jews, who served as a contrasted racial unity, served as a call to violent, protective action by Germans. In other words, such a Nazi creation myth results not only in value-laden, dichotomous thinking (pure/dirty, legitimate/illegitimate, self/other) that repairs earlier pejorative insults; it also yields a lack of empathy or status for the imagined different other as a threat to existence (Lester, 1986). This dichotomous discriminative pattern fits the historic progression of changes in Nazi propaganda and laws through successive wars (Bytwerk, 2004) and accounts for the establishment of *Mein Kampf* as a Nazi sacred text. It also fits the historical pattern of the origin myths of many other nations that have committed genocide.

Modern nation states may be distinguished by the degree to which they reify their essential, imagined difference and superiority (Hinton, 2002), believe in their imaginary origins and homogeneity, and seek to exclude or punish non-believers or imagined and real aliens. It is important to recognize that the secret of modern state power lies precisely in the interpenetration of laws and potential suppressive violence and, in addition, to recognize how the nation state operates through the production of fear and threat as well as through practices of hope and security. The trajectory of the Nazi state reveals this dual process gone awry.

For example, from 1933 to 1945 the Nazis constructed a fictitious German mytho-archeology to create an image of historical Aryan superiority and to support pseudo-scientific ideas of racial hygiene that re-imagined European history (B. Anderson, 2016). In that effort the Nazis made an enhanced claim as an imaginary anthropological entity, not just a political one; one that on the surface had less inherently to do with ideologies than with racial superiority and religion. At its ideological base, this claim is more similar to unquestioned religious belief than to rationalist political institutions. At its zenith, the Nazi fiction transcended reality for its community of believers, creating a new community of hubris supported by an imaginary history and science. Based on their imaginary racial superiority and true military strength the Nazis constructed legal and scientific justifications to denigrate and eliminate their threats or enemies, and in doing so enhance the viability of their belief system. Violence enforced the everyday notion of citizens that the Nazi German state had power over who would live and who was a citizen. The mutability of national myths, character and historical narratives suggests that Nazi Germany was not the only nation state to use such constructions for systematic racial violence and abuse in the pursuit of a national ideology or purity. Such real and imagined differences in ideology or racial categories rationalized colonial exploitation, slavery and the right to annihilate difference. In such a categorical hierarchy, there exists a second imaginary concept of idealized nationalism: that the organization of its society is natural and inevitable, guided by exalted "high centers" and exalted leaders who rule by prophetic ability or access to special powers. Basic human loyalties and deeper unconscious wishes seek such an omnipotent, central figure, much like a revered sacred script, that was an imagined source of magical and mythic access and direction (Bion, 1961). Hitler was such a designed leader to the Germans, and the Third Reich was his creation. Before and along with the cascade of violent acts in Germany, a Nazi phantasm of race was constructed within an exaggerated nationalist philosophy, in which interactive tropes of blood (genetics), soil (land) and contagion found resonance with past anti-Semitism and remained just below levels of conscious acknowledgement. Such imaginary constructions must find entrepreneurs, followers and violent believers to succeed. For Germans to continually commit the atrocities against other humans that they did during World War II, they must have constructed a rich and directive inner life of imaginary national and racial differences that had deeper meanings. Such constructions served to foster imaginary hierarchical differences among the varied, polyglot people of Europe and Asia through murderous violence and threat. Bartov, a historian (1996), believed that the decimation of World War I was re-enacted in the Holocaust, with Germany reversing its previous victimhood. Again, we encounter the dynamic of violent reversal, not from passive to active, but from threat of catastrophe or destruction to violent attack and murder.

For all the reasons I have laid out, official Nazism was rationalized as a self-protective state policy intimately linked to reparative imperial interests. A defining feature of this style of Fascism was that it was official, emanating from the state and its leaders' imagination. The leaders of the state were positioned to use all the structures of the state for their purposes of wholesale murder and imagined revenge. To that end, Nazi leadership revised the military pomp and circumstance of older dynasts and proto-clans and adopted a model of militarized punitive nationalism. Out of this accommodation came state "Machiavellism" (B. Anderson, 2016), which is a consistent feature of authoritarian regimes that vary in their lies (theories), myths-mystics and imaginary goals. The more the state is naturalized by its elite leaders' imaginary vision, terror and violence, the more the state appears leader-centric or charismatic and Machiavellian. The elite Nazi leaders were autocrats, answerable to no one yet dependent on a wide range of agents, interpreters and implementers: ordinary Germans.[6] Hitler managed a web of facilitators and agents who were accountable yet autonomous, yielding a range of violent perpetrators linked to a bureaucratic, authoritarian hierarchical structure that accepted mass murderous violence or its medical and "scientific" counterpart as a solution and a legal right. This violent structure spread over the territories that had been embroiled in World War I and transformed into a growing empire of Nazi authority and violent ideology supported by willing local co-believers. This was not a matter of either ideology or irrationality but the simple idea that threat and the use of violence was at the core of the Nazi movement (Bessel, 2009) to remake Europe in Hitler's image. This movement was bound up with the death cult of the Nazi movement tied to the passions of war making (Bessel and Schumann, 2003).

To be effective, threats against life must have demonstrations and pageants and this was consolidated by the actions of the SS, Gestapo and Nazi army. Machiavellian corruption and criminality were rampant, along with murderous violence (both casual and planned) and purposeful neglect, even when retreating from the allies. Highly visible elite authorities such Himmler, Eichmann and Mengele became notorious yet obscured by the sheer number of violent advocates and perpetrators of vastly different personalities and occupations who killed by whim and curiosity. Criminal exploitation melded with a Nazi war machine that aimed to exert control over Europe. In this process the definition of crime itself in World War II became dubious. For example the Dirlewanger Brigade, composed of released criminals and led by a man with a PhD in political science, became notorious in fighting partisans, killing for pleasure and crushing the Warsaw uprising. Dirlewanger, "The Butcher of Warsaw," was given medals for his violent leadership.

With the preoccupation with murder and the resources used for these acts, the politicization of deaths or thanatopolitics is evident in the holocaust. Murder impinged on everyday life and extended beyond battlefields, appearing in war films and German heroic poetry. Foucault (2003) describes such a mobilization of an entire population for the purposes of wholesale slaughter to account for the fuel for genocide. On one imaginary level there was the elevation of the eternal Third Reich and on the opposite other the reduction of lives to ashes. There is a remarkable similarity to lynching in the American South that burned victims' bodies after lynching. For another example B. Anderson (2016) also argues that the public honoring of citizens who died in the war, making the ultimate sacrifice for an imagined nation, or are rewarded for brutal killing bears a significant relation to the belief in violence as a solution in war, or a honoring of a *Kriegsideologie*. Though these sacrifices were often not made by choice, they were used to fortify ideological ideals, symbols and structure of an imaginary sacrificial mission for the nation. This exaltation of the sacrifice of life appears to be a layered protective group ritual of honoring the imaginary nations war dead in order to encourage additional devotional sacrifices for the state. This protective wish is also expressed in a variety of ways for the victorious military survivors, who expect their nation to honor them for their service after they have returned home. Here I also make a distinction in the double meaning of "home front," a term of art that creates a combination of home and nation as a proto-container to be defended. A cynical view of the honoring of survivors casts this act as preparation for the next battle.

I believe that such terms as "*Kriegsideologie*" "ultimate sacrifice," thanatopolitics, Bion's "negative container" (Grotstein, 2009) and Sandler's Anti-alpha (2009) encompass and structure the negative in the emotional and developmental struggles associated with the basic anxieties of being alive among one's kin and non-kin. These basic anxieties are not only transformed into the destruction of connections to others, in order to provide some relief, but are often displaced onto an enduring secular national community. *Kriegsideologie* required a secular transformation of the anxiety of individual mortality into a violent and destructive sacrifice for the continuity of the (imaginary) nation state. Individual death could then be honored, yet then this individual death abolishes nothing, as there is only individual death and not that of the imagined greater national body. A related belief was that ultimate sacrifice must be joined with the imagined ideal of purity of belief and honor, establishing a language of sacred honor that offered dissociation from acts of human destruction. Sacrifice was believed to serve historical and future imagined ideologies as well as continued national solidarity and intervention. Absent from B. Anderson's (2016) thesis is the question of the state's pre-emptive abuse, mastery, control and use of weapons that kill at a distance, along with its power to make its citizens conform, submit to threat and volunteer to fulfill their nation's destiny. Anderson's otherwise insightful analysis also ignores that one significant psychological outcome of successful warfare may include the forging of a nation state's identity through threat and the power of mass death making. Such destructive power increased in World War II with the use of the atomic bomb and the saturation bombing of Dresden. Ironically, the destruction of the other is not the brave "triumph of the perpetrator" as presented by Sofsky (2004); instead, it strengthens the sense of national identity by violently conquering death anxiety by acting as perpetrator or savior. Where earlier divinely ordained dynasties were seemingly formed through marital alliances, treaty and warfare, the Nazi state utilized the possible inversion of threat and destruction by the state, with Freudian genitality (libido) almost totally retreating. In sum, for the individual, the imagined nation state and its leader became a pliable entity for violent individual projective needs when at war. Genocides and mass murders usually emerge in or are preceded by warfare. Warfare, such as the invasion of Poland by the Nazis, created a psychic opening to increase and accelerate the expression of the xenophobic wish to eliminate difference and create a pure German Teutonic community that unified German-speaking people. Oddly, at a time when the idea of "nation" was gaining currency with the fall of the major polylingual empires (B. Anderson, 2016), Nazi Germany established a hybrid nation state by seeking to unify German speakers and by making use of slave labor and organized mass murder—actions associated with earlier dynastic empires. Marxist regimes would follow a similar pattern of committing mass murder in their quest for a national identity based on ideological purity, which disguised its bio-racist ideas.

It is important to try to more clearly understand the unique human capacity for false ideas and beliefs. From a developmental perspective, over time humans have developed varied, rich and complicated perceptual mental frameworks to adapt to their changing social and physical environments. In addition to being emotional animals, humans are meaning-making neural machines who need to create meaning in context from their dynamically changing external reality through shared images or language. In addition to creating personal meaning, humans must recognize and become critical concerning cultural meaning, whether it is meaning created by themselves, teacher or by politicians. Because we are essentially vulnerable to harm from a variety of sources, humans are also anxiety-making machines, poised to distinguish and respond to difference, threat, loss and pleasure; humans are also influenced by how and by whom information is presented and organized. These abilities are compounded by the basic human state of temporality. The limited span of a human lifetime plays an important, albeit hidden role in our choices and our need for an instrumental belief system that offers explanations. Temporality is a basic human anxiety that likely arises after the formation of an immature core identity, and it may be partially relieved by the wish or fantasy that the kin group or national community is protected by or aligned with a superior power. One explicit example of such imaginary power is the power of the idea of the Thousand-Year Reich as a new Holy Roman Empire. Homeland, motherland and fatherland, sacred site and mother tongue are all small examples of linguistic symbolic containers that are employed to salve basic human anxieties and wishes The relatively recent formation of imaginary nation states can also be understood as a replacement for earlier belief systems and captures these collective anxieties left by the ebbing of religious states with their reassuring beliefs and rituals. Redemption was to be found in protecting the nation state's continued existence. This embodies a basic paradox, for the very thing that makes the person safe—a representation of the imaginary nation state—also rests on the imaginary. The attention, value and emotion invested in this illusive representation of the nation state are found in the rituals of legitimization of its value and identity. The dynamics of the binding and unbinding of the individual to the existence and goals of a nation state are a powerful dynamic transformation, which has not been carefully examined. Negative nation state concepts such as patriot, spy, treason and traitor carry enormous emotional group meaning and belief. From a group analytic perspective, the history of the nation state reveals that the citizen's passionate belief and attachment to its ideology, dependency on the nation state and fear for its safety can be magnified into persecution and violence, rebellion and secession. Protective violence is thought of as necessary to defend an ideology (belief system), a symbol or guard against a real or imagined threat to an imaginary construct: a nation. The dynamic changes and challenges within an individual after a nation loses a war, or returns from a war for which imaginary histories are constructed, have not been properly examined. Central national belief systems are destroyed when a nation loses in war and must be mourned before the national psyche is reconstructed.

It is necessary to summarize our knowledge about false or imagined beliefs, as it informs the dynamics of mass murder during World War II. When Hitler assumed dictatorial control of Germany it appears that the latent dynamics of mass exploitation, which are inherent in the psychological structuring of a nation state during periods of transition, occurred in a distorted and exaggerated violent form. The German latent cult of predatory law and violence emerged as a deep and widespread national solution. The establishment of a toxic false belief of exclusive racial and ideological imaginations formed an ongoing dynamic necessary for the collective "denial" of responsibility for the earlier loss of its vital status among other states. This dynamic played a central role in inciting the malignant forces and the justification for extreme genocidal violence from below. Such an imagined "pure" or sacred Nazi social identity required construction of an exalted racial myth of origin, a threat of pollution and an illusionary millennial promise of utopian renewal through a melding of sacrifice and extreme violence. This violent combination of the sacred purification of Germany to remove imaginary pollutants through violence remained an imaginary solution. State sanctified violence is a transformative act of devotion to an imaginary belief in a vengeful divine calling authored by a prophetic leader.

Significantly, for mass murder to occur within such a predatory culture, there had to be an underlying cultural preoccupation of a cluster of values and attitudes about death and violence as a solution. These death cult elements are imagined as a personal and national social solution, often expressed in conditions that create an earlier history of violent warfare or rebellion (B. Anderson, 2016). This constellation emerged as an overt form of thanatopolitics the politics of death and purification. Where cultures offer imagined symbolic immortality to those who live up to their death-transcending standards, the Nazis constructed a culture that depended on sacrificing others that threatened contagion in their fantasy of creating a pure and sacred race.

Genocide as an expression of this Nazi thanatopolitical stance cannot occur without a leader establishing imaginary solutions to remove the source of the contagion and disorders while offering a path to purity and sacredness—a visionary authoritarian leader offering an emotionally exciting and appealing array of remedial false beliefs and possessing the authority and control of weapons or mechanisms that threaten, terrorize and kill. These false beliefs must offer a magical solution to some basic humiliation or deep fear in the culture concerning real and imaginary threats to survival. The leader must be able to attract ideological and violent predatory oracles and implementers by offering imaginary solutions and/or a contrasting visible or ideological enemy that resonates with deep fears within the culture. That imagined enemy usually lacks the power and means to protect themselves and is cast as helpless prey. Hitler and Himmler repeatedly cast Poles, Jews, Roma and Bolsheviks as prey and Nazi Germany as a death-transcending culture.

Bion broadened the psychoanalytic field by focusing attention on events that might otherwise be overlooked. For Bion, hallucinosis is that event that occurs when a core of fantasy interdicts reality after it is projected outward. The important distinction between reality and fantasy collapses in the direction of fantasy so that inner pressures transform individual or collective group perception. The internal mechanisms or elements of experience take on or are subjected to an intrusion that reconstructs them in a distorted, illusionary manner. In Bion's description, this represents a failure in normal symbol formation in which the perception of something in reality is transformed to be powerful, dangerous, exciting or gratifying external presence. Following the process of distortion of reality, a bizarrely reconstituted perception can exist simultaneously with normal perceptions of the external world. This presupposes a greater degree of unconscious functioning in perception and splitting as a defense that creates the transformation in hallucinosis described by Bion (Sandler, 2009). In hallucinosis internal and external perceptions of reality are pre-determined by an unconscious influence in which they fit a fixed dangerous relationship to a superior or threatening person or group. The potential for a hallucinotic experience is always present to a greater or lesser extent in thinking. The perceived object is distorted as a normal mental functioning of the automatic projective elements of perception, and the perceiver may or may not be aware of distortion. Often overlooked is that the perceiving self is also transformed in the hallucinosis while the realness of external people has its emotional significance or intention changed. This is particularly evident in the dynamics of perversion that generates excitement and sexualized bodily arousal.

Bion also points out that in any group experience a hallucinatory phenomenon transformation, to a greater or lesser extent, is always present, since he considers that one of the mind's functions is to establish and continually correct perceptions and their context. He also maintains that rivalry, envy, greed and thieving—together with a sense of being blameless—deserve consideration as invariants of hallucinosis (1965, pp. 132–133). Group hallucinosis is a byproduct of a shared group transformation of an object or idea that exists in reality into something inauthentic and infiltrated with projected elements. The group members treat the original object or idea as unknowingly transformed into a "desired" object or idea that bonds the members together in that belief. Group members may join that group to ameliorate some anxiety, frustration or developmental absence in reality. A hallucinotic social belief system requires ignoring some elements in reality. One example was accepting the Nazi propaganda poster that " Jews bring Typhus" as true.

The nature of the threat to the German Nazi nation-as-container for individuals, as well as the nature of the propaganda used by the Nazis, was constructed to describe a lethal threat to the German nation state constructed in the minds of its citizens of to a human body (Cariola, 2014). The nation (among other large structures or groups), as an imaginary entity, is often represented as a corpus or body, and attacks upon it are experienced as assaults on the conjoined body of the primal parents (Cariola, 2014)[7] represented as a proto-home "home."

With the Nazis, the distorted threatening object was created on the outside of the individual as a penetrating or polluting threat, a threat to the life of the individual and his imaginary state. The Nazi solution was organization to violently remove the external imagined threatening object. In contrast, the perverse individual creates a distorted internal model of what constitutes sex and sexual pleasure, which psychically changes the "actual" representations of the body and the arousing other. The external Jew at the time of the violence is hallucinotically perceived as representing an immediate polluting danger, although the danger does not exist in realty. Violence and removal of the dangerous body, mind and traces of the other were imagined to avoid any threat to the self, the Nazi state and the future. In the perpetrator's mind, these threatening representations may not exist as separate entities and may mirror internal feared unconscious fantasies. An externalization of the origin of the threat is particularly significant for the perpetrator, as the threat must be kept on the outside.

Placing the mass traumatic event of the Holocaust into a psychoanalytic narrative serves a number of important functions. Foremost among them is erasing the Nazi silence and efforts to conceal their actions and the motivations of individuals within the Nazi state. The Jewish other as a threat and foreign element in relation to the Nazi nation was an imaginary creation made violently real in a culture vulnerable to a death cult. In addition, this Jewish catastrophe has remained outside of psychoanalytic reach, creating a "radical incomprehension that inadvertently contributes to the … rhetoric of silence or unspeakability" (Haidu, 1992, p. 48). Haidu resolved that Himmler's themes are familiar to us and that the Holocaust was not a unique, singular occurrence but a potentially repetitive event that has the power to return. The Nazis did not willingly give up their secret motivations and mostly gave implausible explanations.

The decisions to remain silent contributes to make these events un-representable and beyond comprehension, placing it in a negative thought container. If we cannot bear to face this horror, we have lost an important battle for meaning. Adorno (1997) noted that the representation or rendering into narrative form of any aspect of the Holocaust necessarily implies the possibility of an alternative representation or counter-narrative. This is a profound dilemma that appears to set a moral limit on the ability of psychoanalysts to honestly represent Nazi intentions and motivations. While there is a profound obligation towards the Nazis' victims and survivors, who are essentially ignored in this effort, this does not mean the victims were not considered. There are no cruel perpetrators without victims. To understand Nazism from a psychoanalytic perspective is not to justify it. However, it does place this author at the limits of psychoanalysis. Bartov (1996, p. 111) quotes Primo Levi, who insisted that the history of the Third Reich could be reread as a war against memory, an Orwellian falsification of memory and reality. Orwellian falsification is hallucinosis at work. We are not all murderers.

Notes

1 The ability to conceive of mental states and to use mental state concepts to interpret and predict one's own and other people's behavior.
2 Carveth extends some notions of hysterias to a range of hysterias that they refer to as Hystero-paranoid. This includes a retreat from the "capacity for concern" for the other combined with repression and projection of hatred and envy of the other.
3 Beta elements are the mental representation of the thing-in-itself, undigested mentally. Alpha elements are the processed elements of the betas on which thought, dreams and memory depend.
4 Winnicott's holding environment bears a close relationship to Bion's (1962) notion of container. To become a human object, the infant must encounter a series of reciprocating objects. First among them is the mother. Bion's concept refers to the psychic nature of the capacity for thinking and communicating.
5 I use the term self as a generic term to stand for the "I."
6 Here I make a distinction between Browning's "ordinary men" and ordinary Germans. Browning's implication is that anyone can become a mass murderer. I believe that there are unique conditions that lead to the emergence of genocidal cooperation in Germany. For example, if a non-violent movement had faced the Nazis as happened in India to the British, the Nazis would have annihilated the movement. The Germanic or Teutonic mythology is likely different from the Roman and Greek mythology.
7 Cariola approached the language pattern of *Mein Kampf* (1943) through body boundary imagery, primordial though and emotional language.

9
ADDENDA

> It is forbidden to kill; therefore all murderers are punished unless they kill in large numbers and to the sound of trumpets.
> *Voltaire,* Questions sur l'Encyclopédie *(1770–1774)*

> Lodz itself a beautiful city. Drive through the ghetto. We got out and looked everything over closely. It is indescribable. These are not human beings, these are animals. Therefore it is not a humanitarian operation it is a surgical one … Otherwise some day Europe will perish from the Jewish disease.
> *J. Goebbels* Diary, *p. 628 entry, November 2, 1939*

The dynamics of very large groups are often very difficult to discern and this is particularly so within large political entities that become violent. Much of what we find repulsive about violence cannot be directly explained by individual psychoanalytic theory, particularly since ideas of sanity and democracy were closely bound together following 1945 (Pick, 2012). Certain post-war psychoanalytic models and ideas were formed on the renunciation of Nazism and the linking of the political struggle between freedom and tyranny and the political psychoanalysis of both Hitler and other individual Nazis as exemplar. With the coming of the Cold War totalitarianism was seen as an authoritarian "sickness" (Pick, 2012). The psychological health of the citizen and the robustness of the polity were thereafter linked. Insanity, it was argued, could be found not only in political leaders, but also in communities, groups and nations. Aggression in development rather than violence and sadism became an abiding concern but its study was confounded by its conceptual vagueness. Child developmental theories came into prominence and the nurturing mother was seen as the bulwark against authoritarian politics and a sadistic superego assumed to be present with violence. The latter being the source of both totalism and warfare could only be countered by nurturance, security and secure attachment. War was defined as mad, likely meaning beyond psychoanalytic concepts, and fought by the obedient, patriotic and sacrificially devoted. Yet a great proportion of our literature, film and art, museums and monuments are directly related to violence, war and criminal activity. Absent was a greater understanding of the psychological components of systems of beliefs or ideology and violence role in culture. While other disciplines will continue to have their distinctive concerns regarding the continued appearance of genocidal murder, my concern here was to peer beneath the historical reports of the Nazis by the use of group analytic theory to uncover neglected dynamics of violence and mass murder. Continued reliance on the technology of warfare as a solution may only increase the number of victims and reduce the number of combatants. By bringing ignored dynamics to the surface we decrease the mystery of the will to mass murder.

I now agree with Hoggettt (1998) that, in ordinary language, the forces of life and death, expressed through progress and annihilation, creativity and destructiveness, are active within all of us. In other words terror and fear have an existential status and can become a silent deadly force that makes us all psychically vulnerable individually and in collective groups. I observed that phenomena in New York City in the aftermath of 9/11 when the safe group "context" was radically challenged (Roth, 2007) and responded to with violence. This human vulnerability is internally countered by productive and healthy narcissism as an internal life force. Every emotional attachment between people interacts with the balance of these positive and negative forces, according to the group analytic theories of Bion and Kaes and a few others. Our dilemma is that we emerged as group animals at war with our groupishness and yet dependent upon it. What is at stake is two-fold. That the group I belong to, no matter its status, survives amongst other groups. And, what is also at stake is survival of the individual body and mind while in the group. In other terms the establishment of a safe "I," in the collective "We" (Zahavi, 2015; Turquet, 1975). This dynamic is essential in understanding the impact of different belief systems and ideologies.

Humans possess a capacity for unique forms of shared intentionality, beliefs and cooperation that allows for and contributes to the complex creation of a variety of forms of social aggregates, groups and cooperative working institutions. To accomplish this according to Jacques (1955), emerging individuals in the group psychologically assign the destructive parts of their selves to non-members or other entities outside of the group. In other words the potential inner threat is psychically placed on the outside of the group or when found in the group is expelled or destroyed. These projective displacements of negativity and potential threat allow for the formation of cooperative work groups and roles, which will help start to establish beliefs about the group selves and identity that explain their task and often encourage survival. During this ongoing effort to maintain the group, over time there is often a return of a basic fear or anxiety that an enemy will emerge from within rather than an enemy attacking from the outside the group boundary. As suggested by Meltzer (1986), the group members are caught between a feared inner catastrophic event and one that is externally persecutory. This dilemma prevents or is claimed to prevent access to the generative healing protective process, which ordinarily protects the body and mind from threatening or noxious events. The positive healing force (healthy narcissism) is reliant on a composite of the individual early experiences of safety in development with significant others interacting with individually given psychic inheritance and resilience. This composite is constructed as a unique internal mental establishment with an individual living under its protection. Bion's most profound conjecture concerning groups was that in some way the mind is not the tri-partite model Freud hypothesized, but structured in the manner of a primitive society with the quest for survival involving a constant struggle between antagonistic forces within the psyche. The "I" in conflict with the demands of the "We." Hoggett (1998) expanded Bion's idea by arguing that individuals have continually developed a highly organized "internal agency" operating at an internal fulcrum dealing with continuing presentations of threat and opportunities for healthy progress. This internal agency is also shaped by experiences of safe attachments, nurturance and a capacity for learning from social and intimate experiences that stands against frustrations and threats. This internal agency emerged from humans banding together to form and organize cooperative non-kin societies that served some of the functions needed by individuals within groups to varying degrees while providing basic safety in the environment. Individuals identified with and recognized these functions and were adversely affected when these protective functions failed. Banding into non-kin groups must have enhanced chances of survival while creating other interactive problems and competitions. Sociality also decreases the risk of falling prey while increasing the possibilities of finding food and other resources. The emergence of strong pair bonding (male and female partnership) to produce an ongoing division of labor to offset the high costs of raising human children eventually led to the emergence of hierarchical social structures. Pair bonding also allowed for between kin group alliances afforded by female bonding to other females and family of origin when females transferred to other human groups and brothers remained in the original group. Social success in securing mates was linked to competition between males that was potentially destructive to the group but provided a foundation for the modern family (Gavrilets, 2012). The theory of the evolution of pair bonding illuminates the unconscious underpinning of the exclusionary Nuremberg Laws prohibition against the mixing of the "races" and restricting kin selection. Imposing a restriction on mating systems by Nazi law was a legal strategy for transforming a social-racial structure of exclusion and citizenship that has psychosocial significance.

When individuals live in large working groups of any size that invite us to live under its protection of its "us" or "we," the innate tension between being granted primary safety, being expelled, excluded and finding an enemy must constantly be resolved. It is within these governed groups that awareness of like-me emerges and the "other" is created. Group selection theory posits that self-evaluation and reflection requires the interpretation of the person from the perspective of their peer group and family. In modern political life this is no longer only presumed as given but is constituted within the moral authority of national sovereignty: of bio-political regulation and authority (Murray, 2005).

At an individual psychological level ongoing unique group participation, with its competing rewards and threats, finds expression, and this expression will always be mediated by the biographical circumstance of the individual participants interacting with the character and goals of leaders. In other words the various internal agents will draw their character from the real external experiences with other significant people that have been involved in encounters with the individual during the course of his or her life. Individuals will always have unique ways of enacting and resolving their identification, cooperation or competition within the group "We." Shared group social identities and recognition of emotions sharpen differences within the group (you-we) as well as the identification (empathy) with each other. Alterity or radical difference is part of all group dynamics and covers a spectrum of real and imagined differences among the group members and emotional responses to that difference affect the emotional status of the links in the group.

Hoggett's extension of Bion's theory has not been applied to a psychoanalytically informed analysis of the individual's relation to the unique imaginary idea of a nation (B. Anderson, 2016), in particular to the negative or destructive emotions and actions that are anti-linkage or attachment, anti-truth, anti-knowledge (learning), violent (Meltzer, 1986) and anti-reality (Sandler, 2009). The basic negative mechanism by which the groups maintain their status appears to be by the mechanisms of expulsive projective identification. This form of projective identification is an unconscious defensive process that exteriorizes incompatible aspects of the self or group psychic organization into a representation in ways that permit "an unburdening of an unacceptable attribute or the preservation of an aspect of one self away from hostile primary process presence" (Appry and Stein, 1993, p. 77). One result of a co-joined group projective process is that there is a change in the collective perception of the group, its members and the boundary between that group and the other defined groups. It is through this collective process in groups that ontological hate that creates danger and threat is temporarily established and directed outside of the group. "Normal" projective process within the group fosters group cohesion and safety. When other than normal projective defenses are employed there is a concurrent search for an obedient relationship with the leader as the sense of separateness may be weakened and a need for group identity exaggerated (Bion, 1961).

Returning to the idea of nation as a large group, every imagined nation has its own imagined history that establishes an antagonist, a justification or an enemy that helps define its physical borders and ideology. It is through this process that nations occupy that potential space where nothing is simply real or is hallucinated. But this space is difficult to sustain without an external agency that has been established to govern and protect, even if it may not behave that way. It supplies the socially structured avenues that "make sense" to an elite governing structure to continue its "work" and self-definition. When functioning as a work group, the nation is engaged with real and necessary political tasks in reality, there is cooperation among its members and awareness of the issues of time and security. In this book, I am concerned with the emergence of part of the elite establishment that becomes negative, untruthful and established a violent, dramatic reality; one that created a pathological or negative organization that demands the existence of an internal or an external enemy that was real and/or imagined. If the individual members' latent fear of annihilation is exaggerated and marshaled in this group they will accept a suitable "lie" or threatening illusion (hallucinosis) as an explanation for their determination of a required enemy. With this dynamic untruth the leader(s) also establishes dominance by offering an imaginary solution to the real or imagined terror and threat posed by this enemy. The leaders then may propagandize making false statements regarding a solution but their dominance does not depend on the "truth" as in a work group but on whether the rest of the people in the nation believe in these false untrue (hallucinotic) statements. In other words collusion lies at the heart of any openly repressive regime that does not hide its bias and violence, and honors its capacity for destructiveness by creating an imaginary enemy. This repressive dynamic seeks or allows the formation of an informative elite group that controls information, monopolizes terror and capitalizes on some of its subjects' willingness to accept lies and to be its violent agents. This leads to progressive violentization in the manner that Athens (1992) describes. Individuals who do not accept their leader's mystifications as true in a totalistic state must behave as if they do or at least be silent bystanders giving up their confidence in language as conveying true or false. The violent leaders may argue that the "I" individual identity within the nation is not necessary in an attempt to censor forms of independent thinking. For the other individuals the normal internal state of "I fear" or "I am vulnerable" is transformed into "I hate" and "I attack and must destroy." The individual and collective psychodynamic struggle in these punitive situations was to relocate the force for destruction and annihilation from the psychic inside to outside: that is to locate it in the psychosocial (Hoggett, 1998). This group hallucinosis is accomplished by the rejection of a clear division between truth and illusion necessary to create a dangerous group alterity.

I return to the Nazi ideology that I referred to as *Kreigsideologie* or death cult that transforms citizens into a willing "community of murderers." For the Nazis, war between competing states in Europe was destiny; it was an all-encompassing and unavoidable undertaking waged by mobilizing all the energy, devotion and organizational sophistication of an industrial state (Bessel, 2009). War was no longer a mythical chivalrous encounter (Bartov, 2000) but one that would change the relationship between war, citizens and state. War lust militarized the German state and its citizens making them tools for ruthless destruction, an effort that was augmented by racist ideology and laws, with illusions of eugenic and magical providence. Hitler was symbolized as a man who came back from the dead (Bartov, 2003b) seeking vengeance for the imagined national betrayal that nearly killed him and coming to stand for Germany and its future, past guilt and revenge. War became a Nazi mission to destroy real and imaginary national or ideological enemies that had victimized or threatened Germany. War became a state form of spreading violentization in "large dimensions" (Wildt, 2009) and finding necessary geographic space. Any distinction between fighting enemy troops, political commissars, massacring Jews, wiping out villages and shooting or starving prisoners collapsed: all became honorable if for the nation state or its units. Enemies in war were declared on the basis of the political, ideological and the biological with pity or empathy constructed as betrayal of the imaginary "Volk." As Bartov puts it, massacre and genocide became synonymous with glory, while perpetrators remained clean and decent (2000, p. 130). Nazi Germany was in a national transformation into a *community of murder* that believed they were purging the world of evil that in fantasy threatened its very existence. Depravity and criminality on a grand scale were transformed into morality, honor and heroism in the manner that Alexander (1949) described in medical practice. War and racial politics were openly merged (Bessel, 2009). If the Nazis had an imaginary explanation based on a racial ideology it was not criminal.

What is insufficiently understood is this Nazi war created an international gulf formed by vastly different conscious ideologies: toward life and learning embedded in a ruthless disregard for life and democratic values of the rule of law. An ideology of "Volk" based on a magical Nazi reversal of logic to use violence and sadism to ensure the existence of a Nazi Empire based on racial superiority and the celebrity of Hitler. In war, the winners usually see their victory as just and the defeated as evil. In World War II the gulf widened between those who believed in the sanctity of life and the rule of law and those who used the state's power over life to organize and commit mass murder. My psychoanalytic colleagues, who, in their manner, sanctify life, have not been able to stare into that gulf in which state power is levied against lives.

While studying violent individuals, Athens (1992, 2003) described the stages of a process of violetization that has some application to the extensive Nazis use of force. According to Athens the cause of criminal violence is not poverty or genetic inheritance or psychopathology, but active violentization is the cause of criminal violence. One problem in applying the stages of the violentization model to the Holocaust is there was millions murdered creating astonishingly millions of unique murder events. The Nazi capacity and zest for murder required multifaceted organs of violence that were applied differently in various countries and within the different Nazi structures constructed specifically for this murderous purpose. For example 876–1370 individual Jews were killed per day at Auschwitz-Birkenau Concentration Camp and this was not the only location where such murders took place. Forty thousand people were killed in two weeks in the suppression of the Warsaw uprising by specialized Nazi militia.

In the death camps the violence against life was an everyday experience of horror or hell while in the countryside violence took the form of public murderous ethnic cleansing. However, there is still something to understand about the culture and stages of preparation for violence in large groups that "normalizes" and routinized mass and individual murder. Violentization takes place in the following stages described by Athens (1992) that may not be discrete in groups.

Brutalization: In this stage, individuals are taught to engage in violent behavior through observation and demonstration. Athens breaks this down to violent subjugation, personal horrification and violent coaching. Future genocidal victims are physically assaulted or threatened and their legal rights are under rhetorical or actual physical attack.

Defiance: A belief system that justifies violent behavior is presented to the individual or group as a just or necessary act, although the nature of the justification is imaginary. Ideology attracts the agents of extermination and certain individuals' amplifiers in the unfolding of these monstrous events.

Violent performances: This marks the transition from a resolution to use murder-violence to its actual use. This is a crucial phase: intentionally and gravely injuring another human being for the very first time in one's life is not as casual a matter as those who have not seriously contemplated, much less performed, such action might not realize. Once the murder occurs it must be explained to the self and the person is no longer innocent or "ordinary": killing again may be easier.

Virulency: A continuing willing readiness to use extreme violence against other individuals with minimal or little provocation. The violence occurred in the absence of preventative protection for the victims.

Extreme virulence: Mass murder or genocide by collective perpetrators.

Athens (1992) also found that violent individuals had three types of self-images and these were violent, incipiently violent and non-violent. Each individual in each type had a matching " phantom community" used internally to construct their self-image. This finding poses a possibility of understanding how an external political organization can replace the individual "internal community" (Hoggett, 1998) and accept or authorize murder. There are inherent problems in applying Athens' stages to the Holocaust. The first is that war and militarization are usually present in nation building and this political movement often justifies various forms of violence. The second is that the mass killings by Germans were state sponsored complicating the dynamics of Athens' phantom community by supplying a reciprocal source of ongoing state approval and honoring for violence. Thirdly, the Nazi genocide was not a unitary event. The German death camps annihilated tens of thousands over years and in rural areas mass slaughters were commonplace in occupied areas. Single acts of murder that likely were not recorded included beating, starvation, sadistic experiments and random episodes of violence for the rewards of cruelty. Finally, the actual dynamics of the individual murderous acts are lost. Retaliatory murders by Nazis found fantastic and real causes. No one in Germany or the conquered areas was safe from the contagion of violentization, which created an imaginary community of murderers and accomplices acting over a wide range of territories from the annexation of Austria in 1938. The contagion of violentization on a small physical scale has been noted in Rwanda and Bosnia, where because of their geographic size the effects of contagion were apparent. In Nazi Germany there was an invisible multifaceted group force of ideologically driven social expectancies, sleeper needs and behaviors of potential victims that likely drove a chain of violence across a much wider geographic area. The conclusion of these factors was that the perpetrators found cause to believe the authorization of imaginary beliefs that the victims were evil, polluting and dangerous. This perception of contagion incited violence easily in certain individuals within a militarized group to commit violence and murders. Once violence was ignited in areas where elite military control was strong and unchallenged, the violence continued without seeming conscious constraints. In forcefully segregated communities opportunists and extremist entrepreneurs exploited the targeted group members, serving as role models or authorizing and escalating group violent behavior within their domain of influence. One documented report of such violence was reported in Nanking as officers demonstrated killing techniques on unarmed civilians for soldiers (Chang, 1998). Given this range of effects over time it is best to see violentization as a massive pressure system from which storms of action emerge. A kind of gang offering protection by murdering that keeps the imagined other permanently devalued or eliminated.

All genocides have a violentization process and its psychic goals can be understood to first move the latent internal psychic danger within the individual, while under the influence of the group, on the outside of the individual. Once this danger is located in the other on the outside, the violentization state process uses various techniques to create circumstances under which the murder of the imagined dangerous is necessary, justified and carried out. The energy of violent entrepreneurs along with exhorting propaganda skillfully elicits confirmation bias that the external danger was removable and justified serving as a confirming community for a community for violence.

The Nazi murdering process was unique in its scope in place and time and in the dark constellations of murderous violence that it spread across Europe. The Nazis consciously constructed unspeakable policies that openly identified millions of people as being without positive value then found devices that murdered them. I must conclude that genocide is a state of lucid consciousness that conceives of the world as possessing infinite dangers that must be violently removed. The dangers are a mental constructions spread in a prepared and "willing" political group that accepts its premises and seeks to verify them. The radicalization of Bion's group theory, and those inspired by Bion, informs the explanation of hallucinotic beliefs that have taken on this political meaning and its violent consequences. To paraphrase Rosenfeld (1971) I believe that there is some deadly force that emerges inside certain groups resembling that which Freud attributed to the death instinct that exists and can be clinically observed as murderous violence. A "willing" political group is one that shares this deadly belief, that accepts violence and murder as a solution to real and imagined political and social problems. A narcissistically organized active death cult was established among the Nazis that embraced the belief that killing unarmed others was an essential part of a remedial fantasy of relief from some danger or to attain an imaginary future goal. In regard to the Nazi leaders with different character structures having a shared Nazi personality, clinical evidence indicates they shared a particular personality character structure that made them especially dangerous. And, that this personality structure was not unique to Nazis, but rather is typical of people who occupy positions of leadership in a variety of rigidly hierarchical institutions. Accepting these two propositions, Resnick and Nunno concluded by warning that:

> Such personalities are not rare. They can be found, not only in totalitarian regimes, but commonly in the upper echelons of most closed systems that make their own rules—such as the civil service, government, intelligence agencies, the military, and large public and private corporations.
> *(Resnick and Nunno, 1991, p. 28)*

These structures have to do with justifications for a variety of violent acts in many forms. Fortunately only a few have access to power and weapons.

APPENDIX A

From a speech by Himmler before Senior SS Officers in Poznan, October 4, 1943

Evacuation of the Jews

I also want to speak to you here, in complete frankness, of a really grave chapter. Amongst ourselves, for once, it shall be said quite openly, but all the same we will never speak about it in public. Just as we did not hesitate on June 30, 1934, to do our duty as we were ordered, and to stand comrades who had erred against the wall and shoot them, and we never spoke about it and we never will speak about it. It was a matter of natural tact that is alive in us, thank God, that we never talked about it amongst ourselves, that we never discussed it. Each of us shuddered and yet each of us knew clearly that the next time he would do it again if it were an order, and if it were necessary. I am referring here to the evacuation of the Jews, the extermination of the Jewish people. This is one of the things that is easily said: "The Jewish people are going to be exterminated," that's what every Party member says, "sure, it's in our program, elimination of the Jews, extermination – it'll be done." And then they all come along, the 80 million worthy Germans, and each one has his one decent Jew. Of course, the others are swine, but this one, he is a first rate Jew. Of all those who talk like that, not one has seen it happen, not one has had to go through with it. Most of you men know what it is like to see 100 corpses side by side, or 500 or 1,000. To have stood fast through this – and except for cases of human weakness – to have stayed decent, that has made us hard. This is an unwritten and never-to-be-written page of glory in our history, for we know how difficult it would be for us if today – under bombing raids and the hardships and deprivations of war – if we were still to have the Jews in every city as secret saboteurs, agitators, and inciters. If the Jews were still lodged in the body of the German nation, we would probably by now have reached the stage of 1916–17.

The wealth they possessed we took from them. I gave a strict order, which has been carried out by SS Obergruppenfuehrer Pohl, that this wealth will of course be turned over to the Reich in its entirety. We have taken none of it for ourselves. Individuals who have erred will be punished in accordance with the order given by me at the start, threatening that anyone who takes as much as a single Mark of this money is a dead man. A number of SS men – they are not very many – committed this offense, and they shall die. There will be no mercy. We had the moral right, we had the duty towards our people, to destroy this people that wanted to destroy us. But we do not have the right to enrich ourselves by so much as a fur, as a watch, by one Mark or a cigarette or anything else. We do not want, in the end, because we destroyed a bacillus, to be infected by this bacillus and to die. I will never stand by and watch while even a small rotten spot develops or takes hold. Wherever it may form we will together burn it away. All in all, however, we can say that we have carried out this most difficult of tasks in a spirit of love for our people.

And we have suffered no harm to our inner being, our soul, our character ...

Documents on the Holocaust, Selected Sources on the Destruction of the Jews of Germany and Austria, Poland and the Soviet Union, Yad Vashem, Jerusalem, 1981, Document no. 161.pp. 344–345

APPENDIX B

Friedrich Jecklen

S-Obergruppenfuhrer Friedrich Jeckeln (1895–1946) is not an everyday name among students of the Holocaust. However, he played a key role during the first phase of the Holocaust, when German policy towards Jews in occupied Eastern Europe was to identify and ghettoize them, and then kill as many of them as possible, often in semi-public mass-shootings on the outskirts of town. Latvian auxiliaries assisted the murders. Himmler's motive was to eliminate the Latvian Jews in Riga so that Jews from Germany and Austria could be deported to the Riga ghetto and housed in their place. Jeckeln and eight other defendants in Riga were found guilty, sentenced to death and hanged at Riga on February 3, 1946 in front of some 4000 spectators.

SS General Friedrich Jeckeln's system worked as follows:

1. The Security Service (SD) men rousted the people out of their houses in the Riga ghetto.
2. The people to be murdered (typically Jews) were organized into columns of 500 to 1,000 people and driven to the killing grounds about 10 kilometers to the south.
3. The Order Police (Orpo) led the columns to the killing grounds.
4. Three pits had already been dug where the killing would be done simultaneously.
5. The victims were stripped of their clothing and valuables.
6. The victims were run through a double cordon of guards on the way to the killing pits.
7. The killers forced the victims to lie face down on the trench floor, or more often, on the bodies of the people who had just been shot.
8. Each victim was shot once in the back of the head with a Russian submachine gun. The shooters either walked among the dead in the trench,

killing them from a range of two metres, or stood at the lip of the excavation and shot the prone victims below them. Anyone not killed outright was simply buried alive when the pit was covered up.

In the western Ukraine, SS General Friedrich Jeckeln noticed that the haphazard arrangement of the corpses meant an inefficient use of burial space. More graves would have to be dug than absolutely necessary. Jeckeln solved the problem. He told a colleague at one of the Ukrainian killing sites, "Today we'll stack them like sardines." This system was called "sardine packing" (*Sardinenpackung*). It was reported that even some of the experienced *Einsatzgruppen* killers were horrified by its cruelty.

At Rumbula, Jeckeln watched on both days of the massacre as 25,000 people were killed before him. There was a division of labor among the German troops according to the presence or absence of "skills with specialists in killing."

In 1943, apparently concerned about leaving evidence behind, Himmler ordered that the bodies at Rumbula be dug up and burned.

On January 27, 1942 Jeckeln was awarded the War Merit Cross with Swords for killing 25,000 at Rumbula "on orders from the highest level" (Friedlander, 2007).

Some of the Rumbula murderers were brought to justice. Hinrich Lohse and Friedrich Jahnke were prosecuted in West German courts and sentenced to terms of imprisonment. Victors Arajs, a Latvian collaborator, evaded capture for a long time in West Germany, but was finally sentenced to life imprisonment in 1979. Herberts Cukurs escaped to South America, where he was assassinated, it is said by agents of Mossad. Eduard Strauch was convicted in the Einsatzgruppen case and sentenced to death, but he died in prison before the sentence could be carried out. Friedrich Jeckeln was publicly hanged in Riga on February 3, 1946 following a trial before the Soviet authorities.

APPENDIX C

The Kovno Massacre (from various published sources)

Kovno's Jewish life was disrupted when the Soviet Union occupied Lithuania in June 1940. The occupation was accompanied by arrests, murders, confiscations and the elimination of all free institutions. Jewish communal organizations disappeared almost overnight. Soviet authorities confiscated the property of many Jews. Meanwhile, the Lithuanian Activist Front, founded by Lithuanian nationalist émigrés in Berlin, clandestinely disseminated anti-Semitic literature in Lithuania. Among other themes, the literature blamed Jews for the Soviet occupation. Hundreds of Jews were exiled to Siberia. As the Soviets retreated they murdered Lithuanian nationalists and took Jewish possessions.

Following Germany's invasion of the Soviet Union on June 22, 1941, Soviet forces fled Kovno. Immediately before and following the German occupation of the city on June 24, anti-Communist, pro-German Lithuanian mobs began to attack Jews (whom they unfairly blamed for Soviet repression), especially along Jurbarko and Krisciukaicio streets. These right-wing vigilantes murdered hundreds of Jews and took dozens more Jews to the Lietūkis Garage, where detachments of German Einsatzgruppen, together with Lithuanian auxiliaries, began murdering the Jews. Groups of partisans, civil units of nationalist-rightist anti-Soviet affiliation, initiated contact with the Germans as soon as they entered the Lithuanian territories. A rogue unit of insurgents headed by Algirdas Klimaitis and encouraged by Germans from the *Sicherheitspolizei* and *Sicherheitsdienst*, started anti-Jewish pogroms in Kaunas (Polish: Kovno) on the nights of June 25–27, 1941. Over a thousand Jews perished over the next few days in what was the first pogrom in Nazi-occupied Lithuania.

The most infamous incident occurred in what was later known as the Lietūkis Garage Massacre. and was photographed. During the Lietūkis Massacre, carried out before the invading Germans had actually set up their administration, 40–60 people were killed and publicly humiliated in the process. Jews were forced to gather on the afternoon in the courtyard of a garage at 43 Vitautas Avenue, in the center of the city. Some of them were killed with shovels, iron bars or by other barbaric methods. Lithuanian children were lifted onto the shoulders of their parents to catch a glimpse of the "Death Dealer of Kovno," a sight that one German regular army officer later described as the most frightful event he'd witnessed in the course of two world wars.

> On the concrete forecourt of the petrol station a blond man of medium height, aged about twenty-five, stood leaning on a wooden club, resting (allegedly Algirdas Antanas Pavalki). The club was as thick as his arm and came up to his chest. At his feet lay about fifteen to twenty dead or dying people. Water flowed continuously from a hose washing blood away into the drainage gully. Just a few steps behind this man some twenty men, guarded by armed civilians, stood waiting for their cruel execution in silent submission. In response to a cursory wave the next man stepped forward silently and was beaten to death with the wooden club in the most bestial manner, each blow accompanied by enthusiastic shouts from the audience.

Once the mound of the bodies at his feet had reached 50, the Death Dealer fetched an accordion, climbed to the top of the pile of the corpses, and played the Lithuanian national anthem. It was reported that the parents of the blond man who carried out the brutal murders were murdered by the Russians retreating from a German advance. Photos can be found on the internet.

The following excerpts are all from the translations from Lithuanian in the English edition of Joseph Levinson's *The Shoah (Holocaust) in Lithuania* (Vilnius: Vilna Gaon Jewish State Museum of Lithuania, 2006).

Excerpts

After centuries of slavery, Fellow Lithuanian, join the struggle for freedom. The hour of reckoning has come. Someone is on our side. Let us wreak hundredfold vengeance on the Jews and Communists for shedding the innocent blood of our countrymen. Enough of the Jews baking their matzos in Lithuanian blood.

[before 22 June 1941]

At the hour of reckoning all degenerates, traitors, sellouts, Communists, and Jews will be repaid at the price they themselves have set. [...] Judases, your days are numbered. The final hours of enslavement by Jews and Bolsheviks are approaching. After being ravaged and mauled by you, Lithuania is ready to rise up. Freedom will come to us over your corpses. Away with the Jews, Communists and Lithuanian Judases. All hail an independent new Lithuania.

[before 22 June 1941]

Our Lithuanian Brothers and Sisters!

[…] The fateful hour of final reckoning with the Jews has come. Lithuania must be liberated not only from Asiatic Bolshevik slavery but also from the age-old yoke of Jewry. In the name of the entire Lithuanian nation, the Lithuanian Activist Front most solemnly declares […]:

1 The ancient right of refuge in Lithuania, granted to the Jews during the times of Vytautas the Great, is completely and finally revoked.

2 Every Lithuanian Jew without exception is hereby sternly warned to abandon the land of Lithuania without delay.

3 All those Jews who exceptionally distinguished themselves with actions of betraying the Lithuanian state and of persecuting, torturing, or abusing our Lithuanian countrymen will be separately be held accountable and receive the appropriate punishment. It should become clear that at the fateful hour of reckoning and of Lithuanian rebirth especially guilty Jews are finding opportunities to escape somewhere in secret, it will be the duty of all honorable Lithuanians to take their own measures to apprehend such Jews, and if necessary, carry out the punishment. […]

The Jews are to be expelled completely and for all time. If any one of them should dare to believe that in the new Lithuania he will nevertheless find a refuge of sorts, let him learn today the irrevocable judgment on the Jews: in the newly restored Lithuania not even one Jew will have either the rights of citizenship or the means of earning a living. In this way, we will rectify past mistakes and repay Jewish villainy. In this way, we will lay a strong foundation for the happy future and creative work of our Aryan nation.

[not later than 22 June 1941]

APPENDIX D

The *Einsatzgruppen*

By the spring of 1943, the *Einsatzgruppen* and Order Police battalions had killed over a million Soviet Jews and tens of thousands of Soviet political commissars, partisans, Roma and institutionalized disabled persons

The *Einsatzgruppen* following the German army into the Soviet Union were composed of four battalion-sized operational groups.

Einsatzgruppe A. Franz Walter Stahlecker, commander (10 October 1900–23 March 1942). It fanned out from East Prussia across Lithuania, Latvia and Estonia toward Leningrad (now St. Petersburg). It massacred Jews in Kovno, Riga, and Vilna.

Einsatzgruppe B. Arthur Nebe (13 November 1894–21 March 1945). It started from Warsaw in occupied Poland, and fanned out across Belorussia toward Smolensk and Minsk, massacring Jews in Grodno, Minsk, Brest-Litovsk, Slonim, Gomel and Mogilev, among other places.

Einsatzgruppe C. SS-Brigadeführer Emil Otto Rasch earned 2 PhDs (7 December 1891–1 November 1948). It began operations from Krakow (Cracow) and fanned out across the western Ukraine toward Kharkov and Rostov-on-Don. Its personnel directed massacres in Lvov, Tarnopol, Zolochev, Kremenets, Kharkov, Zhitomir and Kiev, where famously in two days in late September 1941 units of *Einsatzgruppe* detachment 4a massacred 33,771 Kiev Jews in the ravine at Babi Yar.

Einsatzgruppe D. Otto Ohlendorf, a German economist (4 February 1907–8 June 1951). It operated farthest south. Its personnel carried out massacres in the southern Ukraine and the Crimea, especially in Nikolayev, Kherson, Simferopol, Sevastopol, Feodosiya and in the Krasnodar region.

There were fourteen additional *Einsatzgruppen* and two that were proposed: the United Kingdom and Tunis.

BIBLIOGRAPHY

Abel-Hirsch, N. (2015) *Bion on Sexuality*. London, UK: Melanie Klein Trust.
Aberbach, D. (1989) Creativity and the Survivor: The Struggle for Mastery. *International Review of Psycho-Analysis*, 16, 273–286.
Adair, M. J. (1993) A Speculation on Perversion and Hallucination. *International Journal of Psycho-Analysis*, 74, 81–92.
Adorno, T.W. (1973) Freudian Theory and the Pattern of Fascist Propaganda. In P. Roazen, *Sigmund Freud*. Princeton, NJ: Da Capo Press, pp. 82–102.
Adorno, T.W. (1997) *Aesthetic Theory*. Trans. R. Hullot-Kentor. London, UK: The Athlone Press.
Adorno, T.W., Fenkel-Brunswick, E., Levinson, D.J. and Sanford, R.N. (1950) *The Authoritarian Personality*. New York, NY: Norton.
Akhtar, S. (2009) *Comprehensive Dictionary of Psychoanalysis*. London, UK: Karnac Books.
Akhtar, S. and Parens, J. (eds) (2009) *Lying, Cheating, and Carrying On: Developmental, Clinical, and Sociocultural Aspects of Dishonesty and Deceit*. New York, NY: Aronson Inc.
Akpan, U. (2009) My Parents Bedroom. In *Say You're One of Them*. London: Little Brown and Company.
Alexander, L. (1948) War Crimes and Their Motivation: The Socio-Psychological Structure of the SS and the Criminalization of a Society. *Journal of Criminal Law and Criminology*, 39, 298–326.
Alexander, L. (1949) Medical Science Under Dictatorship. *Massachusetts Medical Society*, 241, 39–47.
Alford, C.F. (1994) *Group Psychology and Political Theory*. New Haven, CT: Yale University Press.
Allen, J.G. and Fonagy, P. (eds) (2006) *Handbook of Mentalization-Based Treatment*. Chichester, UK: Wiley.
Aly, G. (1999) *"Final Solution": Nazi Population Policy and the Murder of the European Jews*. London, UK: Arnold.
Aly, G. (2007) *Hitler's Beneficiaries: Plunder, Racial War, and the Nazi Welfare Hitler's Beneficiaries State*. New York, NY: Metropolitan Books.

Aly, G., Chroust. P. and Pross, C. (1994) *Cleansing the Fatherland: Nazi Medicine and Racial Hygiene*. Baltimore, MD: The Johns Hopkins University Press.

Aly, G. and Helm, S. (2002) *Architects of Annihilation: Auschwitz and the Logic of Destruction*. Trans. W. Templer. Princeton, NJ: Princeton University Press.

Anderson, B. (2016) *Imagined Communities: Reflections on the Origin and Spread of Nationalism*. London, UK: Verso.

Anderson, R. (ed.) (2016) Clinical Lectures on Klein and Bion. *The New Library of Psychoanalysis*, 14, 34–45.

Antonakis, J. (2012) Transformational and Charismatic Leadership. In *The Nature of Leadership*, ed. D.V. Day and J. Antonakis. Thousand Oaks, CA: Sage Publications, pp. 256–288.

Appry, M. and Stein, H. (1993) *Intersubjectivity, Projective Identification and Otherness*. Pittsburgh, PA: Duquesne University Press.

Arendt, H. (1951) *The Origins of Totalitarianism*. New York, NY: Harcourt Brace.

Arendt, H. (2014) *On Violence*. Fort Washington, PA: Harvest Books.

Asch, S.S. (1980) Suicide and the Hidden Executioner. *The International Review of Psychoanalysis*, 7, 51–60.

Athens, L. (1992) *The Creation of Dangerous Violent Criminals*. Urbana, IL: University of Illinois Press.

Athens, L. (2003) Violentization in Larger Social Context. In *Violent Acts and Violentization: Assessing, Applying, and Developing Lonnie Athens' Theories*, ed. L. Athens and J.T. Ulmer. Boston, MA: Elsevier Science, pp. 1–41.

Bae, S.H. and Ott, A.F. (2008) Predatory Behavior of Governments: The Case of Mass Killing. *Journal of Defense and Peace Economics*, 19, 107–125.

Bak, R.C. (1968) The Phallic Woman; The Ubiquitous Fantasy in Perversions. *Psychoanalytic Study of the Child*, 23, 15–36.

Balint, M. (1968) *The Basic Fault: Therapeutic Aspects of Regression*. New York, NY: Bruner Mazel.

Baranger, W. and Goldstein, N. (1980. About the Perverse Structure. *Revista de Psicoanálisis*, 37, 653–670.

Barkun, M. (1996) *Millennialism and Violence*. London, UK: Frank Cass and Co.

Baron-Cohen, S. (2011) *Zero Degrees of Empathy: A New Theory of Human Cruelty*. Bristol, UK: Penguin/Allen Lane.

Baron-Cohen, S., Golan, O., Chakrabarti, B. and Belmonte, M. (2008) Autism Spectrum Conditions. In *Social Cognition and Developmental Psychopathology*, ed. C, Sharp, P. Fonagy and A. Goodyer. New York, NY: Oxford University Press, pp. 29–56.

Bartov, O. (1996) *Murder in Our Midst*. New York, NY: Oxford University Press.

Bartov, O. (2000) *Mirrors of Destruction: War, Genocide, and Modern Identity*. New York, NY: Oxford University Press.

Bartov, O. (2003a) *Germany's War and the Holocaust: Disputed Histories*. Ithaca, NY: Cornell University Press.

Bartov, O. (2003b) The Roots of Modern Genocide. In *The Spectre of Genocide*, ed. R. Gellately and N. Kiernan. New York, NY: Cambridge University Press.

Baum, S. (2008) *The Psychology of Genocide*. New York, NY: Cambridge University Press.

Bentall, R.P. and Kaney, S. (2005) Attributional Lability in Depression and Paranoia. *British Journal of Clinical Psychology*, 44, 475–488.

Berger, B. (1986) *History and Hate: The Dimensions of Anti-Semitism*. Philadelphia, PA: The Jewish Publication Society.

Berreby, D. (2005) *Us and Them: The Science of Identity*. Chicago, IL: University of Chicago Press.

Bessel, R. (2009) *Nazism and War.* New York, NY: Modern Library.
Bessel, R. and Schumann, D. (2003) *Life After Death: Approaches to a Cultural and Social History of Europe.* New York, NY: The German Historical Institute, Cambridge University Press.
Bettelheim, B. (1943) Individual and Mass Behavior in Extreme Situations. Journal of Abnormal and Social Psychology, 38, 417–452.
Biess, F., Roseman, M. and Schissler, H. (2007) *Conflict, Catastrophe and Continuity: Essays on Modern German History.* Brooklyn, NY: Berghan Books.
Bingham, P.M. and Souza, J. (2009) *Death from a Distance and the Birth of a Humane Universe.* South Carolina, USA: BookSurge.
Bion, W.R. (1957) *Differentiation* of the Psychotic from the Non-Psychotic Personalities. International Journal of Psycho-Analysis, 38, 266–275.
Bion, W.R. (1961) *Experiences in Groups and Other Papers.* London, UK: Tavistock Publication.
Bion, W.R. (1962a) *Learning from Experience.* London, UK: Heinemann.
Bion, W.R. (1962b) The Psycho-Analytic Study of Thinking. *International Journal of Psycho-Analysis, 43,* 306–310.
Bion, W.R. (1965) *Transformation: Change from Learning to Growth.* New York, NY: Basic Books.
Bion, W.R. (1970) *Attention and Interpretation.* London, UK: Tavistock Publications.
Bion, W.R. (1984a) *Second Thoughts: Selected Papers on Psychoanalysis.* London, UK: Tavistock Publications.
Bion, W.R. (1984b) *Transformations.* London, UK: Karnac Classic.
Bion, W.R. (1997) *War Memoirs 1917–1919.* Ed. F. Bion. London, UK: Karnac Books.
Binion, R. (1979) *Hitler Among the Germans.* New York, NY: Elsevier.
Birksted-Breen, D. (1996) Phallus, Penis and Mental Space. *International Journal of Psychoanalysis, 77,* 649–657.
Birksted-Breen, D. (2016) *The Work of Psychoanalysis: Sexuality, Time and the Psychoanalytic.* London, UK: Routledge.
Bisi, N.E. (1969) About Male Perversion. *Revista de Psicoanálisis, 26(2),* 301–341.
Blos, P. 1984. Son and Father. *Journal of the American Psychoanalytic Association, 32,* 301–324.
Bloxham, D. (2009) *The Final Solution: A Genocide.* New York, NY: Oxford University Press.
Bohleber, W. (1992) Identity and the Self. The Importance of Recent Developmental Research for the Psychoanalytic Theory of the Self. *Psyche (Stuttgart), 46(4),* 336–365.
Boot, M. (2006) *War Made New: Technology Warfare and the Course of History.* New York, NY: Gotham Books.
Britton, R. (1992) The Oedipus Situation and the Depressive Position. In *Clinical Lectures on Klein and Bion,* ed. R. Anderson. London, UK: The New Library of Psychoanalysis, Vol. 14, pp. 34–45.
Britton, R. (1998) *Belief and Imagination: Explorations in Psychoanalysis.* London, UK: Routledge.
Britton, R. (1999) Preface. In *Psychoanalytic Understanding of Violence and Suicide,* ed. R.J. Perelberg. London, UK: The New Library of Psychoanalysis, pp. xviii–ixx.
Britton, R. (2003) Sex and Death. In Sex, Death and the Super-Ego. London, UK: Karnac, pp. 1–5.
Britton, R. (2004) Subjectivity, Objectivity, and Triangular Space. *Psychiatric Quarterly,* 5–46
Bromberg, N. and Small, V. (1983) *Hitler's Psychopathology.* New York, NY: International University Press.
Brown, L. (2005) The Cognitive Effects of Trauma Reversal of Alpha Function and the Formation of a Beta Screen. Psychoanalytic Quarterly, 74, 397–420.

Browning, C. (1992) *Ordinary Men: Reserve Police Battalion 101 and the Final Solution in Poland*. New York, NY: Harper Collins.
Browning, C. (2004) *The Origins of the Final Solution: The Evolution of Nazi Jewish Policy, September 1939–March 1942*. London, UK: William Heinemann.
Brunner, J. (2000) Eichmann's Mind: Psychological, Philosophical, and Legal Perspectives. *Theoretical Inquiries in Law*, 1(2), Article 7, 429–464.
Bytwerk, R.L. (2004) *Bending Spines: The Propaganda of Nazi Germany and the German Democratic Republic*. East Landing, MI: Michigan State University Press.
Campana, P. and Varese, F. (2013) Cooperation in Criminal Organizations: Kinship and Violence as Credible commitments. Rationality and Society, 25(3), 263–289.
Cariola, L.A. (2014) A Corpus-based Psychodynamic Analysis of Body Boundary Imagery in Hitler's Mein Kampf. Journal of Applied Psychoanalytic Studies, 11(4), 318–338.
Cartwright, D. (2002) *Psychoanalysis, Violence and Rage-Type Murder: Murdering Minds*. New York, NY: Bruner-Routledge.
Carveth, D.L. and Carveth, J.H. (2003) Fugitives from Guilt. Postmodern De-Moralization and the New Hysterias. American Imago, 60, 335–479.
Cath, S.H. (ed.) (1982) *Father and Child*. Boston, MA: Little, Brown.
Chalk, F. and Jonassohn, K. (1990) *The History and Sociology of Genocide: Analysis and Case Studies*. New Haven, CT: Yale University Press.
Chang, I. (1998) *The Rape of Nanking: The Forgotten Holocaust of World War II*. New York, NY: Penguin Books.
Charny, I.W. (1986) Genocide and Mass Destruction: Doing Harm to Others as a Missing Dimension in *Psychopathology*. *Psychiatry, 49*, 144–157.
Charny, I.W. (1991) Genocide Intervention and Prevention. Social Education, 55, 124–127.
Chasseguet-Smirgel, J. (1974) Perversion, Idealization and Sublimation. *International Journal of Psycho-Analysis*, 55, 349–357
Chasseguet-Smirgel, J. (1981) Loss of Reality in Perversions—With Special Reference to Fetishism. *Journal of the American Psychoanalytic Association*, 29, 511–534.
Chasseguet-Smirgel, J. (1984) *Creativity and Perversion*. New York, NY: W.W. Norton and Co.
Chasseguet-Smirgel, J. (1990) Reflections of a Psychoanalyst upon the Nazi Biocracy and Genocide. The International Review of Psycho-analysis, 17, 167–176.
Civitarese, G. (2008) "Caesura" as Bion's Discourse on Method. *International Journal of Psycho-Analysis*, 89, 1123–1143.
Coetzee, J.M. and Kurz, A. (2015) *The Good Story: Exchanges on Truth, Fiction and Psychotherapy*. New York, NY: Viking.
Confino, A. (2014) *A World Without Jews: The Nazi Imagination from Persecution to Genocide*. New Haven, CT: Yale University Press.
Cornwell, J. (2003) *Hitler's Scientists: Science, War and The Devils Pact*. New York, NY: The Penguin Group.
Crowe, D.M. (2004) *Oskar Schindler: The Untold Account of His Life*, Wartime Activities, and the True Story Behind the List. Boulder, CO: Westview Press.
Cunliffe. B. (2009) The Roots of Warfare. In *Conflict*, ed. M. Jones and A.C. Fabian. New York, NY: Cambridge University Press, pp. 63–81.
Daly, M. and Wilson, M. (1988) *Homicide: Foundations of Human Behavior*. New York, NY: Aldine Transaction.
Davidowicz, L. (1975) *The War against the Jews 1933–1945*. New York, NY: Holt, Rinehart, Winston.
Dicks, H.V. (1972) *Licensed Mass Murder: A Socio-Psychological Study of Some SS-Killers*. London, UK: Heinemann. For Sussex University Press.

De Bianchedi, E. et al. (2000) The Many Faces of Lies. In W.R. Bion: Between Past and Present. London, UK: Routledge, pp. 220–236.
Dederichs, M.R. (2009) *Heydrich: The Face of Evil*. Drexel Hill, PA: Casemate.
Diamond, M.J. (1995) Someone to Watch Over Me: The Father as the Original Protector of the Mother-Infant Dyad. *Psychoanalysis and Psychotherapy*, 12, 89–102.
Diamond, M.J. (1998) Fathers with Sons: Psychoanalytic Perspectives on "Good Enough" Fathering through the Life Cycle. *Gender and Psychoanalysis*, 3, 243–299.
Diamond, M.J. (2009) Masculinity and Its Discontents: Making Room for the "Mother" inside the Male—An Essential Achievement for Healthy Male Gender Identity. In *Heterosexual Masculinities: Contemporary Perspectives from Psychoanalytic Gender Theory*, ed. B. Reis and R. Grossmark. London, UK: Routledge, pp. 23–54.
Drescher, S. (1996) The Atlantic Slave Trade and the Holocaust: A Comparative Analysis. In *Is the Holocaust Unique? Perspectives on Comparative Genocide*, ed. A.S. Rosenbaum. Boulder, CO: Westview Press, pp. 103–124.
Eley, G. (2013) *Nazism as Fascism: Violence, Ideology, and the Ground of Consent in Germany 1930–1945*. Kindle Locations, pp. 539–541.
Elias, N. (1969) *The Civilizing Process, Volume 1*. London, UK: Blackwell Publishing.
Eller, J.D. (2006) *Violence and Culture: A Cross Cultural and Interdisciplinary Approach*. Belmont, CA: Belmont Wadsworth.
Enoch, S. (2004) The Contagion of Difference: Identity, Bio-politics and National Socialism. *Foucault Studies*, 1, 53–70.
Erikson, E. (1942) Hitler's Imagery and German Youth. *Psychiatry*, 5, 475–593.
Erikson, E. (1953) Wholeness and Totality: A Psychiatric Contribution. In *Totalitarianism*, ed. C.J. Friederich. Cambridge, MA: Harvard University Press, pp. 156–171.
Erikson, E. (1956) The Problem of Ego Identity. *Journal of the American Psychoanalytic Association*, 4, 96–121.
Erikson, E. (1980) *Identity and the Life Cycle*. New York, NY: W.W. Norton and Co.
Erikson, K. (1996) On Pseudospeciation and Social Speciation. In *Genocide, War and Human Survival*, ed. C.B. Strozier and M. Flynn. Lanham, MD: Bowman and Littlefield, pp. 51–58.
Eshel, O. (2005) Pentheus rather than Oedipus: On Perversion, Survival and Analytic "Presencing." *International Journal of Psycho-Analysis*, 86, 1071–1097.
Esteban, J., Mayoral, L. and Ray, D. (2012) Ethnicity and Conflict: An Empirical Study. *American Economic Review*, 102, 1310–1342.
Estaban, J. Morelli, M. and Rohner, D. (2010) Strategic Mass Killings. *Institute for Empirical Research in Economics, University of Zurich Working Paper No. 486*.
Etchegoyen, A. (1997) Inhibition of Mourning and the Replacement Child Syndrome. In *Female Experience: Three ~Generations of British Women Psychoanalysts on Work with Women*, ed. J. Raphael-Leff and R.J. Perelberg. London, UK: Routledge, pp. 195–251.
Etchegoyen, A. (2002) Psychoanalytic Ideas about Fathers. In *The Importance of Fathers: A Psychoanalytic Re-Evaluation*, ed. J. Trowell and A. Etchegoyen. New York, NY: Brunner-Routledge, pp. 20–41.
Evans, R.J. (2008) *The Third Reich at War*. New York, NY: Penguin.
Falk, A. (2006) Collective Psychological Processes in Anti-Semitism. *Jewish Political Studies Review*, 18, 1–2.
Federn, P. (1940) Psychoanalysis as a Therapy of Society. *The American Imago*, 1, 125–131.
Ferencz, B.B. (1979) *Less than Slaves. Jewish Forced Labor and the Quest for Compensation*. Cambridge, MA: Harvard University Press.
Fonagy, P. (1999) Final Remarks. In *Psychoanalytic Understanding of Violence and Suicide*, ed. R.J. Perelberg. London, UK: The New Library of Psychoanalysis, pp. 161–168.

Fonagy, P. (2003) Towards a Developmental Understanding of Violence. *The British Journal of Psychiatry*, 183(3), 190–192.

Fonagy, P. (2008) A Genuinely Developmental Theory of Sexual Enjoyment and Its Implications for Psychoanalytic Technique. *Journal of the American Psychoanalytic Association*, 56, 11–36.

Fonagy, P., Gergely, G. and Target. M. (2007) The Parent-Infant Dyad and the Construction of the Subjective Self. *Journal of Child Psychology and Psychiatry*, 48(3–4), 288–328.

Fonagy, P., Gergely, G., Jurist, E. and Target, M. (2002) *Affect Regulation, Mentalization and the Development of the Self*. New York, NY: Other Press.

Fonagy, P. and Target, M. (1995) Towards understanding violence: The use of the body and the role of the father. *International Journal of Psychoanalysis*, 76, 487–502.

Fornari, F. (1974) *The Psychoanalysis of War*. New York, NY: Doubleday Anch Books.

Foucault, M. (1976) *The History of Sexuality*. Trans. D. Macey, ed. M. Bertani. London, UK: Penguin Books.

Foucault, M. (1978) Part 5: Right of Death and Power over Life. *The History of Sexuality*, Volume 1. London, UK: Allen Lane.

Foucault, M. (2000) Power. In *Essential Works of Michel Foucault 1954–1984* Volume 3, ed. J. D. Faubion. New York, NY: New Press.

Foucault, M. (2003) Michel Foucault: "Society must be defended." Lectures at the Collège de France. London, UK: Picador.

Frankfurter, D. (2006) *Evil Incarnate: Rumors of Demonic Conspiracy and Ritual Abuse in History*. Princeton, NJ: Princeton University Press.

Franks, B., Bangerter, A. and Bauer M.W. (2013) Conspiracy Theories as Quasi-religious Mentality: An Integrated Account from Cognitive Science, Social Representations Theory, and Frame Theory. *Frontiers in Psychology*, 4, 424.

Freeman, T. (2008) Psychoanalytic Concepts of Fatherhood: Patriarchal Paradoxes and the Presence of an Absent Authority. *Studies in Gender and Sexuality*, 9, 113–139.

Freud, A. (1937) *The Ego and the Mechanisms of Defense*. London, UK: Hogarth Press.

Freud, S. (1896) *Beyond the Pleasure Principle: Group Psychology and Other Works—Sigmund Freud*. Trans. J. Strachey (1986). London, UK: The Hogarth Press and the Institute of Psycho-Analysis.

Freud. S. (1915) *Totem and Taboo. The Standard Edition of the Complete. Psychological Works of Sigmund Freud*, ed. J. Strachy. London, UK: The Hogart Press.

Freud, S. (1932–1936) *Why War? The Standard Edition of the Complete Psychological Works of Sigmund Freud*, Volume XXII. London, UK: The Hogart Press.

Friedlander, H. (1995) *The Origins of Nazi Genocide: From Euthanasia to the Final Solution*. Chappell Hill, NC: The University of North Carolina Press.

Friedlander, S. (2007) *The Years of Extermination: Nazi Germany and the Jews 1939–1945*. New York, NY: Harper Collins.

Frosh, S. (2005) *Hate and the "Jewish Science": Anti-Semitism, Nazism and Psychoanalysis*. London, UK: Palgrave McMillan.

Gaddini, E. (1982) Early Defensive Fantasies and the Psychoanalytical Process. *International Journal of Psycho-Analysis*, 63, 379–388.

Gailbraith, J.K. (2006) *The Predator State*. San Francisco, CA: Mother Jones.

Gallese, V. (2008) Empathy, Embodied Simulation, and the Brain: Commentary on Aragno Zepf/Hartmann. *Journal of the American Psychoanalytic Association*, 56, 769–780.

Ganzarain, R. (2000) Group-as-a-whole Dynamics in Work with Traumatized Patients. In *Group Psychotherapy for Psychological Trauma*, ed. R. Klein and V. Schermer. New York, NY: Guilford Press, pp. 89–115.

Gass, R.H. and Seiter, J.S. (2013) *Persuasion: Social Influence and Compliance Gaining*. London, UK: Routledge.

Gavrilets, S. (2012) Human Origins and the Transition from Promiscuity to Pair-bonding. *Proceedings of the National Academy of Sciences of the USA*, 109(25), 9923–9928.

Geddes, B., Wright, J., and Frantz, E. (2014) Authoritarian Regimes: New Data Set: Autocratic Breakdown and Regime Transitions. *Perspectives on Politics*, 12(1), 313–331.

Gellately, R. (2001) *Backing Hitler*. New York, NY: Oxford University Press.

Gellately, R. and Kiernan, B. (2003) *The Spector of Genocide: Mass Murder in Historical Perspective*. New York, NY: Cambridge University Press.

Gerlach, C. (2010) *Extremely Violent Societies*. London, UK: Cambridge University Press.

Gerlach, C. (2016) *The Extermination of the European Jews*. New York, NY: Cambridge University Press.

Gibson, J.J. (1977) The Theory of Affordances. In *Perceiving, Acting, and Knowing Towards an Ecological Psychology*, ed. R. Shaw and J. Bransford. Hoboken, NJ: John Wiley and Son, pp. 67–82.

Gilbert, G.M. (1950) *The Psychology of Dictatorship: Based on the Leaders of Nazi Germany*. New York, NY: Ronald Press.

Gilbert, G.M. (1995) *Nuremberg Diary. New York*. New York, NY: Da Capo Press Liveright Pub. (Original work published 1961.)

Girard, R. (1977) *Violence and the Sacred*. Baltimore, MD: Johns Hopkins University Press.

Girard, R. (1987) *Oedipus Unbound: Selected Writings on Rivalry and Desire*. Stanford, CA: Stanford University Press.

Glasser, M. (1979) Some Aspects on the Role of Aggression in the Perversions. In *Sexual Deviations*, ed. I. Rosen. Oxford, UK: Oxford University Press, pp. 278–305.

Glasser, M. (1986) Identification and Its Vicissitudes as Observed in the Perversions. *International Journal of Psycho-Analysis*, 67, 9–17.

Glover, E. (1938) A Note on Idealization *International Journal of Psycho-Analysis*, 19, 91–96.

Goldensohn, L. (2004) *The Nuremberg Diary*. Ed. R. Gellately. New York, NY: A.A. Knopf.

Goldhagen, D.J. (1996) *Hitler's Willing Executioners: Ordinary Germans and the Holocaust*. New York, NY: A.A Knopf.

Goldhagen, D.J. (2009) *Worse than War*. New York, NY: Public Affairs.

Gonen, D. (2000) *The Roots of Nazi Psychology: Hitler's Utopian Barbarism*. Lexington, KY: The University of Kentucky Press.

Gorman, S. and Gorman, J. (2017) *Denying to the Grave: Why We Ignore Facts that Will Save Us*. New York, NY: Oxford University Press.

Green, A. (1999) *The Work of the Negative*. Trans. A. Weller. London, UK: Free Association Books.

Green, A. (2000) *The Chains of Eros: The Sexual in Psychoanalysis*. Trans. L. Thurston. London, UK: Karnac. (Originally published 1997.)

Green, A. (2001) *Life Narcissism, Death Narcissism*. Trans. A. Weller. London, UK and New York, NY: Free Association Books.

Green, A. (2002) A Dual Conception of Narcissism: Positive and Negative Organization. *Psychoanalytic Quarterly*, 71, 631–649.

Greenacre, P. (1987) *Trauma, Growth and Personality*. London, UK: Karnac Books.

Griffin, R. (2012) *Terrorist Creed: Fanatical Violence and the Human Need for Meaning*. New York, NY: Springer Publishing.

Gross, J.T. (2001) *Neighbors: The Destruction of the Jewish Community in Jedwabne, Poland*. Princeton, NJ: Princeton University Press.

Grossman, D. (2009) *On Killing: The Psychological Cost of Learning to Kill in War and Society*. Boston, MA: Back Bay Books.

Grotstein, J.S. (1985) *Splitting and Projective Identification*. New York, NY: Jason Aronson.

Grotstein, J.S. (1996) Bion's "Transformation in 'O'", the "Thing-in-itself", and the "Real": Toward the Concept of the "Transcendent Position". *Melanie Klein & Object Relations, 14* (2), 109–141.
Grotstein, J.S. (1998) Bion W.R. War Memoirs 1917–1919 Francesca Bion (ed.) London: Karnac Books, 1997. Journal of Analytic Psychology, 43, 610–614.
Grotstein, J.S. (2009) *A Beam of Intense Darkness: Wilfred Bion's Legacy to Psychoanalysis.* London: Routledge.
Haidu, P. (1992) The Dialectics of Unspeakability: Language, Silence and the Narratives of Desubjectification. In *Probing the Limits of Representation: Nazism and the "Final Solution"*, ed. S. Friedländer. Cambridge, MA: Harvard University Press, pp. 277–299.
Haralambos, M., Heald, R.M. and Holborn, M. (2004) *Sociology Themes and Perspectives.* London, UK: Collins Educational.
Harari, Y.N. (2014) *Sapiens: A Brief History of Humankind.* London, UK: Harvill Secke.
Harff, B. and Gurr, T.R. (1988) Toward Empirical Theory of Genocides and Politicides: Identification and Measurement of Cases Since 1945. *International Studies Quarterly*, 32, 359–371.
Harris, M. (2010) *The Aesthetic Development: The Poetic Spirit of Psychoanalysis Essays on Bion, Meltzer, Keats.* London, UK: Karnac Books.
Hasselbach, I. and Reiss, T. (1996) How Nazis are Made. *The New Yorker*, January, 36–57.
Hatch, J. M. and Cunliffe, A. L. (2013) *Organization Theory: Modern, Symbolic and Postmodern Perspectives.* Oxford, UK: Oxford University Press.
Hatzfeld, J. (2003) *Machete Season: The Killers in Rwanda Speak.* New York, NY: Farrar, Strauss and Giroux.
Haynal, A., Molnar, M. and de Puymehe, G. (1983) *Fanaticism: A Historical and Psychoanalytic Study.* New York, NY: Shocken Books.
Hebb, D.O. (1949) *The Organization of Behavior: A Neuropsychological Theory.* New York, NY: John Wiley & Sons.
Hedges, C. (2002) *War Is a Force That Gives Us Meaning.* New York, NY: Perseus Book Group.
Herzog, J.M. (1982) On Father Hunger: The Father's Role in the Modulation of Aggressive Drive and Fantasy. In *Father and Child*, ed. S.H. Cath, A.R. Gurwitt and J.M. Ross. Boston, MA: Little, Brown, pp. 163–174.
Herzog, J.M. (2002) *Father Hunger: Explorations with Adults and Children.* Hillsdale, NJ: Analytic Press.
Hinshelwood, R.D. (2005) The Individual and the Influence of Social Settings: A Psychoanalytic Perspective on the Interaction of the Individual and Society. *British Journal of Psychotherapy*, 22, 155–166.
Hinshelwood, R.D. (2008) Repression and Splitting: Towards a Method of Conceptual Comparison. *The International Journal of Psychoanalysis*, 89(3), 503–521.
Hilberg, R. (1961) *The Origins of Nazi Genocide: From Euthanasia to the Final Solution* (first edition). Chapel Hill, NC: University of North Carolina Press.
Hilberg, R. (1985) *The Destruction of the European Jews.* New York, NY: Holmes & Meier.
Hinton, A.L. (2002) *Annihilating Difference: The Antropology of Genocide.* Berkeley, CA: University of California Press.
Hirsch, H (1995) *Genocide and the Politics of Memory: Studying Death to Preserve Life.* Chapel Hill, NC: University of North Carolina Press.
Hoggett, P. (1998) The Internal Establishment Bion's Legacy to Groups. In *Selected Contributions from the International Centennial Conference on the work of W.R. Bion* ed. P. Bion, F. Talamo, S. Borgogno and A. Merciai. London, UK: Karnac, pp. 9–24.
Hohne, H. (2000) *The Order of the Deaths Head: The Story of Hitler's SS.* Trans. R. Barry. Classic Military History. London, UK: Penguin Books.

Hopper, E. (2003) *Traumatic Experience in the Unconscious Life of Groups: The Fourth Basic Assumption: Aggregation/Massification of (ba) I:A/M*. London, UK: Jessica Kingsley.
Hunt, L. (2007) *Inventing Human Rights: A History*. New York, NY: W.W. Norton and Co.
Huntington, S. (1996) *The Clash of Civilization: Remaking of World Order*. New York, NY: Simon and Schuster.
Hyatt-Williams, A (1998) *Cruelty, Violence, and Murder: Understanding the Criminal Mind*. New York, NY: Jason Aronson.
Jackson, K.D. (1992) *Cambodia 1975–1978 Rendezvous with Death*. Princeton, NJ: Princeton University Press.
Jacques, E. (1955) Social Systems as a Defense against Persecutory and Depressive Anxiety. In *New Directions in Psychoanalysis*, ed. M. Klein, P. Heiman and R.E. Money-Kyrle. New York, NY: Basic Books.
Jacques, E. (1990) A Contribution to the Discussion of Freud's Group Psychology and the Analysis of the Ego. In *Creativity and Work*. New York, NY: International Universities Press, pp. 361–371.
Jones, M. and Fabian, A.C. (eds) (2009) *Conflict*. New York, NY: Cambridge University Press.
Kaes, R. (1993) *Le groupe et le sujet du groupe*. Paris, France: Dunod.
Kaes, R. (2007) *Linking, Alliances and Shared Space*. London, UK: International Psychoanalysis Library.
Kaplan, J.T., Gimbel, S.I. and Harris, S. (2016) Neural Correlates of Maintaining One's Political Beliefs in the Face of Counterevidence. *Scientific Reports*, 6, 39589.
Kaplan, M. (1999) *Between Dignity and Despair: Jewish Life in Nazi Germany*. New York, NY: Oxford University Press.
Katz, S.T. (1994) *The Holocaust in Historical Context: The Holocaust and Mass Death Before the Modern Age* Vol. 1. New York, NY: Oxford University Press.
Keeley, L.H. (1997) *War Before Civilization: The Myth of the Peaceful Savage*. New York, NY: Oxford University Press.
Kegan, R (1982) *The Evolving Self: Problem and Process in Human Development*. Cambridge, MA: Harvard University Press.
Keller, J. and Anderson, H. (1937) *Der Jude als Verbrecher*. Berlin, pp. 11–12. Quoted in Confino, A. (2014) *A World Without Jews: The Nazi Imagination from Persecution to Genocide*. New Haven, CT: Yale University Press.
Kelly, M. (1995) The Road to Paranoia. *The New Yorker*, June 19, pp. 62–64.
Kelman, H.C. and Hamilton, L. (1989) *Crimes of Obedience. Toward a Social Psychology of Authority and Responsibility*. New Haven, CT: Yale University Press.
Kemperer, V. (2013) *The Language of the Third Reich*. Trans. M. Bady. London, UK: Bloomsbury.
Kernberg, O.F. (1998) *Ideology, Conflict, and Leadership in Groups and Organizations*. New Haven, CT: Yale University Press.
Kernberg, O.F. (2003a) Socially Sanctioned Violence: Part 1. The Large Group as Society. In *The Large Group Revisited*, ed. S. Schneider and H. Weinberg. International Library of Group Analysis. Vancouver, BC: UBC Press, pp. 126–149.
Kernberg, O.F. (2003b) Sanctioned Social Violence: A Psychoanalytic View Part II. *International Journal of Psychoanalysis*, 84, 953–968.
Kershaw, I. (1987) *The Hitler Myth. Image and Reality in the Third Reich*. New York, NY: Oxford University Press.
Kershaw, I. (1991) *Hitler: Profiles in Power*. Essex, England: Pearson Education Limited.
Khan, M.M.R. (1979) *Alienation in Perversions*. New York, NY: International University Press.

Khuene, T. (2010) *Belonging and Genocide: Hitler's Community, 1918–1945*. New Haven, CT: Yale University Press.

Kiernan, B. (2007) *Blood and Soil: A World History of Genocide and Extermination from Sparta to Darfur*. New Haven, CT: Yale University Press.

Klee, E., Dressen, W. and Riess, V. (eds) (1991) *"The Good Old Days": The Holocaust as seen by its Perpetrators and Bystanders*. New York, NY: Konecky & Konecky.

Kogon, E. (2006) *The Theory and Practice of Hell: The German Concentration Camp and the System Behind It* (2nd edn). New York, NY: Farrar, Strauss and Giroux.

Koonz, C. (2003) *The Nazi Conscience*. Cambridge, MA: Harvard University Press.

Krausnick, H. and Broszat, M. (1982) *Anatomy of the SS State*. London, UK: Granada Publishing.

Kris, E. and Speier, H. (1944) *German Radio Propaganda: Report on Home Broadcasts during the War*. New York, NY: Oxford University Press.

Kuehne, T. (2010) *Belonging and Genocide: Hitler's Community, 1918–1945*. New Haven, CT: Yale University Press.

Kuhl, S. (2016) *Ordinary Organization: Why Normal Men Carried out the Holocaust*. Malden, MA: Polity Press.

Kuran, T. (1995) *Private Truths, Public Lies: The Social Consequences of Public Preference Falsification*. Cambridge, MA: Harvard University Press.

Lacan, J. (1955–1956) *The Psychoses, The Seminar of Jacques Lacan*. Ed. J.-A. Miller. Book III trans. R. Grig. London, UK: Routledge (1993 edition).

Lang, B. (1990) *Act and Idea in the Nazi Genocide*. Chicago, IL: The University of Chicago Press.

Langer, W.C. (1972) *The Mind of Adolf Hitler: The Secret War Time Report*. New York, NY: Basic Books.

Langerbein, H. (2004) *Hitler's Death Squads, the Logic of Mass Murder*. College Station, TX: Texas A. & M. University Press.

Larner, C. (2000) *Enemies of God: The Witch Hunt in Scotland*. Edinburgh, UK: John Donald Publishers.

Lawrence, W.G., Bain, A. and Gould, L.J. (1996) The Fifth Basic Assumption. *Free Associations*, 6(37), 28–55.

Lemkin, R. (1944) *Axis Rule in Occupied Europe: Laws of Occupation, Analysis of Government, Proposals for Redress*. Washington, DC: Carnegie Endowment for International Peace, Division of International Law.

Lester, E.P. (1986) Narcissism and the Personal Myth. *Psychoanalytic Quarterly*, 55, 452–473.

Levi, P. (1986) *The Drowned and the Saved*. London, UK: Abacus Books.

Liebman, S.J. and Abell, S.C. (2000) The Forgotten Parent No More: A Psychoanalytic Reconsideration of Fatherhood. *Psychoanalytic Psychology*, 17, 88–105.

Lifton, R.J. (1986) *The Nazi Doctors. Medical Killing and the Psychology of Genocide*. New York, NY: Basic Books.

Lifton, R.J. (1987) The Image of "The End of the World": A Psychohistorical Review. In *Facing Apocalypse*. Dallas, TX: Spring Publication, pp. 25–48.

Lifton, R.J. (1991) *Death in Life: Survivors of Hiroshima*. Chapel Hill, NC: North Carolina Press.

Lifton, R.J. (1999) *Destroy the World in Order to Save It. Aum Shinrikyo, Apocalyptic Violence, and the New Global Terrorism*. New York, NY: Henry Holt and Co.

Lifton, R.J. and Markusen, E. (1988) *The Genocidal Mentality: Nazi Holocaust and Nuclear Threat*. New York, NY: Basic Books.

Lochner, L.P. (1943) *What about Germany*. New York, NY: Dodd Mead and Company.

Marcia, J.E. (1988) Common Processes Underlying Ego Identity, Cognitive/Moral Development, and Individuation. In *Self, Ego, and Identity: Integrative Approaches*, ed. D. K. Lapsley and F.C. Power. New York: Springer-Verlag, pp. 211–266.

Mann, M. (1995) *The Dark Side of Democracy: Explaining Ethnic Cleansing*. Cambridge, UK: Cambridge University Press.

Mann, M. (2000) Were the Perpetrators of Genocide "Ordinary Men" or "Real Nazis"? Results from Fifteen Hundred Biographies. *Holocaust and Genocide Studies* 14, 331–366.

Marcuse, H. (2001) *The Legacies of Dachau: The Uses and Abuses of a Concentration Camp, 1933–2001*. New York, NY: Cambridge University Press.

Mazower M. (2009) *Hitler's Empire: How the Nazis Ruled Europe*. New York, NY: Penguin Books.

McDougall, J. (1972) Primal Scene and Sexual Perversion. *International Journal of Psycho-Analysis*, 53, 371–384.

McDougall, J. (1986) Identifications, neo-needs and neo-sexualities. *International Journal of Psycho-Analysis*, 67, 19–31.

McElhaney, K.B. and Allen, J. P. (2001) Autonomy and Adolescent Social Functioning: The Moderating Effect of Risk. *Child Development*, 72, 220–235.

Meltzer, D. (1968) Terror, Persecution, Dread—A Dissection of Paranoid Anxieties. *International Journal of Psychoanalysis*, 49, 396–400.

Meltzer, D. (1973) *Sexual States of Mind* (first edition). Perthshire: Clunie Books.

Meltzer, D. (1981) The Kleinian Expansion of Freud's Metapsychology. *International Journal of Psycho-Analysis*, 62, 177–185.

Meltzer D. (1986) Clinical Application of Bion's Concept "Transformations in Hallucinosis". In *Studies in Extended Metapsychology*. London, UK: Clune Press for the Roland Harris Trust Library, pp. 105–115.

Meltzer, D. (1994) *Sincerity and Other Works: Collected Papers by Donald Meltzer*. Ed. A. Hahn. London, UK: Karnac Books.

Meltzer, D. (2008) *Sexual States of Mind* (revised edition). London. UK. Karnac Books.

Meyer, J. (2011) The Development and Organizing Function of Perversion: The Example of Transvestism. *International Journal of Psycho-Analysis*, 92, 311–332.

Miale, F. and Selzer, M. (1975) *The Nuremberg Mind*. New York, NY: Quadrangle Books.

Midlarsky, M. (2005) *The Killing Trap: Genocide in the Twentieth Century*. New York, NY: Cambridge University Press.

Mitscherlich, A. and Mitscherlich, M. (1975) *The Inability to Mourn: Principles of Collective Behavior*. New York, NY: Grove Press.

Mizen, R. and Morris, M. (2007) *On Aggression and Violence: An Analytic Perspective*. New York, NY: Palgrave.

Mohamed, S. (2015) Of Monsters and Men: Perpetrator Trauma and Mass Atrocity. *Columbia Law Review*, 115. Berkeley Law School Repository.

Moore, R.I. (1990) *The Formation of a Persecutory Society*. Oxford, UK: Blackwell Publisher.

Money-Kyrle, R.E. (1951) *Psychoanalysis* and Politics A Contribution to the Psychology of Politics and Morals. London, UK: Gerald Duckworth.

Money-Kyrle, R.E. (2015) *The Collected Papers of Roger Money-Kyrle*, ed. R. Money-Kyrle, D. Meltzer, E. O'Shaughnessy and M. Harris Williams. London, UK: UK Meltzer Trust.

Moses, A.D. and Stone, D. (2007) *Colonialism and Genocide*. London, UK: Routledge.

Muller-Claudius, M. (1948) *Der Antisemitismus und das deutche*. Frankfurt au main: Verhangnis.

Murray, S.J. (2005) Thanatopolitics: The Use of Death for Mobilizing Political Life. Available at: www.academia.edu/186168/Thanatopolitics_On_the_Use_of_Death_for_Mobilizing_Political_Life

Musia, B. (2000) The Origins of "Operation Reinhard": The Decision Making Process for the Mass Murder of the Jews in the General Government. *Yad Vashem Studies*, XXVIII. Jerusalem, Israel: Shoah Resource Center, pp. 113–153.

Nadelson, T. (2005) *Trained to Kill: Soldiers at War*. Baltimore, MD: The Johns Hopkins University Press.

Narroll, R. (1964) On Ethnic Unit Classification. *Current Anthropology*, 5, 283–312.

Neitzel, S. and Welzer, H. (2012) *Soldaten: On Fighting, Killing, and Dying*. New York, NY: A Knopf.

Nolzen, A. (2011) *The Nazi Party and its Violence against Jews, 1933–1939*. Yad Vashem, The Holocaust Martyrs' and Heroes' Remembrance Authority

Ogden, T. (1986), The Matrix of the Mind. Northvale, NJ: Jason Aronson.

Ogden, T. (1988) Misrecognitions and the Fear of Not Knowing. *Psychoanalytic Quarterly*, 57, 643–666.

Ogden, T.H. (1996) The Perverse Subject of Analysis. *Journal of the American Psychoanalytic Association*, 44, 1121–1146.

Ogden. T.H. (1998) *Reverie and Interpretation: Sensing Something Human*. New York, NY: Jason Aronson.

Ornstein, A. (2012) Mass Murder and the Individual: Psychoanalytic Reflections on Perpetrators and Their Victims. *International Journal of Group Psychotherapy*, 62, 1–20.

O'Shaughnessy, E. (1990) Can a Liar be Psychoanalysed? *International Journal of Psycho-Analysis*, 71, 187–195.

Ostow, M. (1986) The Psychodynamics of Apocalyptic: Discussion of Papers on Identification and the Nazi Phenomenon. *International Journal of Psycho-Analysis*, 67, 277–285.

Ostow, M. (1988) Apocalyptic Thinking in Mental Illness and Social Disorder. *Psychoanalysis and Contemporary Thought*, 11, 285–297.

Otterbein, K.F. (ed.) (1994) *Feuding and Warfare: Selected Works of Keith F. Otterbein*. Langhorne, PA: Gordon and Breach.

Otterbein, K.F. (2004) *How War Began*. College Station. TX: Texas A. & M. University Anthropology Series.

Overy, R. (2001) *Interrogations: Nazi Elite in Allied Hands 1945*. New York, NY: Penguin Books.

Patterson, O. (1990) *Slavery and Social Death; A Comparative Study*. Cambridge, MA: Harvard University Press.

Pearlman, M. (1987) When Heaven and Earth Collapse: Myths of the End of the World. P 170–195. In *Facing Apocalypse*, ed. R. Bosnack. Dallas, TX: Spring Publication.

Perelberg, R.J. (1999a) The Interplay Between Identifications and Identity in the Analysis of a Violent Young Man: Issues of Technique. *International Journal of Psycho-Analysis*, 80, 31–45.

Perelberg, R.J. (1999b) *Psychoanalytic Understanding of Violence and Suicide*. London, UK: The New Library of Psychoanalysis.

Perelberg, R.J. (1999c) Psychoanalytic Understanding of Violence and Suicide: A Review of the Literature and Some New Formulations. In *Psychoanalytic Understanding of Violence and Suicide*. London, UK: The New Library of Psychoanalysis, pp. 1–16.

Pergher, R. and Roseman, M. (2013) Holocaust: An Imperial Genocide? *Dapim; Studies on the Holocaust* 27(1): 42–49.

Pick, D. (1993) *War Machine: The Rationalization of Slaughter in the Modern Age*. New Haven, CT: Yale University Press.

Pick, D. (2009) In Pursuit of the Nazi Mind. The Development of Psychoanalysis in the Allied Struggle Against Germany. *Psychoanalysis and History*, 11, 137–157.

Pick, D. (2012) *The Search for the Nazi Mind*. London, UK: Oxford University Press.

Pinker, S. (2011) *The Better Angels of Our Nature*. New York, NY: Viking.
Plesch, D. (2017) *Human Rights after Hitler: The Lost History of Prosecuting Axis War Crimes*. Washington, DC: Georgetown University Press.
Polak, J. (2014) *After the Holocaust the Bells Still Ring*. New York, NY: Urim Publications.
Poliakov, L. (1996) *The Aryan Myth* (3rd edn). New York, NY: Barnes and Noble.
Power, S. (2002) *A Problem from Hell*. New York, NY: Harper Collins.
Prince, R. (2009) Psychoanalysis Traumatized: The Legacy of the Holocaust. *The American Journal of Psychoanalysis*, 69(3), 179–194.
Proctor R.N (1988) *Racial Hygiene: Medicine Under the Nazis*. Cambridge, MA: Harvard University Press.
Quinn, N. (2003) Cultural Selves. In *The Self: From Soul to Brain*, ed. J. LeDoux, J. Debiec and H. Moss. *Annals New York Academy of Sciences*, Vol. 1001. New York: New York Academy of Sciences, pp. 145–176.
Quinn, N. (2005) Universals in Child Rearing. *Anthropological Theory*, 5, 477–516.
Rank, O. (1971) *The Double. A Psychoanalytic Study*. Trans. and ed. with an Introduction H. Tucker, Jr. Chapel Hill, NC: The University of North Carolina Press.
Reich, W. (1933) *Massenpsychologie des Faschismus*. Published in English in 1970. New York, NY: Farrar, Strauss and Giroux.
Reich, W. (1980) *The Mass Psychology of Fascism*. Trans. V. Carfago. New York, NY: Farrar, Strauss and Giroux.
Redles, D. (2008) *Hitler's Millennial Reich: Apocalyptic Belief and the Search for Solution*. New York, NY: New York University Press.
Rees, L. (2012) *The Charisma of Hitler*. London, UK: Ebury Press.
Resnick, M.N. and Nunno, V.J. (1991) The Nuremberg Mind Redeemed: A Comprehensive Analysis of the Rorschachs of Nazi War Criminals. *Journal of Personality Assessment*, 57(1), 19–29.
Rey, H. (1994) *Universals of Psychoanalysis: In the Treatment of Psychotic and Borderline States*. London, UK: Free Association Books.
Rey, J.H. (1986) Reparation. *Journal of the Melanie Klein Society,* 4(1), 5–35.
Ricoeur, P. (1981) *Hermeneutics and the Human Sciences*. New York, NY: Cambridge University Press.
Rioch, M.J. (1970) The Work of Wilfred Bion on Groups. *Psychiatry*, 33, 56–66.
Roseman, M. (2002) *The Wannsee Conference and the Final Solution: Reconsideration*. New York, NY: MacMillan.
Roseman, M. (2007) Beyond Conviction? Perpetrators, Ideas and Action in the Holocaust in Historiographical Perspective. In *Conflict, Catastrophe and Continuity: Essays on Modern German History*, ed. F. Biess, M. Roseman and H. Schissler Brooklyn, NY: Berghan Books, pp. 83–103.
Rosenbaum, R. (1998) *Explaining Hitler*. New York, NY: Random House.
Rosenfeld, H. (1971) A Clinical Approach to the Psychoanalytic Theory of the Life and Death Instincts: An Investigation into Aggressive Aspects of Narcissism. *International Journal of Psycho-Analysis*, 52, 169–178.
Roth, B. (1991) Some of the Origins of Freud's Paper on Group Psychology. In *Psychoanalytic Group Therapy: Essays in Honor of Saul Scheidlinger*. New York, NY: International University Press, pp. 287–308.
Roth, B. (2007) Second Thoughts at Ground Zero. *Psychoanalytic Review,* 94(2), 245–264.
Roth, B. (2013) Bion, Basic Assumptions, and Violence: A Corrective Reappraisal. International Journal of Group Psychotherapy, 63(4), 524–543.

Roth, B. (2015) Banal No More: An Essay on the Film Hannah Arendt, with Special Reference to Eichmann and the Nazi Killing Groups. *Psychological Review*, 102, 265–289.

Roth, P.A. (2004) Hearts of Darkness: Perpetrator History and Why There Is No Why. *History of the Human Sciences*, 17, 211–251.

Safrian, H. (2010) *Eichmann's Men*. New York, NY: Cambridge University Press.

Sánchez-Medina, A. (2002) Perverse Thought. *International Journal of Psycho-Analysis*, 83, 1345–1359.

Sandler, P.C. (2009) *A Clinical Application of Bion's Concepts*. London, UK: Karnac Books.

Sandler P.C. (2015) *An Introduction to W.R. Bion's A Memoir of the Future*, Volume Two. London, UK: Karnac.

Scaruffi, P. (2006) *The Worst Genocides of the 20th and 21st Century*. Available at: www.scaruffi.com/politics/dictat.html

Schlossberg, R. (2011) *The Einsatzgruppen*. Kindle edition.

Schmitt, K. (1996) *The Concept of the Political*. Chicago, IL: The University of Chicago Press (originally published 1932).

Schulman, K. and Ross, M. (2010) The Benefits, Costs, and Paradox of Revenge. *Journal of Social and Personality Psychology*, 4, 1193–1205.

Schwartz, S. (2001) The Evolution of Eriksonian and Neo-Eriksonian Identity Theory and Research: A Review and Integration. *Identity: An International Journal of Theory and Research*, 1, 7–58.

Seddone, G. (2013) *The Cooperative Filter: Essays on Mind, Intentionality and We Intentionality*. Anchen, Germany: Shaker Verlag.

Seethalret, J., Karmasin, M., Meleschik, G. and Wohlert R. (eds) (2013) *Selling War: The Role of the Mass Media in Hostile Conflicts from World War I to the "War on Terror"*. Chicago, IL: Intellect Books, University of Chicago Press.

Segal, H. (1972) A Delusional System as a Defence against the Re-emergence of a Catastrophic Situation. *International Journal of Psycho-Analysis*, 53, 393–401.

Segal, H. (1996) From Hiroshima to the Gulf War and After: A Psychoanalytic Perspective. In *Psychoanalysis in Contexts: Paths between Theory and Modern Culture*, ed. A. Elliott and S. Frosh. London, UK: Routledge, pp. 191–204.

Segev, T. (1987) *Soldiers of Evil. The Commandants of the Nazi Concentration Camps*. Jerusalem, Israel: Domino Press.

Segev, T. (1993) *The Seventh Million. The Israelis and the Holocaust*. New York, NY: Hill and Wang.

Semelin, J. (2009) *Purify and Destroy: The Political Uses of Massacres and Genocide*. New York, NY: Columbia University Press.

Sharp, C. and Fonagy, P. (2008) Social Cognition and Attachment related Disorders. In *Social Cognition and Developmental Psychopathology*, ed. C. Sharp, P. Fonagy and I. Goodyer. New York, NY: Oxford University Press.

Showalter, E. (1997) *Hystories: Hysterical Epidemics and Modern Media*. New York, NY: Columbia University Press.

Sofsky, W. (1999) *The Order of Terror: The Concentration Camp*. Princeton, NJ: Princeton University Press.

Sofsky, W. (2004) *Violence: Terrorism, Genocide, War*. London, UK: Granta Books.

Spitz, R.A. (1957) *No and Yes*. New York, NY: International Universities Press.

Spitz, V. (2005) *Doctors from Hell: The Horrific Account of Nazi Experiments on Humans*. Boulder, CO: Sentient Publications.

Stanton, G. (1996) *The Eight Stages of Genocide*. Genocide Watch Briefing Paper to US State Department. Available at: www.genocidewatch.org/images/8StagesBriefingpaper.pdf

Staub, E. (1989) *The Roots of Evil: The Origins of Genocide and Other Group Violence*. New York, NY: Cambridge University Press.

Stein, H. (2003) *Beneath the Crust of Culture: Psychoanalytic Anthropology and the Cultural Unconscious in American Life*. Amsterdam-New York, NY: Rodopi.

Steiner, J.M. (1980) The SS Yesterday and Today: A Sociopsychogical View. In *Survivors, Victims and Perpetrators: Essays in the Nazi Holocaust*, ed. J.E. Dimsdale. New York, NY: Hemisphere Publishing Corp, pp. 405–445.

Steiner, J. (1982) Perverse Relationships between Parts of the Self: A Clinical Illustration. *International Journal of Psychoanalysis*, 63, 241–251.

Steiner, J.M. (2011) *Seeing and Being Seen: Emerging from a Psychic Retreat*. London, UK: Routledge.

Steuber, K. (2006) *Rediscovering Empathy*. Cambridge, MA: MIT Press.

Stoller, R. (1975) *Perversion: The Erotic Form of Hatred*. New York, NY: Pantheon.

Stoller, R. (1986) *Sexual Excitement: The Dynamics of Erotic Life*. London, UK: Routledge.

Stone, M. (2009) *The Anatomy of Evil*. Amherst, NY: Prometheus Books.

Strauss, S (2016) *Fundamentals of Genocide and Mass Atrocity Prevention*. Washington, DC: United States Holocaust Memorial Museum.

Summers, K., Szanto, T. and Crespi, B. (eds) (2013) *Human Social Evolution: The Foundational Works of Richard D. Alexander*. New York, NY: Oxford University Press.

Sutherland, J. D. (1994) Bion's Group Dynamics. In *The Autonomous Self: The Work of John D. Sutherland*, ed. J. S. Scharff. Northvale, NJ: Jason Aronson.

Symington, J. and Symington, N. (1996) *The Clinical Thinking of Wilfred Bion*. London, UK: Routledge.

Szanto, T. and Moran, D. (2015) *Empathy and Collective Intentionality: The Social Philosophy of Edith Stein*. Human Studies, 38, 445–461.

Szykierski, D. (2010) Shaping the Group Relations Discourse: Bion's Position Regarding Freud's View on Groups. *Organizational and Social Dynamics*, 10, 56–78.

Tang, S. (2009) The Security Dilemma: A Conceptual Analysis. *Security Studies*, 18, 587–582.

Tarantelli, C.B. (2010) The Italian Red Brigades and the Structure and Dynamics of Terrorist Groups. *International Journal of Psycho-Analysis*, 91(3), 541–560.

Tarrow S. (1994) *Power in Movement: Collective Action, Social Movements and Politics*. New York, NY: Cambridge University Press.

Taylor, J.L. (2006) *From Weimar to Nuremberg: A Historical Case Study of Twenty-two Einsatzgruppen Officers*. Masters Thesis. Ohio University.

Taylor, K. (2009) *Cruelty: Human Evil and the Human Brain*. New York, NY: Oxford University Press.

Tomasello, M. (2009) *Why We Cooperate*. Boston, MA: MIT Press.

Tomasello, M. (2014) *A Natural History of Human Thinking*. Cambridge, MA: Harvard University Press.

Tuomela, R. (2013) *Social Ontology: Collective Intentionality and Group Agents*. Oxford Scholarship online.

Turquet, P. (1975) Threats to Identity in the Large Group. In *The Large Group: Dynamics and Therapy*, ed. L. Kreeger. London, UK: Constable, pp. 87–144.

Trevor-Roper, H. (1988) *Hitler's Table Talk 1941–1944*. New York, NY: Oxford University Press.

Twemlow, A. (2003) A Crucible for Murder: The Social Context of Violent Children and Adolescents. *Psychoanalytic Quarterly*, 3, 659–698.

Tyrell, A. (1999) Seizure and Consolidation of Power: Towards Dictatorship: Germany 1930 to 1934. Chapter 2. In *The Third Reich: The Essential Readings*, ed. C. Leitz. New York, NY: Oxford University Press.

Usó-Doménech, J.L. and Nescolarde-Selva, J. (2016) What are Belief Systems? *Foundations of Science*, 21(1), 147–152.

Van den Berghe, P.L. (1985) Paternalism, Patronage, and Potlatch: The Dynamics of Giving and Being Given to. *Current Anthropology*, 26(2), 262–263.

Van Den Bosch, J. (2015) Personalism: A Type or Characteristic of Authoritarian Regimes? *Politologická Revue*, 1, 11–30.

Volkan, V. (1997) *Bloodlines: From Ethnic Pride to Ethnic Terrorism*. Boulder, CO: Farrar, Straus & Giroux Publishing.

Von Leer, J. (1937) *The Criminal Nature of the Jews*. Berlin and Leipzig: Nibelungen-Verlag.

Wachsmann, N. (2015) *Volume 1: A History of the Nazi Concentration Camps*. New York, NY: Farrar, Straus and Giroux.

Waite, R.G. (1977) *The Psychopathic God*. Cambridge, MA: Da Capo Press (rev. edn 1993).

Waller, J. (2002) *Becoming Evil, How Ordinary People Commit Genocide and Mass Killings*. New York, NY: Oxford University Press.

Weiss, J. (1996) *The Ideology of Death: Why the Holocaust Happen in Germany*. Chicago, IL: Ivan R. Dee Publisher.

Welch, D. (2002) *The Third Reich: Politics and Propaganda*. London, UK and New York, NY: Routledge.

Welldon, E.V. (1988) *The Idealization and Denigration of Motherhood*. London, UK: Karnac.

Welldon, E.V. (1991) Psychology and Psychopathology in Women – A Psychoanalytic Perspective. *British Journal of Psychiatry*, 158, 85–92.

Welldon, E.V. (2011) *Playing with Dynamite: A Personal Approach to the Psychoanalytic Understanding of Perversions, Violence, and Criminality*. London, UK: Karnac.

Westen, D. (1985) *Self and Society: Narcissism, Collectivism and the Development of Morals*. New York, NY: Cambridge University Press.

Westen, D. (1992) The Cognitive Self and the Psychological Self. Can We Put Our Selves Together. *Psychological Inquiry*, 3, 1–13.

Wildt, M. (2009) *An Uncompromising Generation: The Nazi Leadership of the National Security Main Office*. Madison, WI: The University of Wisconsin Press.

Williams, M.H. (2005) The Three Vertices: Science, Art and Religion. *British Journal of Psychotherapy*, 21, 429–443.

Wilson, D.S. (2015) *Does Altruism Exist: Culture Genes and the Welfare of Others*. New Haven, CT: Yale University/Templeton Press.

Winnicott, D.W. (1965) *Maturational Processes and the Facilitating Environment: Studies in the Theory of Emotional Development*. London, UK: Hogarth Press.

Winnicott, D.W. (1974) Fear of Breakdown. *International Review of Psycho-Analysis*, 1(1–2), 103–107.

Wrangham, R.W. (2006) Why Apes and Humans Kill. In *Conflict*, ed. M. Jones and A. Fabian. New York, NY: Cambridge University Press, pp. 43–62.

Yahil, L. (1990) *The Holocaust: The Fate of European Jewry, 1932–1945*. New York, NY: Oxford University Press.

Zahavi, D. (2015) You, Me, and We: The Sharing of Emotional Experiences. *Journal of Consciousness Studies*, 22, 84–101.

Zahavi, D. and Michael, J. (2016) *Beyond Mirroring: The Oxford Handbook of 4E Cognition*. Ed. A. Newen, L. de Bruin and S. Gallagher. Oxford, UK: Oxford University Press.

Zimbardo, P. (2007) *The Lucifer Effect: Understanding How Good People Turn Evil*. New York, NY and London, UK: Random House.

INDEX

accommodation 18
addictive perversion 77
adolescent stage development 35
affine intervention 43
aggression 16, 117; and mass violence, difference between 16
Anderson, Benedict 104, 111
anti-Jewish legislation 47
Anti-Jewish policy 4
Anti-Semitic culture, latent 24
Anti-Semitism 44, 46, 47, 82; source of violence in 44
Arendt Hannah 86
Aryans 40, 46, 48, 52, 61, 65
Asch, Solomon 69
Asian history 103
Athens, Lonnie 122
Aum Shinrikyo 67
Austria 54
Auschwitz-Birkenau Concentration Camp 122
authoritarian leaders 38
authoritarian societies 36
automatic group identity 38

Bartov, Omer 122
"the balance of power" 19
belief 58
belief function, disorders of 20
beliefs 19; causal component 21; conceptual and abstract 21; contradictory 20; existence of 20–21; fabricated 44; false 24, 25, 27, 28 (*see also* false beliefs);

imaginary system of 23–24, 26–27; and psychic impairments 20; role of 20–21; shared 21
belief system 123
Bingham, Paul. *Death from a Distance* 17
Bion's system 59
Bion's theory 120, 124
bizarre object, formation of 81, 82
Blitzkrieg 104, 105
body image 71
Bolsheviks 24, 55, 64, 65
Britton, Ronald 19
bullying 30

cadavers 56
Cambodia 54
catastrophe 73
charisma 61
charismatic effect, leader 59
child rearing, aim of 31, 33
choice, concept of 34
clan warfare 43
closed mindedness 60
coercive laws 7
coercive violence 19
cognitive distortions 72
Cambodian revolution 88
common enemies 37
competition 19
complex statement 62
confirmation bias 20
conspiracy theories 25–26

conspiring agents, imagined 25
constitutional and environmental traumas 62
cooperating groups 8
counter-democratic violence 10
criminal perversion 77
cruelty 123
cultural and family values 31–32
cultural diversity 3
cultural evolution, multilevel 2
cultural suppressors 6

Darwin's evolution theory 5
death anxiety 66
death camps 66
death constellation 66
death threat 62–63, 66
default identification, in non-kin groups 35
delusional belief 65
democratic cultures 33
disconfirmation bias 20
disgust 21
disruptive behavior, suppression of 18
distortions of perception 81
disturbed thinking 58
double messages 61

ego identity 32
Eichmann, Adolph 37
elite status 18
Erikson, Kai 11
Erikson's theory 34–35
ethnic cleansing 53
ethnic familiarity 4
ethnic minorities 47
ethnic vulnerability 47
euthanasia program 49
evacuative projection 82
existential-depressive affect 66
"extremely violent societies" 28

faith 58 *see also* belief
false beliefs 24, 25, 27, 28, 56, 58, 63, 64, 69, 70, 80
false emotional belief 61
family groups 17
fantasy: and reality 60; of revenge 66
final solution 27, 48, 49, 52
foreclosed identities 36
foreignness of Jews 48
formal warfare 88
French Revolution 107
free riders 17, 32

Freud: on father in kin related family 18, 19; group theory, problems with 1–14; on life in horde 1, 4–5
Fuhrer's destructive violent wishes 26

Gender identity 105
genetic "pruning" of inferiors 48
genocide 2, 14, 28, 30, 43, 45, 61–62, 82, 84, 113; categories of 87, 93; definition 86; element of 93; historical 87. *see also* mass murder; and perversions 82
Gerlach, Christian 28
German euthanasia movement of purification 63
German Teutonic community 112
German Jews 44
Germans 23–24, 49, 53
German social identity, creation of 38
Germany 14, 22–27, 36, 37, 39–41, 43, 54, 64
governmental genocide 14
group behavior, dynamics of 29
group beliefs 59; indoctrination to 59
group boundaries, protection of 38
group coalitions, intrapsychic relationships in 11
group conformity, influence of 69
group cooperation 18
group fitness 17
group identity 31, 32, 88; complex 32; development 34; individual identity and 33, 34, 37
"groupishness" 31
group hallucinosis 114
group killing 2
group leader 59; charisma 61; negative anti-reality delusional belief by 61
group mentality 31
group oriented behavior 31
group selection theory 5, 119
group violence 2, 10, 34, 62

habitual perversion 77
hallucinations 69
hallucinosis 60, 64, 69, 78, 97; destructive power of 65
hallucinotic beliefs 23, 44
hallucinotic collusions/hysterias, in group 69
hallucinotic leader 67
hallucinotic thinking 67–68
Hamburg 55
harmful violence 16
Hegemonial genocide 87
hereditary rulers 18
Himmler, H. 1, 12

Hitler 14–27, 22, 38–41, 44–45, 46–52, 59, 62; false belief utterances 67; laws of exclusion 47; murder driven messages 67; plan for racial cleansing 48; public and written verbal statements 54, 61; style of leadership 47; visionary prophetic national leader, position of 65
Hitler's Aryanization of Germany 105
Hitler youth *(HitlerJugend)* 39
Hoess, Rudolf. 50
holocaust 45, 88
human culture 30
human group: coalitions 16; evolution of 3
human infants, development of 30
human moral development 31
Hyatt-Williams, Arthur 62, theory of violence 63
hyper-competitive/hyper-patriotic behavior 30
hyper-groupism 46

identification with aggressor 53
identity foreclosure 36
identity formation 33–35; and sociocultural context, link between 33
illusory and conspiratorial belief system 26
imaginary beliefs 7–, 68
imaginary belief system of Germans, emergence of 23–24
Imaginary Nation-State 101
imaginary enemy 45
imaginary threat 61
individual identity 33, 34; and group identity development 33, 34; and social identity 35
individual killing 2
infantile polymorphism 76
injustice 30
intrusive projective identification 92
internal identity 34
interpersonal violence 70

Japanese warrior ethic 91
Jeckeln, Friedrich 128-129, Rumbula Massacre 129
Jewish agitators 54
Jewish threat, imaginary 25
Jewish women 44
Jews 21–27, 40, 43, 44–45, 46–47, 52, 61

killing: anthropologists on 2; and destruction 19; group 2; individual 2; to remove negative 52
"kin-ness" 21
kinship 4

Klimaitis, Algirdas 130
Kriegsideologi 37, 38, 63, 111

Lacan's law of the father 73, 76
landowners 18
law enforcement 7
laws of exclusion 47
Lifton, Robert 26
longitudinal splitting of the ego 78

male monarchies 15
Manson group 67
massification 55
mass killing 88
mass murders 21, 27, 43, 45, 52, 55, 63, 65; by Nazis 4, 44; without risk 43
medical research 49–50
megalomaniacal violent eliminative fantasy 27
Meltzer, Donald 60
membership: in social groups 18; in violent and non-violent authoritarian/ millennial groups 34
mental health interventions in Western societies 32
mentalization 79, 80
mentalizing 79
mentally ill and retarded, planned killing of 53
mental space 76
military and social order 16
military warfare systems, creation of 10
Minus K (Knowledge) 59
misconceptions 80–81
misrepresentation, process of 79
modern states, emergence of 4
morals 31–32
mortal enemies 63
multilevel group selection theory 17
multinational cooperation 45
Munich 54
murder 30

national group crises 36
natural selection theory 18
Nazification of eugenics 22
Nazification of judicial systems 23
Nazified eugenic practices 46
Nazi hallucinotic negative basic assumption 65
Nazi leadership 110
Nazi mission 121
Nazi movement 104, 110
Nazi propaganda 108

Nazis 21–28, 37, 39–41, 44, 48–50, 53; criminal acts and organized exploitation by 23; false belief system 22–23; goal of 23; mass murders 44, 53; megalomaniac utopian goals 27; murderous phenomenon 70; path to violence 42–56; political movement 39; violent empire by, creation of 26; "we" identity, purification of 32
Nazi social identity 113
Nazi solution 115
Nazi terrors 16
"the negative," destruction of 46
negative personal identity 36
neonatal brain 30
non-cooperation 17
non-intimate violence 17
non-kin coalitions and groups, violence between 32
non-kin communities 16
non-kin groups 4, 10, 33
non-kin humans 2
non-kin security and safety 4
non-kin social group development 33
nuclear warfare 43
Nuremberg Trials 56, 119

object representation 79
Oedipal trilogy 1
Omniscience 82
oscillating core complex 70, 71

pair bonding, children 30
paranoid/schizoid national large group formation 40
parent-offspring conflict 6
parents and children, conflicts of interests between 17
paternity, in human groups 5
path of violence 66–67
peace between states 43
peer group identity 32
Peoples Temple 67
persecutory anxiety 62
persecutory violence 65
personal identity 33
personalist dictatorship 47
personalist leaders 47
personality disorders 34
perverse distortions 77
perverse fantasies 72
perverse internal nucleus 75
perverse person 73
perversion: body distortion in 78; dynamic process leading to 75; psychoanalytic model of 75; sexual excitement in 81; and violence 70–72
phantom community 123
plastic neural systems, infant 30
Poland 28, 48, 49, 52, 54
"policy" 90
political affinity 44
political beliefs 85
political cleansing 52
political community, concept of 5
political opposition, elimination of 46
political racial discrimination 45
political revolutions 107
political violence and terror 46
political will 10
polity 5; destruction of 8
poly-ethnic group coalitions, emergence of 4
"power" 91
predator-prey model of Nazi and Jew 53–54
predatory basic assumption group mentality 64
predatory killing 3, 53
predatory rulers, loyalty to 41
predatory society 53, 86
predatory states 54
preference falsification 12
prejudice 33
prejudicial transformations 60
premature or precocious closure 73
prey group 54
prey, unarmed 56
priestly castes 18
primary couple 74
primary pair 76
primary sexual identity 77
primitive war vs. organized warfare 3
privilege subgroups 18
process of distortion of reality 114
process of violetization 122
projection of an internal organization 78
propositional logic 64
prosocial beliefs 19, 20
protective violence 65
proto-mental phantasy 82
proto-mental system 74–75
psychic cluster 75
psychic pain 69, 78
psychic sexual life 80
psychoanalytic theory 98
public purposes 54

racial beliefs of Hitler 24
racial-genocidal society, creation of 40
racial warden 51

racist behavior 22
reactions to contamination 21
regression, concept of 73
Reich Institute for Ancestry Research 48
religion 43
religious groups 67
remote killing techniques, evolution of 19
repressive politicide 87
restrictive practices in families and cultures 31
retaliatory violence 65
retributive politicide 87
return to order 45
reversal of function 78
revitalization movement for Germans 60
revolutionary politicide 87
right to fair trial 17
right to life 56
risk, absence of 43
role and identity 36
RSHA (Reich Main Security Office) 49, 52–55
rule of law 17
Russia 28, 49, 53, 64, 65

sadistic acts 71
Sandler, Paolo 64
Schmitt's complex political theory 96
security bonding rituals 12
Security Service (SD) 128
self-interested coalitions 18
self-interest groups 33, 34
selfish self-interest, suppression of 7
selfish strategies 17
self-preservative acts 71
self-protective acts 71
self-reflective capacities 32
self-representations, unstable 72
semi-paranoid process 25
sense of self 18
sense of trust 34
serial murders 67
sexual excitement 78
sexuality 71, 72, 74
sexual maturity 6
sexual perversions 73; and violent acts 74
shared beliefs 7, 21, 59
shared illusion 61
shared language within groups 9
"sleeper needs" 27
social (rule bound) behavior 18
social behavior, regulation of 17
social cognitive capacity 18
social confirmation bias 60
social conflict 71

social constraint, breaking of 3
social cooperation 17, 30, 33; in human groups 17
social deterrents 16
social groups 17
social growth of cooperative societies 19
social identity 4, 32, 35, 37; recognition of 9
social interactions 30
social IQ 31
social minority 32
social mores 17
social/political crises 37, 38
social safety 16
social stratification and conflicts 18
social suppressors 6–7
social violence 25–26
Soviet Union 53
specialized work groups 4, 13
splitting 72–73
SS 12, 13, 49, 53, 55
state authorized coercive force 19
state genocide 52
state organized false beliefs 21
state organized perpetrated violence 11
state-organized warfare 3
state sponsored murder 66
status, formation of 18
super-ego integrity 38
surplus killing 56
surrender and helplessness in mass 55
Soviet authorities 130
symbols, use of 9

Thanatopolitics 89-90
Third Reich 26, 50
threat of violence 16
threats 87
totalistic cultures 33
totalitarian leaders 38
transcendent conversion 62
transformational technologies, development of 13
transformation in action 74
"a transient experience of depersonalization" 37
"treacherous" 88
triangular link 76
true believers 59, 60

universal developmental goal 33
unlawful violence 16
us/them beliefs 64
utopian future 46

valence 44
Vietnam 49

violence 16, 37, 44, 93; aggression and 16; against group "outsiders" 38; humans and 17; against Jews 45; organized 16; and perversion 70–72; and sexual impulses 72, 74; suppression of 16, 17
violent behavior, state organized 46
violent competition 6
violent coercion 89
violent group: behavior 2; dynamics 45; individuals in 38
violent impulses 7
violentization 27
violent military coalitions 7
violent society 23
Volksgemeinschaft 40, 50

walking dead 55
war 2, 10, 30, 43, 117; between coalitions 7; culture 7–8; and genocide 11; human losses from violent conflict 8; ritualization of 12–13; violence 43

warfare 2, 19, 33, 43, 53; predatory killing and 53; tools of 7
warring social group 7
warrior class 10
weaponry 19, 33; advances in 19; non-kin aggregates and group violence 19; storage and use of 19
weapons 9; development of 9; of mass destruction 43
"we" identity 32–34, 37
Weltanschauung 39
witch hunts 11
within-group identity 12
within-group violence 14
"World Bolshevism" 24
"World Jewry" 24
World Trade Center 98
World War I 2, 10, 37, 47, 64
World War II 13, 21, 64, 84, 86, 99, 109

xenophobia 85
Xenophobic genocide 87

Printed in Great Britain
by Amazon